THE IMMIGRANT CHURCH AND COMMUNITY

The Immigrant Church and Community

Pittsburgh's Slovak Catholics and Lutherans, 1880–1915

June Granatir Alexander

UNIVERSITY OF PITTSBURGH PRESS

Published by the University of Pittsburgh Press, Pittsburgh, Pa., 15260
Copyright © 1987, University of Pittsburgh Press
All rights reserved
Feffer and Simons, Inc., London
Manufactured in the United States of America

Library of Congress Cataloging-in-Publication Data

Alexander, June Granatir, 1948–
    The immigrant church and community.

    Bibliography: p. 181
    Includes index.
    1. Slovak Americans—Pennsylvania—Pittsburgh—History.   2. Lutherans—
Pennsylvania—Pittsburgh—History.   3. Catholics—Pennsylvania—Pittsburgh—
History.   4. Pittsburgh (Pa.)—Church history.
I. Title.
F159.P69S642   1987   282′74886′0899187   86-30843
ISBN 0-8229-3821-9

For John

Contents

Tables

Acknowledgments

I<small>N THE COURSE</small> of this study I have relied on the help of many persons. I cannot thank each one publicly but I am, nonetheless, grateful to them. A special few, however, made substantial contributions, and I wish to acknowledge their kind assistance.

Several individuals commented on various versions or segments of the manuscript. During its dissertation stage at the University of Minnesota, Rudolph J. Vecoli provided gentle, yet demanding, guidance. His probing questions during the research and writing helped give direction to what, at times, seemed an insurmountable mass of material. His own commitment to the study of immigration history and his support for my research have been sources of inspiration and encouragement throughout my scholarly career. John Modell offered incisive comments and suggestions for revisions. John Bodnar did the same. I especially wish to thank Michael P. Weber for his careful, thoughtful reading of a later version of the manuscript. His candid remarks and suggestions proved invaluable as I made final revisions. I benefited from commentary by Randall M. Miller on a paper that, in revised form, appeared as "The Laity in the Church: Slovaks and the Catholic Church in Pre-World War I Pittsburgh," *Church History* 53 (Sept. 1984): 363–78, and has been incorporated into this work. No person offered more advice and constructive criticism than did John K. Alexander. A perceptive historian in his own right, he has generously lent his keen analytic skills to my work. For nearly a decade, he has cheerfully served as first reader, critic, editor, and, when necessary, as research and technical assistant. I am grateful that, although John is my most

xi

enthusiastic supporter, he remains, above all, the historian—analyzing, questioning, criticizing. He never has permitted his desire to be supportive to outweigh the need to be critical. I can dedicate this work to him, but I can never fully express my appreciation for all that he has done.

Research for this study was supported in part by a grant-in-aid from the Immigration History Research Center, University of Minnesota. The International Research and Exchanges Board awarded a grant for research in Slovakia.

The staffs of the Immigration History Research Center, the Archives of Industrial Society, and the Slovak Museum and Archives offered friendly, capable assistance. Father Edward McSweeney of the Archives of the Diocese of Pittsburgh made special arrangements for me to use records held in that archives. I wish to thank the staff at the National Slovak Society headquarters for allowing me access to the fraternal's early records. Joseph Stefka, now president of the National Slovak Society, took time from his busy schedule to help me. I want to express special thanks to Robert E. Wilson, former director of the Ethnic Resources Inventory for the Pittsburgh Council on Higher Education, who helped me locate some records and made arrangements to facilitate my use of them.

Church and diocesan records were indispensable sources for this study. The Most Reverend Anthony T. Bosco, general secretary and auxiliary bishop of Pittsburgh, graciously permitted me access to diocesan records as well as offered general support for my research. The Reverend John Drzik, former pastor of Holy Emmanuel Lutheran Church, and the Reverend Paul D. Weber, the church's current pastor, made special arrangements for me to use church records. The Reverend Mr. Drzik was particularly generous with his time and tried to locate additional records that might be useful to me.

Members of Pittsburgh's Slovak community also assisted me. The Holovanisin family merits special thanks. Margaret and her late husband, Andrew, extended their kind hospitality to me while I was doing research in Pittsburgh. In addition, Mr. Holovanisin helped me obtain fraternal records and interviews vital to this study. Important among these interviews were those with Mary and the late John Ciganik, and with the late Ferdinand Dvorsky. Mr. Dvorsky's son and daughter, the late Ray and late Anastasia Dvorsky, also provided assistance as well as their hospitality. His daughter, Helen Dvorsky, continues to help and share information when I call upon her. Other immigrants and their children whose interviews were used in this study are listed in the Bibliographical Essay. To these and to all of the individuals who granted me interviews in the course of my research, I owe a debt that can not be repaid: the debt of a historian seeking information preserved only in the memories of immigrants and their children.

Introduction

Ferdinand Dvorsky left his native Slovak village of Lisková in 1905 for the United States. He wanted a better job than the one he had in a textile mill. He went directly to Woods Run in Allegheny City, Pennsylvania, where his brother resided. Other immigrants from his village and several nearby villages also lived in the Woods Run area. Obtaining work was not a problem: Ferdinand got a job at the Pennsylvania Casting and Machine Works, where his brother was already employed. Although there were several Slovak fraternal lodges in the Woods Run region, Ferdinand did not immediately join one. He was young, unmarried, and did not see any pressing need for the insurance they offered. A pious Catholic, Ferdinand did, however, immediately join the Slovak Catholic parish in Woods Run. The congregation had no permanent building in 1905 and church services were temporarily being conducted in a foundation. This simple basement lacked the warmth and beauty of the church he had attended in his homeland. But Ferdinand said he preferred the basement to attending other Catholic churches in Woods Run because "you know how it is, you'd just as soon go to your own." When a church building was finally completed in 1906, Ferdinand did want it to have the interior beauty and elegant furnishings he believed a place of religious worship should have. Morever, he felt that his fellow villagers now living in western Allegheny City ought to contribute to that beauty. So, Ferdinand took up a collection among former Lisková residents to provide a cross for the church's altar. The cross bore a plaque that identified it as the gift of immigrants from Lisková.

Although Ferdinand Dvorsky labored long hours at his job, his life in Woods Run clearly involved more than going to work. In 1909, at the urging of a friend, he changed his mind about fraternal societies and joined Branch 2 of the First Catholic Slovak Union. In later years, he served as vice-president of the lodge. Ferdinand also played the clarinet in a small Slovak band that regularly performed for socials sponsored by Saint Gabriel's parish and by various Slovak organizations in the Pittsburgh area. At one of these socials he met Anna Matlon, a Slovak woman from his native Liptov County. They were married in 1912 at her church, Saint Elizabeth's, and then took up residence in Woods Run. Ferdinand and Anna's eight children were all christened at Saint Gabriel Church. Ferdinand and Anna remained fervent Catholics and active in parish life. Indeed, taking up the early collection for the altar cross signaled only the beginning of Ferdinand's continued interest in church affairs. He was later elected one of Saint Gabriel's collectors, whose duty it was to visit parishioners' homes to collect their monthly assessments. For Ferdinand, supporting his church was a new responsibility he willingly accepted.[1]

John Ciganik, another Slovak immigrant, left Zlatá Bana in 1913 and followed his father to the Detroit area. Because so many people from his village and neighboring villages had already immigrated there, "it was just like home." A short time later, John's father left Michigan for a better job in Pittsburgh's North Side. John was accustomed to seeing his father leave in search of work; he had previously journeyed four or five times to the United States. Since John had a good job, he chose to remain in Michigan. But in 1915, at his father's request, John finally moved to Pittsburgh to work so that "the family would be together." By the time he arrived, other Slovaks John knew from the old country, including his godfather, had settled in Pittsburgh's North Side, formerly Allegheny City.

Although John Ciganik had not gone directly to Pittsburgh from his village, he stayed in the "Steel City" for the remainder of his life. At a wedding reception, his father pointed out a young American-born Slovak woman and told John she would make a good wife. John agreed and courted her. The courtship consisted mainly of attending church services together and chatting afterward. They were married in 1916 at Saint Gabriel Church. All four of John and Mary Ciganik's children were baptized at Saint Gabriel's, where John served on the Church Committee. He was, at the same time, active in Branch 2 of the First Catholic Slovak Union and held elected office as its secretary for over half a century.[2]

Ferdinand Dvorsky's and John Ciganik's descriptions of their emigration from Europe embody underlying influences affecting Slovak immigration to the United States. In both cases, the push to leave northern Hungary was influenced in part by the fact that family and countrymen had emigrated before them. Both men were seeking jobs and both ultimately moved to where family and countrymen already lived. Neither man felt uprooted from his homeland. They had, after all, followed family and friends to the United States. Moreover, their decisions were justified by the fact that emigration was a standard practice among fellow villagers and, at least for John, a family tradition. His father and uncles had all traveled several times between Hungary and the United States.

The reasons these two immigrants left their homeland were based on pragmatic assessments of their economic situations and futures. Once in the United States, Ferdinand Dvorsky and John Ciganik did not fit the stereotype conjured up by the image of a "floating proletariat."[3] While John did not immediately immigrate to Pittsburgh's North Side, there was definitely direction in his geographic mobility. He did not simply wander in search of employment; he followed family and friends and settled with them. Both men became part of that contingent of immigrants who lived out their lives in the same locale. There were more immigrants like them. These permanent, essentially "immobile," immigrants resided in culturally diverse urban neighborhoods and mill towns among populations comprising permanent immigrants as well as mobile sojourners.

In their new country, John Ciganik and Ferdinand Dvorsky remained fiercely loyal to their homeland faith. In this regard, both men were typical of the majority of Slovak immigrants who came to America in the pre–World War I era. Amid the flux created by the coming and going of transient immigrants and despite the dislocation generated by the immigration process, these Slovak immigrants voluntarily and successfully founded national churches.[4] Founding churches and adjusting to enhanced lay responsibilities became part of the Slovak "immigration experience."

Slovaks were part of the immigration at the turn of the century that heightened the ethnic diversity of industrial cities like Pittsburgh. Throughout the period 1880–1910, the foreign-born accounted for more than one-fourth of Pittsburgh's population, while the proportion of immigrants living in Allegheny City consistently totaled just slightly less. However, the origins of these newcomers shifted over the period. In 1880, approximately 1 percent of the two cities' foreign-born came from eastern Europe and Italy. By 1910, persons from these regions made up about one-half of the foreign population.[5] But as the soot that covered Pittsburgh revealed no more than that it was an industrial city, the numbers and geographic origins of immigrants provide only surface indicators of the impact that immigration had on the city's metropolitan area.

This study considers people like Ferdinand Dvorsky and John Ciganik who were part of the pre–World War I Slovak immigration to Pittsburgh.[6] Slovak Lutheran and Roman Catholic churches are the focal points of this investigation. The approach is partially comparative, but the comparison is based on religion and is intraethnic, not interethnic. By placing the formation of national churches within the broader context of the Slovak immigration into Pittsburgh, the analysis seeks to bring to light the complex interplay of factors that led to the creation of ethnic parishes in American cities at the turn of the century.

For nearly two decades, scholars have been working to rescue immigration and ethnicity from the "neglected dimension" of American history.[7] In the history of immigration, researchers have discovered a rich terrain for exploring the American past, especially the impact of urbanization and industrialization on individuals, groups, and families as well as on American society as a whole. A significant number of these studies have focused on the mobile aspects, both spatial and socioeconomic, of the immigration experience.[8] But immigrants did more than go to work, look for a place to live, and perhaps seek advancement on the socioeconomic scale. And their impact on American society went beyond aggravating urban housing conditions and providing sturdy hands and strong backs for America's burgeoning industries. Indeed, there were many sides to the immigration experience; for Slovaks, founding and supporting national churches became an integral part of their adjustment process.

This analysis runs counter to interpretations that see the development of ethnic organizations as a defensive reaction resulting from conflict with or alienation from American society.[9] These views oversimplify the adjustment by immigrants to their new society. Moreover, such interpretations downplay the fact that establishing ethnic institutions could grow out of an assessment by practical persons of their needs. Because religion had been an intrinsic part of life in their homeland, once in the United States, Slovaks organized national churches to serve their particular religious needs. At the same time, the formation of these churches represented an adjustment by Slovaks to their new environment. Establishing ethnic churches in

Pittsburgh was an example of the accommodation by Slovak immigrants to American society—not conflict with it, alienation from it, or assimilation into it.

Founding churches was also an attempt by Slovak Catholics and Protestants to transplant a premigration institution. Typically pious people, most Slovak immigrants wanted to remain loyal to their premigration faith and to continue the system of religious practices attached to that faith. Slovaks had preconceived notions not only about religious worship but also about the function of churches and lay involvement in church affairs. As "institutions in motion," churches propelled immigrants into direct contact with established religious hierarchies in the United States.[10] In the course of this encounter immigrant laities and church hierarchies fashioned a response to each other. Thus immigration involved more than a meeting of different cultures: it was also a meeting of institutions. Sometimes conflict was generated; at other times, it was not.

The formation of ethnic parishes by immigrants and their interaction with established church hierarchies are important aspects of American immigration and religious history. But they are aspects that have not been extensively explored. Due in large measure to views of immigration history that stress the assimilation of ethnic groups into American society or into religious denominations, scant attention has been given to the interaction of most immigrant groups with their church leaders in the United States. Many analyses have looked at the response by church leaders *to* immigrants or, on the other hand, the reaction of immigrants *to* church hierarchies. In general, however, little stress has been placed on the interaction *between* immigrants and church officials in the United States. In the recent past, historians have delved more deeply into the relations between immigrants and church leaders and have shown that these relations were less amicable than traditional histories would have us believe.[11] Still, with some notable exceptions, these analyses focus on crises or those incidents of clear conflict and confrontation. They pay less attention to the ongoing relations between immigrants and their church leaders.[12] The purpose here is to look beyond the crisis events to examine the dynamics that underlay the formation of ethnic churches and to determine how Slovak ethnic parishes fit into and functioned within the established religious structures in the United States.

The picture of immigrant-church relations that emerges from an analysis of Pittsburgh's Slovak parishes is complex. For Slovak Catholics, relations with diocesan officials were not characterized by conflict. The Slovak laity accepted the bishop's authority in the diocese. The response by Slovak Roman Catholics to their bishops grew partially out of their premigration respect for clerical authority. At the same time, these lay Catholics were not always docilely submissive but, instead, demonstrated an assertive deference toward bishops. The reaction by Pittsburgh's bishops to Slovaks was based on a fear of "leakage," meaning the loss of the foreign-born to the Catholic church. The diocese's church officials aimed to keep immigrants within the established diocesan structure. Hence, the competition with Protestant churches for immigrants as well as abhorrence of independent Catholic churches were factors influencing relations between Slovak immigrants and Catholic church officials in Pittsburgh.

For Slovak Lutherans the situation was quite different. Since Lutherans in America were already divided along ethnic and confessional lines, there was no single Lutheran church structure in the United States. Slovak immigrants formed the independent Slovak Synod, which in 1908 affiliated with the Evangelical Lutheran Synodical Conference of America. The association led to conflict between Pittsburgh's Slovak Lutherans and their clerical leaders. This examination thus shows that there could be variations of the "immigration experience" within a single ethnic group.

A comparison between the Slovak Catholic and Lutheran experiences can also help clarify the nagging issue of how ethnicity influenced immigrant-church relations. This study joins those that question the validity of blaming conflicts between American Catholic church leaders and immigrants squarely on an "Irish" hierarchy that wanted to Americanize Catholic newcomers. In Pittsburgh, the Irish-dominated Catholic church enjoyed more success in its dealings with Slovak Catholics than the Missouri Synod, a member of the Evangelical Lutheran Synodical Conference of America, did with its Slovak coreligionists. This analysis suggests that the nationality of church leaders was less important than their position regarding the religious practices of immigrant groups. Fitting into Pittsburgh's Catholic church structure did not require Slovak Catholic immigrants fundamentally to alter their system of religious practices. Influenced by the Missouri Synod, however, the Slovak Synod set out to reform Slovak Lutherans in a way that would change some of their traditional religious practices. Conflict resulted. Indeed, relations between Pittsburgh's Slovak Lutherans and their clerical leaders were comparable to those between Italian Catholic immigrants and some American bishops.[13] Their similar experiences show that attacks by American churches on premigration religious practices created conflict. This was a problem for some Protestant denominations as well as for the Catholic church.

An examination of the Slovak experience reveals that the objective of preserving the faith was a potent factor influencing the relations between American denominations and Slovak immigrants. However, preservation of faith took on different meanings. For Pittsburgh's Catholic diocesan officials, it meant keeping Slovaks loyal to the Catholic church and responsive to diocesan authority; for the Slovak Synod and the Evangelical Lutheran Synodical Conference of America, it meant reforming Slovak Lutherans.

This study is in some ways traditional institutional history. But it is institutional history that attempts to view immigrant churches from two perspectives: that of lay immigrants and that of the established religious hierarchies. A second but not secondary goal is to assess the role of the church in Slovak community life. This assessment necessarily begins with a discussion of Slovak fraternal societies. Although founded to give mutual aid, the religious fraternals quickly established the broader objective of organizing Slovak churches. By instigating these efforts and, subsequently, by helping to support the new churches, these societies helped encourage the development of Slovak communities in several Pittsburgh neighborhoods.

Over time, the Slovak lay perspective on churches and fraternal societies and on their functions changed. As laities had to assume enhanced roles in church affairs, they had to develop a new sense of community based on a shared interest and mutual obligation toward their churches. The necessity that churches be self-supporting meant that Catholic parish life took on added dimensions. Indeed, Slovak Catholic churches became social institutions in part because a congregation's social activities often centered on garnering funds for church operating expenses. Religious restrictions prevented a similar development in Pittsburgh's Slovak Lutheran church.

Lay involvement in parish matters was not a continuation of roles that Slovak lay persons had or were assuming prior to emigration. Claims that such involvement was an extension of the laity's changing role in Europe glide too facilely over how conditions in America affected the role of immigrant lay persons.[14] A focus of this study is what happened to churches and laities as immigrants tried to transplant this premigration institution. There was continuity between Old World churches and New World churches, but continuity accompanied by change.

The creation of national churches signified the emergence of Slovak communities in Pittsburgh, and each church acted as a kind of mirror of those communities. In such mirrors, we see not the disintegration of ethnic communities but, rather, the development of their institutional structure. These mirrors reveal that ethnic institutions were neither static in function nor in the immigrants' perceptions of them. Moreover, Pittsburgh's Slovak communities were multidimensional and defy narrow definitions based simply on territory or religion.

An examination of Pittsburgh's Slovak churches also provides some opportunity to investigate the elusive issue of the development of ethnic consciousness among immigrants who, in their homeland, had identified themselves by local origins.[15] Slovak churches encouraged the development of a "consciousness of kind" among Slovak immigrants; however, in the prewar years, these institutions did not by themselves foster the development of a strong ethnic consciousness among Pittsburgh Slovaks as members of a unique people or nation.[16]

The following discussion does not offer a comprehensive history of Pittsburgh's Slovak communities in the pre–World War I era. The focus is on the religious lives of these Slovaks. Given this, the dynamics of ethnic church formation, the interaction between immigrants and church hierarchies, and the social relationships among parishioners and between them and their clergy are explored. Questions of the impact of industrialization on these immigrants or the emergence of social classes among them await additional research. This study then, as much as the sources allow, attempts to provide an internal view of Slovak congregations and communities before these immigrants faced the knotty questions of ethnic identity that the creation of an independent homeland raised and that, unavoidably, became entangled with their religious identities.

THE IMMIGRANT CHURCH AND COMMUNITY

From Village to City:
Slovak Immigration to Pittsburgh

Sʟᴏᴠᴀᴋ ɪᴍᴍɪɢʀᴀᴛɪᴏɴ to the United States was a dichotomous process. It involved at once a diffusion of Slovaks from villages throughout northern Hungary and a coming together in American mill towns or industrial cities like Pittsburgh. Sometimes this coming together was merely a reunion of family and friends; in other instances, it meant a meeting of countrymen who were nonetheless strangers.

During the pre–World War I era, Slovaks were neither pushed nor pulled to Pittsburgh. Instead, the Slovak immigration into Pittsburgh sprang from an interplay between cultural traditions and economic factors in Hungary and economic conditions in the United States. The society that Slovak immigrants left was characterized by localisms and steeped in religious traditions. Resilient local identities and a deep-seated religious heritage had an impact on institutional and community development among Pittsburgh Slovaks. That impact was not yet evident during the early stages of their movement into the "Steel City." Indeed, for nearly the first decade and a half of the Slovak immigration into Pittsburgh, there was little evidence that a recognizable Slovak community would develop. During these early years, Slovaks did not cluster in a specific section of the city.[1] But despite this dispersion, Slovaks were coming together and forging a framework for the development of Slovak ethnic institutions and communities.

Slovaks were one of several cultural minorities that inhabited the Kingdom of Hungary. The largest Slavic group, Slovaks accounted

3

for approximately 12 percent of Hungary's 1880 population.[2] Most Slovaks lived in sixteen counties in the northern agricultural region of Hungary. This area was by no means ethnically homogeneous. The larger villages and towns of Upper Hungary were often culturally diverse, but this diversity varied by region as well as by county.[3]

The counties inhabited by Slovaks also had various religious denominations. Approximately 70 percent of all Slovaks were Roman Catholic, while about 7 percent followed the Greek Rite. Lutherans accounted for 13 percent, Calvinists 5 percent, and Jews and "other" religious groups another 5 percent.[4] Although the Edict of Toleration (1781) extended freedoms to recognized religious denominations, Catholicism remained the state religion of Hungary, and religion was a state affair. The government paid clerical salaries, appointed church officials, and passed laws regarding church governance and religious matters such as mixed marriages.[5] For Slovaks, however, such legislation had little to do with their perceptions of religion and the role it played in their lives. For them, religion was a system of practices and beliefs that profoundly affected their daily existence. Religion involved observing designated holy days, but it was also a blend of Christian liturgy and peasant superstitions.

Regular communal worship constituted part of the routine of Slovak village life. On religious feasts, Slovaks of different persuasions passed one another as they traveled to devotions. Because not every village had churches for all denominations represented among its inhabitants, some neighboring communities shared a church.[6] Still, churches dotted the countryside and towns of northern Hungary, and the faithful who wanted to worship or who needed the services of a clergyman typically had easy access to both. Prominently situated among humble peasant cottages, Catholic churches were the most commanding structures in Slovak villages. The steeples and bell towers were visible for miles. Government restrictions prevented Protestant churches from enjoying similar prominence.[7] Some churches, especially Catholic ones, had a significance beyond their function as places of worship. Perhaps an ornate interior or religious work of art such as a statue or altar had historical import and had become part of the community's history. A feature of the church's exterior architecture or interior furnishings could be sources of community pride and even occasionally of fame for the village or town.[8] Nevertheless, churches were above all places for communal and individual worship. The important events in the lives of Slovaks, beginning with their christening, took place at least partially in the church. Wedding celebrations began only after family and friends had witnessed the solemnization of marriage vows in the church. The church was the unavoidable stopover in a funeral procession's march from the deceased's cottage to the cemetery.

For Slovaks, religion involved more than observing designated days, participating in the sacraments, or solemnizing important events in an individual or family's life cycle. Religion was an integral part of daily life and the struggle for existence. Slovak religion was not founded on an understanding of church dogmas; rather it was a system of rituals rooted in a peasant past and tied to the practical concerns and stark realities of a self-subsistent agrarian society. Bent on daily survival, Slovaks knew their success in the fields depended upon forces mightier than themselves. Believing in the direct intervention of God in human affairs, Slovaks appealed to the deity for successful harvests and for the health of their animals as well as themselves. In their religious culture the celebration of the liturgical calendar was closely intertwined with the agricultural seasons of the natural year. For example, the Easter period which marked the Christian celebration of Christ's death also signaled the arrival of spring and the symbolic awakening of the earth for the imminent planting season. Palm Sunday celebrations both welcomed the spring and commemorated Christ's triumphant trip into Jerusalem. During Easter time, Slovaks appealed to the deity for fruitful harvests. On the feast of Saint Mark (April 25) they prayed for rain and favorable growing weather for village crops. Catholic breviaries contained prayers for entreating the Lord throughout the year for changes in the climate that would improve the year's harvest, help the animals, or otherwise benefit the community.[9]

Slovak religion was also a blend of folklore and superstitions.[10] Religious holy days and some saints' feast days were accompanied by rituals as well as church attendance. On saints' feasts Slovaks prayed for a favor legendarily associated with a saint's life or peculiar powers. Individual and communal rituals aimed at protecting the village or its inhabitants were carried out. At times, items thought to bring good fortune or good health were blessed by priests. Ceremonies believed to rid a village of witches or demons or to prevent them from entering the community's confines were conducted. At some feasts the religious significance of the day was subordinate to ceremonial rituals. Indeed, at times customs had nothing apparent to do with the religious meaning of the day. For instance, during the Christmas season, Slovaks followed various rituals that supposedly revealed future spouses, chased away witches, or foretold whether joy or sorrow would befall a family or village during the upcoming year.[11] The religion that permeated the lives of Slovaks was, thus, a religion practiced on various planes. On one level, Catholics and Protestants partook of the sacraments and observed religious feasts dictated by church and state laws. But in their daily lives, religion was guided less by theological doctrines than by a system of beliefs and practices grounded in peasant mystic traditions and affixed to the Christian calendar. The conscious religiosity of Slovaks was evident in their homes. Religious pictures and artifacts hung on the walls of even the poorest Slovak cottages; close by there might be talismans to bring good luck, scare away evil beings, or cure illnesses.[12]

Not all Slovaks, even those of the same religion, practiced in the same way. Variations in rituals, traditions, and some religious ceremonies reflected the regionalism that distinguished northern Hungary's Slovak population. Inhabitants often identified themselves by county, and consequently localisms based on county and region developed. Regionalism was encouraged by the fact that Slovaks spoke one of three distinct dialects: eastern, central, or western. Persons could rather easily identify countrymen by their speech. Slovaks also could often distinguish countrymen by their clothing since differences in dress extended even to the village level. Clothes, especially headdress, revealed a woman's geographical origin as well as her marital status. Peasant costumes could be so distinctive that they simultaneously indicated a person's village and religion. Music, art, and social customs also exhibited regional variations.[13] These distinctions, together with the Hungarian government's Magyarization policies aimed at eradicating cultural pluralism in Hungary, worked against the development of an ethnic identity among Slovaks. In general, Slovaks living in nineteenth-century Hungary were a cultural minority without a sense of separate "peoplehood."[14]

While Slovaks could be distinguished by regional differences, they typically shared a common economic status and backward living conditions. Besides subsistence farmers who owned small plots of land, northern Hungary's classes included cotters, day laborers, and farmhands. Cotters, or cottagers, were usually tradesmen such as shoemakers, weavers, or blacksmiths who owned at least a house and perhaps a "bit of field" but who could not make a living from their land. Day laborers and farmhands most often did not own land and were dependent on regular employment for their daily bread. Even small landowners often needed additional income to subsist.[15] Hence the nature and uncertainty of the Slovak peasant economy required many Slovaks routinely to seek ways to supplement incomes. From at least the mid-eighteenth century on, Slovaks journeyed to other sections of Hungary or nearby countries in search of jobs. Some Slovaks migrated permanently; others sought seasonal work in industry and construction or as farm laborers. In some regions of northern Hungary, the custom of men temporarily leaving their villages to pursue "wandering trades" became a feature of Slovak life. *Drotári* (tinkers) from Trenčin County traveled throughout Hungary and repaired household items and farm implements. Masons from Liptov County did construction work in Budapest. Other Slovaks sold wares. Thus, by the mid-nineteenth century, migration to supplement incomes was an accepted and firmly entrenched custom among Slovaks. And for some Slovak families, seasonal migration had become part of family life and vital to the family economy.[16] Many Slovaks needing jobs, however, would not find them in late nineteenth-century Hungary.

During the latter part of the nineteenth century, Hungary faced severe economic problems. A depression in the 1870s thwarted the government's incipient industrialization programs. The country also suffered an agricultural depression. These economic dislocations were aggravated by demographic factors. As Hungary's population grew, the country's industry could not absorb the labor increase. At the same time, the small landowners of northern Hungary were finding their holdings insufficient to support their larger families. Landless peasants lacked the wherewithal to purchase their own land. Insufficient jobs and low pay for those available caused Hungary's subjects to look elsewhere for employment.[17] Demographic and economic pressures thus combined to create conditions conducive to emigration.

Hungary's economic and social problems coincided with expanding industrialization in the United States that required cheap, unskilled labor. Slovaks, who had traditionally wandered through Europe to find seasonal work, began packing their bags for a much longer journey. This new trip differed in length but not in objective. When Slovaks began coming to the United States in the 1870s, they came *za chlebom*—after bread.

It is not clear how Slovaks first learned of the labor opportunities in the United States. Emily Balch suggested that Slovaks discovered America through Jews who had emigrated earlier.[18] Some contemporaries attributed the early Slovak emigration to steamship and company agents who enticed laborers with promises of high wages and opportunities in the United States.[19] Regardless of how Slovaks first learned about the United States, once immigration was under way less impersonal factors transformed it into a self-generating movement.

Economic forces alone did not govern the Slovak immigration to the United States. Instead, cultural and economic forces combined to shape this migration movement. Initially, for many Slovaks, traveling to America represented a continuation of the tradition of seasonal migration, and they planned to remain only temporarily.[20] As a result, it was common for Slovaks to make several trips between Hungary and America. At least 19 percent of the Slovaks who entered American ports from 1899 to 1910 had been in the United States before.[21] This tendency reinforced the tradition of seasonal migration and thus further strengthened emigration as an acceptable pattern of behavior. Indeed, the importance of the migration tradition is evidenced by the fact that in some areas of northern Hungary persons did not migrate even though the economic, demographic, and social pressures were the same as in regions experiencing emigration.[22]

As immigration to America became a customary practice among Slovaks, family and friendship connections encouraged the movement to spread from village to village. Since Slovaks migrated as well as intermarried between villages, kinship ties could span more than one village.[23] Kinship ties, in turn, encouraged the emigration movement to spread over a wider region that included large numbers of unrelated families.[24] The continued influence of family and friendship ties on Slovak immigration was dramatically demonstrated by the fact that 98.4 percent of the Slovaks entering the United States in 1907 said they were planning to join relatives or friends.[25] As Slovaks increasingly decided to remain in the United States, seasonal sojourners became permanent immigrants and sent for their families or betrothed. In addition, the movement of grown children to America sometimes caused parents to emigrate who might otherwise not have left their homeland.[26]

Because Slovaks were Hungarian citizens, the United States immigration officials initially listed them as "Hungarians" and, therefore, it is difficult to determine how many Slovaks migrated to the United States. Nevertheless, informed observers conclude that Slovaks constituted the majority of Hungary's emigrants before 1900.[27] From 1899, when American officials began enumerating immigrants by nationality instead of by country of origin, to 1914, at least 451,457 Slovaks entered the United States.[28] These statistics do not, however, accurately reflect the number of Slovaks who immigrated to America either temporarily or permanently during this period. The tendency of Slovaks to travel several times between North America and Hungary renders an exact calculation impossible.

Although the number of persons finally choosing to stay in the United States did increase over time, the pendulum motion of Slovak migration continued throughout the prewar era. For every 100 Slovaks who entered the United States between 1908 and 1910, 59 left. These figures include the depression year of 1908, when those leaving America (23,573) actually exceeded those entering (16,170).[29] These drastic fluctuations suggest that a significant number of Slovak immigrants were not committed to staying and, indeed, were quite willing to return to their homeland, especially if they did not have a job and it seemed unlikely they would get one. Some Slovak men who found themselves unable to support their families in the United States sent them back to Hungary while they stayed to earn more money. They intended either to return to their homeland or send for their families when they could afford to support them again.[30]

Securing employment constituted a primary concern for Slovak men and often for single Slovak females, whose number increased as immigration gained momentum. Agents who solicited immigrant labor at ports of entry were only one means that Slovaks just arriving from Hungary had for learning about job opportunities in the United States.[31] As the years passed and the degree and pace of Slovak immigration increased, Slovaks in the United States developed networks, personal and formal, that alerted countrymen to the availability of jobs and helped them obtain employment. These networks built on and reinforced the cultural, economic, and social forces nurturing Slovak emigration.

Slovak newspapers became important sources of information about job opportunities in various regions of the United States. *Slovák v Amerike,* founded in 1889, carried regular "work reports," which contained information about working conditions, wages, and the availability of employment in cities and towns throughout the United States. In 1900, for example, *Slovák v Amerike* observed that work in Pittsburgh was "universally good," while in 1905 the paper warned in bold type: "Do not go to Pittsburgh for work."[32] Other Slovak newspapers, including those published by Slovak fraternal organizations, also carried news about working conditions. Slovak papers reported when new factories would be opening and, consequently, hiring men. Strikes, regardless of whether they involved Slovaks, generally merited coverage in the Slovak press. In addition to work reports or related stories, Slovak newspapers printed readers' letters, which often provided information about employment conditions where they lived.[33]

Slovak newspapers even reached those immigrants who were not subscribers or were perhaps illiterate. Those who lived in boardinghouses shared newspapers and the information in them. Peter Rovnianek recorded that in 1889, when he became editor of the *Amerikánsko-Slovenské Noviny,* he set out to attract a large readership for the paper. In order to get subscribers, Rovnianek and fellow employees personally visited boardinghouses in Pittsburgh and its environs and distributed the newspapers. According to Rovnianek, in some boardinghouses no one could read Slovak, but someone in the house usually bought a Slovak primer. As a result, Rovnianek claimed that when representatives returned to the boardinghouse they found additional subscribers for the paper.[34] Promoters also sent their newspapers to persons they believed could disseminate information. When John Slovensky began printing the Slovak *Bulletin* in 1885, he first distributed it at John Wolf's saloon in Braddock, Pennsylvania. Wolf apparently made it a practice to read the newspaper to his customers. Later, when the *Amerikánsko-Slovenské Noviny* replaced the *Bulletin,* Wolf continued providing this reading service for his patrons.[35]

Slovak newspapers benefited those immigrants already in America who could respond quickly to reports, but Slovaks still in Europe relied on the postal service and on returning countrymen for news. Letters and financial remittances as well as word-of-mouth reports of economic rewards stirred more Slovaks to travel to the United States.[36] Simultaneously, during the latter part of the nineteenth century, Pittsburgh and its environs underwent a period of dynamic industrial growth that required cheap labor. These needs coincided with Slovaks' wants and, consequently, western Pennsylvania became a popular destination for Slovak immigrants.

The first Slovak laborers reportedly came to Pittsburgh in the early 1880s and worked in Allegheny City. They did not work in mills but were employed laying track for the Pennsylvania Railroad. As early as 1880, Andy Kuchar, a fifteen-year-old boy from Šariš County, is recorded as working as a water boy for the railroad.[37] In 1881, three Slovaks from Zemplín County and four from neighboring Šariš arrived in Allegheny City. In 1882, a few more individuals from Zemplín, Šariš, and Abov counties found their way to Allegheny City. In that same year, John Lesniansky, a native of Zemplín County, began working as a "stable boss" for the Pennsylvania Railroad in Allegheny City. He contracted with the company to recruit workers to lay tracks for the railroad. Subsequently, Lesniansky obtained jobs for Slovaks already in America and countrymen in Hungary willing to come to Allegheny and work a twelve-hour day for $1.75.[38]

There is no evidence that John Lesniansky remained permanently in Allegheny City, but his recruiting efforts and the early flow of Zemplín Slovaks made the Manchester–Woods Run section of western Allegheny City a kind of beachhead for future emigration from that county. Records of Saint Gabriel Slovak Catholic Church, which served the Manchester–Woods Run region, show that from 1903 through 1910, 52 percent of the Allegheny Slovaks married at—and 44 percent of those buried from—the church had come from Zemplín County. No other Slovak church in Pittsburgh recorded comparable numbers for Slovaks from Zemplín County.[39]

At the same time, other Slovaks were immigrating to different sections of Pittsburgh. In 1880, Andrew Evanko, a native of Šariš County, settled in the South Side and within a few months sent for his wife and persuaded his brother to immigrate there as well. Slovak immigrants had preceded the Evanko family to the South Side, and during the 1880s more Slovaks moved into that industrial region just south of the Monongahela River. Slovaks who moved to the South Side recalled that at least 150 Slovaks lived in the neighborhood by the end of the 1880s. And over time, the geographic sources of the South Side's Slovak population became quite varied.[40]

A dispersal into different neighborhoods characterized the early Slovak immigration into Pittsburgh. By the early 1890s, Slovaks could be found not only in Woods Run, Manchester, and the South Side, but also in eastern Allegheny City as well as in the industrial region along the southern banks of the Allegheny River and in southeastern Pittsburgh. In 1896, the Pittsburgh Slovak newspaper, *Amerikánsko-Slovenské Noviny,* confirmed that Slovaks were not concentrating in a single section of the metropolitan area. It cited several areas where Slovaks lived and observed that, in addition, some "individuals" were scattered throughout the two cities.[41]

Slovak immigration into Pittsburgh was not, however, haphazard, nor was it governed by purely economic or environmental factors. Since early Slovak immigrants came in search of jobs, finding employment influenced where they lived in the city. Neither Pittsburgh's hilly terrain nor its transit system permitted easy, inexpensive transportation for workingmen.[42] Thus Slovaks wanting to live meagerly and to save money had to settle near where they worked.

But for Slovaks coming later, this consideration was only one factor affecting where they settled. They also tried to live close to countrymen and preferably close to persons from their own villages or neighboring villages in Europe. As a result of this preference, the movement of Slovaks into Pittsburgh was a chain migration.

Although village migrations were evident, the chain migration that characterized the Slovak settlement in Pittsburgh was not simply a migration by villages. Rather, chain migration occurred in three ways: by village, by region, and by county. Regional migration, whereby residents from a cluster of towns and villages moved to Pittsburgh, dominated. Chain migration affected not only the movement of Slovaks to Pittsburgh but influenced their subsequent settlement patterns within the city. Those Slovaks who remained in the same sections of the city continued to link their neighborhoods with Slovak villages. As families, relatives, and countrymen followed the early immigrants, they often moved to the same section of Pittsburgh.[43] This scattering of Slovaks did not portend that they would fail to create ethnic communities. Rather, it was laying the foundation for the emergence of several Slovak neighborhood and church communities in Pittsburgh.

The self-generating nature of the Slovak movement into Pittsburgh was aided by conditions in that city. The availability of work, together with the hiring practices followed by many of Pittsburgh's industries, helped direct and simultaneously encourage Slovak chain migration. Although some Pittsburgh employers may have sent agents to American ports to recruit immigrants, many Pittsburgh factories relied on foremen to hire laborers. These foremen, in turn, relied on their workers as intermediaries to find laborers.[44] At times, if employees agreed to send for their friends or relatives, foremen promised to provide jobs for them. Consequently, the practice of delegating responsibility for hiring workers benefited Slovaks who wanted to help fellow countrymen or family come to the United States. Thus, Slovaks and other immigrant groups came to depend on a system of personal relationships to obtain work.[45]

The relationship between jobs, chain migration, and the choice of destination is dramatically illustrated by an event at Jones and Laughlin Steel in 1901. An explosion at the company's Soho division killed eight Slovaks and injured three others. All of the Slovaks involved had come from five neighboring villages in Užhorod County. Pittsburgh had not been the first destination for some of these men. Three of the victims, all from the same village, had only recently arrived in Pittsburgh after having worked elsewhere in

Pennsylvania. Yet they worked in the same department as country-men from their own or nearby villages who had come to the city before them.[46] It seems that these men did not migrate by chance into Pittsburgh. For these Užhorod natives, family and friendship ties had given direction to successive geographic movements in the United States.

During the 1880s and 1890s, a steady flow of Slovak immigrants moved into Pittsburgh. In 1896, *Amerikánsko-Slovenské Noviny* reported the Slovak population at five to six thousand. This estimate was much too high; the number of Slovak immigrants was probably no more than one-third this amount.[47] The majority of these were men, and nearly all worked in the local factories. In the mid-1890s, the same newspaper indicated that the city's self-employed Slovaks numbered only seven. Besides Peter Rovnianek's ticket and banking services, there was a grocer, a stamp dealer, a tailor, a repairman, a translator, and a saloonkeeper.[48]

Although Slovaks had been immigrating to Pittsburgh since at least 1880, they did not initiate efforts to organize a church until 1894. Dedicated in 1895, this church, Saint Elizabeth's, served all Slovak Catholics in the Pittsburgh metropolitan region. Part of the delay in organizing a church was due to the make-up and the tempo-rary nature of the Slovak immigration. A substantial number of those who came to Pittsburgh were itinerant workers planning to return to Hungary and not concerned about organizing national churches. They were satisfied to attend the city's Czech and Polish Catholic churches. Only a small number of Slovak Lutheran immi-grants migrated to Pittsburgh in the 1890s. Unfortunately, there is no record of where they worshiped before they organized a church in 1904.[49]

During the decade and a half following the dedication of Pitts-burgh's first Slovak Catholic church, Slovaks continued to stream into and out of Pittsburgh. There is no way to determine their num-bers or how many remained. But, over time, some Slovaks did stay and the scattered Slovak settlement areas of the mid-1890s evolved into neighborhood and church communities.

By 1910, Pittsburgh's Slovak population had experienced signifi-cant changes and yet some features remained the same. Although probably an undercount, the 1910 census recorded the city's Slovak population as 5,096; of these persons, 2,780 were foreign-born and the remaining 2,316 were born in the United States of "foreign parentage."[50] While the number of Slovaks had more than doubled since the 1890s, the overwhelming majority of men were still laborers employed in Pittsburgh's factories and mills. Some were still so-journers and had plans to return to their homeland. Others were willing to leave the city if better job opportunities appeared else-where. But some, such as Ferdinand Dvorsky, had decided to remain permanently in the city.

The increased number of Slovak churches represented one of the most noticeable changes for Pittsburgh's Slovaks in the fifteen-year period. By 1910, Pittsburgh's Slovak Lutherans had organized one church and their Roman Catholic countrymen had four parishes in the city. Like the Saint Elizabeth's of the mid-1890s, the newer three Catholic churches were national churches; but unlike the Saint Elizabeth's of early years, these churches were neighborhood institutions that served designated sections of Pittsburgh. The city's Slovak Lutheran church was a national church whose congregation remained dispersed in the metropolitan area. The willingness to establish national churches demonstrated that Slovak immigrants planned to remain in Pittsburgh for a long time. It also demonstrated that they could successfully create stable and permanent institutions even in the wake of the continuing geographic mobility wrought by seasonal migration patterns.

The Slovaks who immigrated to Pittsburgh at the turn of the century had to adapt to an urban, industrial society. This required a number of adjustments, some of them in their religious lives. Slovak immigrants did not simply abandon their superstitious beliefs nor the customs that accompanied many religious feasts. But some traditional prayers, rituals, and even communal worship were no longer relevant in a city where their livelihood was not typically dependent on favorable weather. Nevertheless, religion remained an intrinsic part of Slovak culture. The tenacity of this religious heritage was evidenced by the dogged determination of these immigrants to organize and support national churches. Religious tenacity was only part of the complex interplay of factors that led Slovak immigrants to establish national parishes in Pittsburgh. Forming national churches became part of the broader, ongoing adjustment Slovaks made to their new society. Establishing these churches was also part of the drawing together phase of the Slovak immigration process. This drawing together got under way with the formation of Slovak mutual aid societies.

From Self-Help to Community Development: Slovak Fraternal Societies

EVEN THOUGH the early Slovak immigration into Pittsburgh contained a substantial proportion of temporary laborers, these workers created permanent institutions to cope with the uncertainties of an industrial society. To mitigate the potentially devastating effects of sickness, disability, or death, Slovaks followed the example of other immigrant groups and banded together into mutual aid societies, commonly called fraternals. These societies helped members in the event of economic misfortune or death by providing some financial benefits to the unemployed or bereaved. While establishing fraternal organizations represented an adjustment by Slovaks to an industrial society, these organizations worked to preserve Old World mores regulating social and familial responsibilities. And in a manner akin to premigration communal pressure, the Slovak religious fraternals monitored the religious lives of their members.

From the outset, founders of national Slovak fraternals developed broad goals for their organizations. Ordinary Slovak immigrants, however, were often more pragmatic than these articulate leaders. Laborers viewed the societies as a protection against catastrophes in the workplace and against the economic vicissitudes of a capitalist, industrial economy. But the perceptions that Slovaks had of their fraternals, especially of the religious societies, underwent change. These changing perceptions meant that the functions of religious fraternal organizations did not remain static but rather expanded over time. And, as the Slovak movement into Pittsburgh numbered more permanent immigrants along with transient workers, the fraternal system became a foundation for the development of national churches and Slovak communities.

15

Slovaks in the United States organized both religious and secular fraternal societies. The National Slovak Society, founded in February 1890, was the largest, most influential of the secular organizations. The fraternal's organizers hoped to generate a Slovak ethnic consciousness that would unite Slovaks into a cohesive group. Accordingly, the National Slovak Society welcomed all Slovak Christians, regardless of their denominational affiliation.[1] In contrast, religious fraternals founded by Catholics, Lutherans, and Calvinists limited their membership to Slovaks of a specific religion. In 1890, Father Stephen Furdek and Father Joseph Kossalko cooperated to create the First Catholic Slovak Union, the largest of the religiously oriented Slovak fraternal associations. Father Kossalko, a Slovak Magyarone, which meant he opposed Slovak nationalism, viewed a Catholic society as a way to undermine the secular National Slovak Society.[2] Father Furdek wanted a separate Catholic organization because he feared that as Slovak Catholic immigrants became Americanized, they would convert to Protestantism. He believed a Catholic society would counter this possibility. Hoping to expand the influence of Catholic organizations in the lives of immigrants, Furdek encouraged efforts to establish the First Catholic Slovak Ladies Union in 1892.[3]

Slovak Protestants in the United States followed the lead of their Catholic countrymen. The catalyst for founding a Lutheran association came in part from an article by Father Kossalko in his newspaper, *Zástava* (The Flag). He chided Slovak Lutherans because they lacked their own religious benefit society.[4] Kossalko no doubt hoped to use the strength of Slovak religious identities as a force in his fight with the National Slovak Society, which he detested. His remarks and the model set by their Slovak Catholic countrymen spurred Slovak Lutherans to action. In 1893 they succeeded in consolidating several independent Slovak Lutheran mutual aid societies in the United States into a centralized organization, the Slovak Evangelical Union.[5]

The successful efforts of Slovak Lutherans and Catholics embarrassed some Slovak Calvinists. In 1901, calling for the formation of a Calvinist fraternal society, one Slovak lamented that "every [Slovak] religion has fraternal societies and takes care of themselves; we Calvinists, alone, do not."[6] Certainly to the relief of this Protestant, a few months later Slovak Calvinists followed the path of their Catholic and Lutheran countrymen and established the Slovak Calvinist Union.[7]

Although religious fraternal associations divided Slovak immigrants along denominational lines, these societies had shared goals. Each was committed to insuring that members did not abandon their premigration faith. By dividing Slovaks along religious lines and yet by drawing them together into national organizations, Slovak fraternal societies helped to heighten religious identities and also to encourage the rise of ethnic consciousness among Slovak immigrants.

Both religious and secular fraternals were popular among Slovak immigrants. Until 1898, the National Slovak Society's membership exceeded that of the First Catholic Slovak Union by approximately 1,000. However, by 1902, the First Catholic Slovak Union had surpassed the National Slovak Society's membership by 9,000. The number of persons belonging to the National Slovak Society increased steadily during the next eight years and in 1910, when it began accepting women into membership, it had 36,786 members. In that year, Živena, the secular women's society, had 4,500 members. At the same time, the First Catholic Slovak Union had 32,610 members and its female counterpart numbered approximately 18,000. The combined membership of Protestant male and female societies in 1910 hovered around 10,000 persons.[8]

Despite ideological or religious objectives, Slovak fraternals were primarily insurance societies. Although the amounts varied and changed over time, Slovak male fraternals paid death benefits ranging from three hundred to a thousand dollars. In 1895, the National Slovak Society paid three hundred dollars to workers disabled by accidents. Members forced to miss work because of illness received compensation of five dollars per week.[9] Local lodges also assumed responsibility for the funeral arrangements in the event of a lodge member's death.

Besides providing monetary compensation to members or their families, fraternal societies aided immigrants in their quests for jobs. In addition to work reports published in the fraternal press, the fraternal system itself acted as a communications network. Slovaks who left one locale for another could transfer to a lodge at their new destination. Or a lodge could issue travel letters to members that introduced them and verified that they were in good standing with the organization. Travelers seeking jobs could count on some assistance from other Slovak lodges.[10] Fraternal societies thus served the practical interests of immigrant workers in a foreign and industrial environment.

Slovaks did not model fraternal societies after premigration institutions. These organizations grew out of a combination of conditions encountered in the United States and were part of what became an ongoing adjustment process for Slovak immigrants. As one Slovak fraternalist explained in 1903, "America has trained us [Slovaks] for fraternal life. Our old country is very poor in this sphere and especially the common people, of which our colony [in the United States] consists, have no conception of mutual aid societies."[11] Writing a history of Slovak mutual aid societies formed in the United States before the large national fraternals came into existence, Ignac Gessay speculated that a small minority of Slovak immigrants might have belonged to craft or workers unions in Europe where they could have learned to "a certain degree, the rules of fraternal life."[12] But unions were urban, industrial organizations, while the great majority of Slovak immigrants came from rural, agricultural regions. Moreover, by the early 1880s, the Hungarian government had effectively banned all Slovak organizations as part of its Magyarization program.[13]

Fraternal enthusiasts recognized that lack of familiarity with mutual aid societies hindered Slovak fraternal growth in the United States. "It is true," Father John Liscinsky explained, that "while we lived in the old country, we did not hear about a single [fraternal] society. We came here and life has convinced us that we cannot live without [such] societies." Elaborating on the differences between traditional village life and new circumstances in a foreign country, Liscinsky reminded Slovaks that in Hungary a Slovak woman could rely upon "neighbors with whom she has grown up for help." He pointed out that unfortunately in America Slovaks often did not even know their neighbors.[14] Therefore, Liscinsky was implying that, in order to be prepared for the misfortunes one might encounter, Slovaks had to rely on a new system of mutual aid to replace the communal assistance available in villages or small towns in northern Hungary. In this instance, Liscinsky was directing his appeal to Slovak Catholic women, but inherent in his argument was the recognition that fraternal societies were outgrowths of New World conditions, not merely transplants of premigration institutions.[15]

The appeals that advocates felt compelled to use in order to persuade Slovaks to join fraternals reveal how ordinary Slovak immigrants viewed these societies. During the formative years of the Slovak fraternal movement, the political, cultural, or religious aims of Slovak leaders held little attraction for the Slovak laboring masses. Even the fervid, often idealistic, nationalist, Peter Rovnianek, did not deceive himself into believing that his lofty rhetoric or ideological objectives prompted Slovaks to join his nationalist society. Rovnianek admitted that in order to "interest" the "masses" in the National

Slovak Society, it had to provide them with tangible, practical benefits.[16] He knew Slovak immigrants were, in the main, industrial laborers, not political activists.

The campaigns to attract Slovaks into fraternals further show that these immigrants maintained a concern about personal dignity as defined by their premigration cultural values. Fraternal promoters were fond of pointing out that the societies offered Slovak immigrants more than insurance benefits. They held out the promise of dignified treatment for persons thousands of miles from home, especially in the unfortunate event of death. Revealing the emotional strength of cultural traditions which placed great stress on a proper burial, one Slovak voiced the frightful thought: "Do you think that on this foreign soil anyone besides your close family and the undertaker would come to your funeral if you did not belong to a fraternal society?"[17] His point was clear: if a Slovak immigrant shunned fraternal societies, the dignity of a traditional Slovak burial complete with a cortege of mourners was jeopardized.

The pressure to join a fraternal society differed for the single man compared to the married man. In the case of a debilitating accident, nonfraternalists usually received no monetary compensation to help tide them over. In the event of death, nonfraternalists might have no one to oversee funeral arrangements. But for single men, and especially for young single men, such dangers affected only themselves. Thus Ferdinand Dvorsky probably reflected the attitude of many unmarried Slovak men when he did not join a fraternal immediately upon arriving in Pittsburgh. He lived with a family, friends from his village resided nearby, and, as he said, he was "young and not concerned about insurance."[18]

It was not easy for married men to be unconcerned. It was, after all, familial concerns—a desire to provide a better, more secure life for their families—that had prompted most married Slovaks to leave their homeland. Slovak newspapers routinely reported "sad" incidents of the hardships inflicted upon families, especially widows and young children, when left without death benefits. One Slovak fraternalist unabashedly admitted that he had joined a fraternal because he feared that if he did not and should suddenly die "people would reproach my family" and ask why had "he cared so little about his family that while alive he did not join even one fraternal society."[19] Thus for some Slovak men, belonging to a fraternal was an extension of their familial responsibility.

Slovaks who immigrated to Pittsburgh typically experienced the same fears and felt the same sense of responsibility as other Slovak immigrants in industrial America did. Such feelings certainly spurred Pittsburgh Slovaks to form mutual aid societies. The early history of the city's Slovak fraternal lodges illustrates, however, that these societies were dynamic organizations whose objectives and functions could expand to meet the needs of a changing immigrant population. Over time, Pittsburgh's Slovak fraternals had an impact that went beyond aiding their regular members and that touched the larger Slovak population in the metroplitan area.

Although Slovaks began immigrating to Pittsburgh in the early 1880s, they did not organize a mutual aid society until 1889. Still, this society was among the early groups formed in the United States before the large central organizations came into existence.[20] The creation of this local mutual aid organization exhibited the mix of factors that could prompt the founding of Slovak fraternal societies.

The desire to emulate other ethnic groups acted as a catalyst to organizing a Slovak mutual aid society in Pittsburgh. The precipitating event took place sometime in the mid-1880s. Watching a parade of Czech and Polish fraternalists inspired Slovak spectators waiting to hear mass at Saint Wenceslaus Church. One Slovak onlooker, Martin Slanina, was particularly impressed. In later years, he recalled how he and other Slovaks were "flabbergasted" by the spectacle of fancily dressed fraternalists marching and accompanied by a band.[21] Slanina credited the occasion with prompting his decision to organize a Slovak mutual aid society. As with other early fraternalists, Slanina explained that he had no prior knowledge of fraternal societies. He noted, "we [Slovaks] came from Austria-Hungary. There we did not see such things."[22]

The recognition that other immigrant groups had impressive fraternals pricked Slanina's ethnic pride. He desired such organizations for Slovaks. As Slanina sought more information about their societies from Czech and Polish fraternalists, he became convinced that Slovaks in the Pittsburgh area had to form their own group. He later befriended other Slovaks, including a Slovak member of a Czech fraternal, who cooperated in the endeavor. Their efforts met success in February 1889 when twenty-five men agreed to form a Slovak mutual aid society. Reflecting the religious tradition of seeking saintly protection over their lives, the men named their organization the Society of Saint Michael the Archangel.

The society was not simply a religious or social organization; it was a mutual aid group. The founders established a compensation fund and wrote by-laws governing the dispensing of aid to members. When the First Catholic Slovak Union was created in September

1890, the Saint Michael Society affiliated with it as Branch 2.[23] Just three months after Slanina and his fellow immigrants had formed the Saint Michael Society, Peter Rovnianek succeeded in establishing a secular mutual aid society in Pittsburgh. This success constituted a crucial advance in Rovnianek's push to create the National Slovak Society.[24]

During the next two decades, the number of Slovak fraternal lodges in Pittsburgh and Allegheny City steadily increased. In 1895, the two cities boasted one female and eleven male lodges. By 1915, the total number of such organizations had increased nearly threefold.[25]

Several factors contributed to the Slovak fraternal boom in Pittsburgh. The number of lodges increased in part because some Pittsburgh Slovaks preferred secular lodges while others opted to form religious organizations. The number of lodges naturally grew as the large national secular and religious societies were created. Provincialism also contributed to the growth of Slovak lodges in Pittsburgh; several were started by Slovaks from the same village or village clusters. This practice continued over time as Slovaks from the same village or regions of northern Hungary formed their own branches of national organizations instead of joining an existing lodge.[26]

The increase in lodges further reflected the fact that Slovaks were settling in different sections of Pittsburgh, and each neighborhood had its own fraternal societies. Stefan Fiala, for example, called on Slovaks in the southeastern section of Pittsburgh to support the formation of a branch of the National Slovak Society.[27] In his appeal, he stressed the dangers that constantly lurked in the workplace and poignantly reminded Pittsburgh Slovaks of their moral responsibilities toward their families. Fiala's message must have struck a responsive note. In June 1895 Slovaks did organize a National Slovak Society branch in southeastern Pittsburgh.[28] Thus was added yet another Slovak neighborhood lodge to the growing number of national affiliates in Pittsburgh. The proliferation of fraternal lodges and their location in different parts of Pittsburgh and Allegheny City were early signals that a single area of Slovak concentration, a "little Slovakia," was not in the making in Pittsburgh.

Despite the growing number of Slovak lodges and the continual pleas of fraternal enthusiasts, not all of the city's Slovak immigrants belonged to a fraternal society. In 1895, when Pittsburgh's Slovak population hovered around 2,000, less than 400 Slovak men and women were members of local lodges.[29] In 1910, lodge membership totaled between 1,600 and 1,700; this was probably no more than 50 percent of the city's eligible members.[30]

A number of factors, beyond those expressed by Ferdinand Dvorsky, caused some Pittsburgh Slovak immigrants to shun fraternal societies. Despite the practical reasons for joining a fraternal, belonging to one could pose financial hardships on members. All of the national associations had initiation fees and monthly dues. Slovak fraternalists were also expected to donate to numerous collections instituted by their own society or other national and local Slovak groups.[31] In addition, national societies as well as individual lodges had numerous rules, which, if broken, cost the violator money. The general economic situation could also make it difficult to join or to maintain fraternal membership. According to one Pittsburgh Slovak, bad economic times in 1908 made it extremely difficult to pay fraternal dues.[32] Consequently, some Slovaks may have hesitated to join a fraternal because of the cost. Other Slovaks may have been expelled from a fraternal and decided not to join another. Finally, some Slovaks were simply not convinced of the necessity of joining a mutual aid society. They were used to the tradition of looking to and helping family and friends in the wake of crises. Such immigrants did not accept the arguments that they should substitute an insurance policy for this more traditional and familiar system of extending a helping hand.[33]

Even those Slovaks who joined fraternals did not always remain members. The early records of some Pittsburgh lodges indicate that in general the benefit societies lacked a permanent membership. Moreover, charter members were no more prone to stay in a lodge than new members. In the 1890s, 51 percent of the Slovaks who joined eight of the city's lodges left within five years of their initiation (see table 1). Some members who left transferred to other Pittsburgh lodges. For example, all nine charter members of Branch 97 of the First Catholic Slovak Union had originally been members of that organization's Branch 4. Their membership in Branch 4 and subsequent participation in founding another lodge reveal their support of the mutual aid idea. Nevertheless, by 1900, all of these men had quit Branch 97; one of them was recorded as returning to Branch 4, but there is no evidence that the others joined another Catholic lodge in Pittsburgh. Some Slovaks who left the First Catholic Slovak Union may have joined the National Slovak Society. Others who disappeared from membership rosters returned to Europe; some were expelled; for some, no reason for leaving could be determined. The records also indicate that a few members who withdrew from a lodge subsequently rejoined one or more times. Whether these members remained in the city or left and subse-

Table 1

Membership in Pittsburgh's Slovak Fraternals, ca. 1891–1900

Branch Number	Years	Total Members Joining	Total Members Leaving (no. & % of total)[a]	Total Charter Members	Charter Members Leaving (no. & % of total)[a]
2	1891–1896	153	94 (61%)	67	38 (57%)
4	1891–1895	166	83 (50%)	39	29 (74%)
21	1891–1896	36	17 (47%)	9	5 (56%)
97	1893–1900	35	28 (80%)	9	9 (100%)
159	1894–1900	153	71 (46%)	25	16 (64%)
185	1895–1900	67	24 (36%)	23	12 (52%)
254	1897–1900	41	19 (46%)	24	13 (54%)
3	1892–1893	66	30 (45%)	—	—

Sources: Membership ledgers, branches 2, 4, 21, 97, 159, 185, 254, First Catholic Slovak Union Papers, IHRC. These lists are contained by branch number in five membership ledgers. The ledger containing membership for Branch 50 (Pittsburgh) is missing from the collection. Menoslov [Membership roster], odbor 2–odbor 17, 1892–1894, NSSH.

a. Percentages rounded to the nearest tenth.

quently returned cannot be ascertained. However, not all Slovaks who quit a lodge also left the city.[34]

The rapid turnover in the early membership of Pittsburgh's Slovak fraternal societies in the 1890s did not cause these ethnic institutions to collapse. Although members often drifted out of the lodges, new members were almost constantly being initiated. The turnover rates suggest that, in the early years of the Slovak immigration into Pittsburgh and even later, the city's Slovak fraternals functioned as tide-over societies for both transients and permanent immigrants. The important benefits these societies provided obviously helped them survive the constant, almost dizzying, changes in their membership. Although they could not be described as offering "a place for everyone," these societies had an impact on Slovak community development that numbers alone cannot convey.[35]

Pittsburgh's Slovak fraternals functioned on different yet related levels. They acted as mutual aid societies responsive to the needs of their subscribing members. On this level, fraternals provided Slovaks living in an industrial society with some of the security of village life. However, on another plane, Slovak fraternals became social organizations whose activities touched more than the lives of their own members. Here they offered the conviviality and social benefits of village life as they helped bring Slovak immigrants together in an urban environment.

The chief concern of Pittsburgh's Slovak fraternals was mutual aid. The national organizations had rules governing the dispensation of death and disability benefits, and Pittsburgh's lodges tried to comply with these guidelines. In 1891 Branch 2 of the First Catholic Slovak Union appointed a "committee for the sick" to visit lodge brothers and to determine the validity of their claims. Calls by these committeemen had a dual purpose: they combined the requirement of verifying claims with the compassionate action of visiting sick countrymen who might otherwise have suffered alone.[36] Lodges did maintain some freedom in granting small financial aid and, consequently, members needing short-term or immediate assistance could go directly to their lodge brothers.[37] The by-laws of the Society of Saint Michael the Archangel, for example, had provisions for making loans to members. The decision to lend money was at the discretion of the lodge and dependent upon funds in its treasury.[38] Occasionally local lodges offered assistance to needy immigrants even though such aid was not stipulated in fraternal by-laws. In 1901, a Pittsburgh branch of the First Catholic Slovak Union held a dance to raise money for a Slovak who had lost his hand in an accident.[39] In

Europe, one's family or fellow villagers might have helped someone who suffered such a fate; in Pittsburgh, Slovaks could turn to fraternal societies.

Slovak fraternalists also saw to it that their deceased brothers and sisters received Christian burials reminiscent of the village burial ceremonies. The regulations of both secular and religious organizations stipulated that all members, properly adorned with the association's funeral badge, had to march in a fellow lodge member's funeral. Pittsburgh's lodges obeyed this dictate. In 1900, the First Catholic Slovak Union's Branch 50 went so far as to rule that all members had to attend their lodge brothers' funerals even if it meant losing a day's work.[40] The membership clearly decided that even the necessity of earning money was no excuse for shirking one's traditional moral and now fraternal obligation. Branch 50's rules assured members that, in the event of death, their funeral cortege would include more than their families and the undertaker. As the number of Slovak lodges increased in Pittsburgh, it was not uncommon for more than one lodge to participate in a funeral procession. In several instances, local branches of different Slovak organizations attended a single funeral.[41]

Pittsburgh's Slovak fraternals offered Slovaks more than economic benefits and the promise of a dignified funeral. Lodges quickly evolved into social organizations whose activities extended beyond lodge memberships. These fraternal activities permit a further, even if obscured, glimpse into early social life among Slovak immigrants.

Slovak lodges sponsored dances and other events that typically had social and monetary goals. Although members paid monthly dues with a portion designated for the local treasury, individual branches needed additional money to bolster their coffers. Fundraising events became a means of lessening financial burdens on members. The National Slovak Society also used socials to garner money for Slovak "nationalist causes" aimed at helping Slovaks who opposed the Hungarian government's Magyarization policies. Thus socials sponsored by fraternals became typical occurrences in Pittsburgh, especially in the 1890s. Except during Lent, Slovak newspapers regularly carried notices announcing upcoming dances or picnics and encouraging all Slovaks in the area to attend.[42] For those who did participate, these activities offered relief from the drudgery of the mills or the monotony of being alone and perhaps not seeing family and friends as routinely as they had in Europe. Fraternal events also drew together Slovaks who lived in different parts of the area and who otherwise would have remained unaware of their fellow countrymen in the city. By sponsoring social activities, even if to raise money for the lodge, Slovak fraternals were actually expanding their functions. They were evolving from mutual benefit societies into organizations that also promoted social contact among the larger body of Slovak immigrants in the "Steel City" and its environs.

Pittsburgh's fraternals did more than encourage Slovaks to socialize with one another. Because Slovak fraternalists routinely participated in interlodge social events, these beneficial organizations also worked to bring area lodges together into a cooperative network. On special occasions such as anniversaries, flag blessings, or socials, lodges often sent invitations to other Slovak lodges to join in the festivities. Upon receiving such invitations, members usually voted on whether they should accept or reject the invitation and whether to make attendance mandatory. When a lodge accepted, members generally met at a designated place and then proceeded to the function together, wearing badges identifying their local.[43]

Pittsburgh's Slovak religious, and occasionally secular societies, also participated in ceremonies that accompanied the laying of church cornerstones, church dedications, or other religious celebrations. These activities were not limited to the immediate Pittsburgh metropolitan area; at times Pittsburgh's lodge members traveled en masse to nearby towns.[44] Indeed, in 1895, the Saint Michael Society was unable to attend ceremonies held by a Catholic church in Pittsburgh because the lodge had previously agreed to take part in functions being held in Braddock. In September, the lodge did attend celebrations arranged by the Pittsburgh church and fined its members who failed to come.[45]

In a variety of ways, the large national Slovak organizations acted as nexuses connecting the local Slovak lodges in the Pittsburgh area. Through the nationals and their newspapers, which regularly published the addresses of local lodges as well as invitations to the events they sponsored, Pittsburgh's Slovak lodges developed and maintained contact with countrymen living in the metropolitan area and in the nearby region. The expectation that local fraternal groups would participate in functions held by affiliated lodges helped strengthen the ties among them. Through the fraternal system, Pittsburgh's lodges became part of a larger network that extended beyond their immediate neighborhoods and perhaps past their parochial interests.

The fraternal system, then, helped bring Slovaks into contact with countrymen who not only lived elsewhere in the Pittsburgh area but who had emigrated from different regions of northern

Hungary. In this way, Slovak fraternals helped encourage a "fellow-feeling" among immigrants who had come to the United States with strong provincial identities and had settled in different parts of Pittsburgh.[46] In 1894, this feeling took on added significance for Pittsburgh's Slovak Catholics. At their February meeting, the members of Branch 2 of the First Catholic Slovak Union came to the conclusion that "enough Slovaks" lived in the Pittsburgh area that "it would be good if there were a Slovak church" in the city. They agreed to contact other Slovak lodges in Pittsburgh to enlist their support for founding a Slovak Catholic church.[47] In the following months, fraternalists assumed leadership in drawing Slovak Catholic immigrants together to organize a national church.

By taking the initiative to found a church, Branch 2 was helping to expand further the scope of fraternal activities. This expansion had been taking place almost step by step in the early 1890s. At the outset, the major emphasis of Pittsburgh's Slovak lodges had been the welfare of their members. Attempting to raise money to help members, Slovak mutual aid societies took on an additional role as sponsors of social activities. These fund-raising activities did reach out to a larger segment of Slovak immigrants. Nevertheless, in the early 1890s the influence of fraternal societies on the Slovak population in the Pittsburgh area had been rather limited. In initiating efforts to establish a church, Branch 2 and the lodges that cooperated with it assumed a still more enhanced role as the promoters of institutional and community development among Slovak immigrants.

By organizing a church, these Slovak fraternalists were also adjusting to a culturally diverse society and establishing a means to facilitate the preservation of faith among Slovak Catholic immigrants. Pittsburgh's Slovak Lutheran fraternalists would follow a course similar to their Catholic countrymen and take the lead in organizing a national church. Thus fraternal societies, designed to help Slovaks cope with the uncertainties of an industrial society, became forces for preserving religious heritages by promoting the transplanting of a premigration institution—the church.[48]

Creating Neighborhood Institutions:
Pittsburgh's Slovak Catholic Churches

3 THE CALL for a church by Branch 2 of the First Catholic Slovak Union ushered in an era of Slovak Catholic church formation in Pittsburgh. This era witnessed first the creation of a Slovak mother church, Saint Elizabeth's, as a citywide institution and then its decline with the emergence of Slovak neighborhood churches. These churches grew out of a deep-seated premigration religiosity. At the same time, they were the products of Slovak migration patterns and of Slovak adjustment to an urban, ethnically diverse, society.

Catholic church law dictated that establishing a church required the permission of a diocese's bishop. Therefore, founding churches brought Slovak immigrants into direct contact with Pittsburgh's diocesan hierarchy. Similar, indeed mutual, goals governed relations between these Catholic immigrants and Pittsburgh's Catholic church officials. In essence, Slovak Catholics wanted to continue practicing their homeland faith, and Catholic church leaders wanted to keep all Catholic immigrants within the established Catholic church structure. Thus preservation of faith became an underlying theme influencing relations between Slovaks and their religious leaders. Ultimately, the objective of keeping immigrants within the established Catholic church structure worked to the advantage of assertive Slovak lay Catholics who wanted national churches.

Slovak Catholics who immigrated to Pittsburgh in the 1880s and 1890s found that the city contained a rather large number of Catholics. In 1890, Catholics accounted for nearly 24 percent of Pittsburgh's inhabitants and approximately 13 percent of the population 28 of Allegheny City. The two cities had over fifty churches to serve these Catholics.[1] Since the universal language of Roman Catholic services was Latin, Slovaks could find places to attend holy day and Sunday worship even if they did not understand the sermons, which were in the vernacular of the parish. Slovaks and the Pittsburgh diocese's other Catholics were led by "Irish" bishops. From 1889 to 1904, the Irish-born Richard Phelan served as Pittsburgh's bishop. Phelan became ill, and in 1903 Regis Canevin, the son of Irish immigrants, was appointed coadjutor bishop and took care of the daily administration of the diocese. When Phelan died in 1904, Canevin became the Pittsburgh diocese's first American-born bishop, serving until his retirement in 1921.[2]

During the Phelan and Canevin episcopates, the Pittsburgh diocese in general and Pittsburgh in particular underwent dramatic change. The influx of southern and eastern European immigrants helped swell the diocese's Catholic population and added to its ethnic diversity. In 1890, Pittsburgh claimed a Catholic population of 70,410; by 1906, the total reached 150,545.[3] The "new immigration" concerned diocesan spokesmen. Indeed, the diocese's official newspaper, the *Pittsburgh Catholic*, at times editorialized in favor of curbing immigration into the United States. Nevertheless, Catholic churchmen were acutely aware that nativism and anti-Catholicism could act as mutually reinforcing sentiments.[4] Thus Catholic church leaders found themselves in an uncomfortable situation. On one hand, aware that contemporary xenophobia might intensify the anti-Catholicism in the country, they were forced to try to dispel charges that the Catholic church was a foreign institution. On the other hand, the fear of leakage compelled the bishops, and especially Regis Canevin, to work to keep the foreign-born in the Catholic fold.[5] Pittsburgh's Catholic hierarchy saw the establishment of immigrant churches and Catholic organizations as a means for preserving Catholicism among European immigrants.

The formation of "Catholic" organizations even before the new immigrants came to the United States helped pave the way for a favorable response by Pittsburgh's diocesan officials to ethnic societies. Catholic insurance societies had been created in the United States by the late 1860s. Many of these associations were, in fact, ethnic fraternals as well as "Catholic" organizations.[6] Pittsburgh's Catholic hierarchy viewed such associations as counterforces to the various secret societies being formed at the turn of the century.[7] Moreover, in the wake of the Cahensly controversy, which embarrassed the Catholic church in the early 1890s, Pittsburgh's Catholic spokesmen took pains to single out and praise German Catholic groups.[8]

While America's Catholic church leaders rejected allegations made by Peter Paul Cahensly and his supporters that the American church had suffered huge membership losses, these leaders nevertheless feared that such losses might occur. Specifically, some Catholic leaders feared that the newcomers might succumb to the conversion efforts of Protestant denominations.[9]

Addressing the ongoing issue of keeping immigrants faithful, a Catholic spokesman in the 1910 commemorative issue of the *Pittsburgh Catholic* insisted that one way to forestall this loss of faith came from within the immigrant populations. Eventually, he argued, immigrant communities would wither away; it was then the Catholic church would face its greatest threat. Because, he said, "when the colony begins to disintegrate, when its families and individuals begin to intermingle with the rest of the population, then will come the loss of faith, unless we are prepared to prevent it." He reasoned that "these nationalities are all alive to the importance and benefits of organization. Let us take them in among us by their societies. In this way they will be kept in constant touch with us and we with them, learning our national and religious life, and preventing them from becoming the prey of proselytizers."[10]

The First Catholic Slovak Union thus met a warm reception in the Pittsburgh diocese. When the fraternal held its 1895 convention in Braddock, located in the Pittsburgh diocese, Bishop Phelan presided at the opening ceremonies and addressed the convention.[11] The fraternal expressed its gratitude by subsequently making Phelan an honorary member and presenting him with an embossed copy of the convention's resolutions.[12] The *Pittsburgh Catholic* enthusiastically described the convention and even took the opportunity to confront nativist feelings among the diocese's native-born Catholics, reminding them that they were the descendants of immigrants and urging them not to snub Slovaks as "foreigners." Catholics must, in fact, "take hand of hand with these good Slovak Catholics, make them, as they should be, one with us."[13]

Bishop Canevin continued Phelan's policy of sanctioning Slovak organizations when, in 1913, he became a "protector" of the newly founded Slovak Catholic Federation. Canevin approved of the federation's goal of "cementing the bonds of fraternal union among Slovak Catholics and the Catholic Societies of this country."[14] Besides trying to bring Slovak organizations into the mainstream of American Catholic societies, the federation energetically labored to prevent Slovak Catholics from abandoning their faith.[15]

Pittsburgh's Catholic church hierarchy had good reason to look with favor upon Slovak Catholic societies, especially the First Catholic Slovak Union and the First Catholic Slovak Ladies Union. From their outset, they worked diligently to keep Slovaks faithful to their religion. An objective of the Ladies Union also was to enlist women in this battle to preserve the faith. As one Slovak priest, reflecting on the twenty-year history of the Ladies Union, noted, "we need to have Catholic societies for our women, we want to have mothers faithful to God."[16] By logical extension, these faithful mothers would instill a fidelity to Catholicism in their children.

The First Catholic Slovak Union attempted to regulate the religious lives of its members through rules governing membership. In order to join the fraternal, a Slovak had to submit an application signed by a priest affirming that the prospective member was a Catholic in good standing.[17] Each lodge had the responsibility of insuring that members regularly performed prescribed religious duties. The First Catholic Slovak Union also used its newspaper, *Jednota,* and its yearly almanac, the *Kalendár,* to educate Slovak immigrants about the differences between church law and practices in the United States and those followed in Hungary.[18] The fraternal's press further functioned as a means of communication between the American Catholic church hierarchy and Slovak Catholics. For example, in 1910 *Jednota* published a pastoral letter by Bishop Canevin that explained rules and procedures governing Catholic marriages in the Pittsburgh diocese.[19]

The First Catholic Slovak Union also staunchly supported America's Catholic church hierarchy in its bid to maintain absolute authority in church matters. Through its publications, the fraternal defended the extensive authority of American bishops within their respective dioceses and admonished Slovak Catholics to obey their prelates in all religious matters.[20] It also upheld a bishop's right to hold church property as a trustee and defended this practice as vitally necessary in the United States.[21] It denounced independent Catholic churches as "anarchy"[22] and suspended any member who associated with such a schismatic church.[23] To remain a member of the First Catholic Slovak Union, loyalty to one's bishop was, in fact, more important than loyal payment of fraternal dues. Thus in the Catholic church's campaign to keep immigrants loyal Catholics, the First Catholic Slovak Union and its female counterpart functioned as weapons against Protestant missionary efforts and as champions of America's Catholic church hierarchy.

However, based on membership statistics, the First Catholic Slovak Union monitored the religious lives of perhaps less than 25 percent of the Slovak Catholics who lived either permanently or temporarily in Pittsburgh in the mid-1890s. By venturing to establish a Slovak church, Branch 2 (the Saint Michael Society) was extending the fraternal's influence among the city's Slovak population. Moreover, by creating the means for Slovak Catholic immigrants to practice their religion and thus promoting Slovak fidelity to Catholicism, the lodge was functioning in a manner envisioned by some founders of the First Catholic Slovak Union.

Although Slovaks had been immigrating to Pittsburgh for nearly fifteen years, there is no evidence that Slovak Catholics attempted to organize a national parish there before 1894. In the early 1890s, members of the Saint Michael Society were content to attend Saint Wenceslaus Church and even contributed money to this Czech church.[24] By February 1894, however, they were no longer satisfied with relying on Saint Wenceslaus's. This change of attitude did not result from ill feelings toward the Saint Wenceslaus parish or its pastor. Rather, the lodge members' decision to act was grounded in their own perceptions of Pittsburgh's Slovak Catholic population and its needs. The call for a church signaled their awareness that changes had taken place in the character of the Slovak immigration into the "Steel City." By 1894, a large number of Slovaks had not only immigrated to Pittsburgh but, more important, a segment was remaining.

To succeed in forming a church, the Saint Michael Society needed to draw together the Slovaks who had settled in different quarters of Pittsburgh. The fraternal network provided the means to achieve this. In April 1894, at the urging of branches 2 and 4 of the First Catholic Slovak Union, representatives of Slovak lodges throughout the Pittsburgh metropolitan area met to discuss plans for a church.[25] Participation was not limited to Slovak Catholics affiliated with the First Catholic Slovak Union. Peter Rovnianek, who was a nationalist often embroiled in disagreements with the national leadership of the First Catholic Slovak Union, attended the meeting. Although no longer a practicing Catholic, Rovnianek was even elected president of this gathering and was offered but declined the nomination as permanent head of the five-member Church Committee elected to oversee subsequent planning efforts.[26] Rovnianek's participation suggests that he envisioned a national church as one means of uniting area Slovaks and perhaps of nurturing the Slovak nationalism he so ardently espoused.

Besides electing committees to direct the organizing effort and find a suitable site for the church, the meeting established procedures for mobilizing financial support for the venture. It elected sixteen representatives from different sections of the metropolitan region and charged them with collecting money from Slovaks living in their respective neighborhoods.[27] Through these personal solicitations, Slovak Catholics throughout the Pittsburgh area would be actively brought into the effort.

The Slovaks who joined in the early plans to organize a church were similar in ways beyond their shared desire for a place of worship. The similarities flowed from their fraternal affiliations and economic status. The endeavor was led by Slovak laborers, not businessmen–entrepreneurs. Seven of the seventeen men nominated or elected to a committee post can be identified by occupation. Only two, including Peter Rovnianek, were businessmen. A third man was listed in the city directories as the secretary to the National Slovak Society. If that was his full-time occupation, he could perhaps be called something of a businessman but it is just as accurate to call him a salaried clerk. The four other men whose occupations could be identified were listed in the 1894 city directory as laborers.[28] Therefore, less than half of the committee nominees whose occupations can be determined were businessmen. Since the remaining ten men were not listed in the city directories, they were probably laborers too.[29]

While church organizers were not businessmen, they were fraternal members. Sixteen of the seventeen men considered for a committee post were current members of a local Slovak lodge. The majority belonged to the First Catholic Slovak Union, but three were affiliated with the National Slovak Society. Since the meeting was sponsored by fraternal societies that had invited members of other fraternal societies, it is not surprising that fraternalists dominated the venture. However, those involved shared characteristics beyond their affiliation with a Slovak lodge and their status as laborers. Nine men, again including Rovnianek, were charter members of their lodges and had been in Pittsburgh three years or longer. The evidence strongly suggests that the Slovaks chosen to represent their lodges were men who had lived a comparatively long time in Pittsburgh and had gained prominence through their fraternal activities.[30]

In addition, the men nominated for a church committee position or elected as collectors were older than the average Slovak Catholic fraternalist. In February 1894, 48 percent of the eighty-five men who belonged to four of the five Slovak Catholic lodges in Pittsburgh were between the ages of eighteen and twenty-nine. Yet this age group represented less than 28 percent of the persons considered for a committee post. Taken as a whole, 65 percent of the men nominated to the various committees and chosen as collectors were over thirty years of age.[31]

There is, unfortunately, no available information regarding the marital status of these early lay church leaders. Nor do records reveal whether the families of the married men were in Europe or in Pittsburgh. Still, the available evidence suggests that the prime movers behind the early organizing efforts for a Slovak church in Pittsburgh were older men, lodge members, and typically laborers, who probably believed they would remain permanently in the city. Through interlodge activities these long-time members, and even recently initiated fraternalists, became aware of their countrymen and most likely of their growing numbers in the Pittsburgh region. This awareness caused them to conclude in 1894 that enough Slovaks lived in the area that it would "be good" as well as possible to organize a national parish.

Forming a national church meant that these Slovaks would have to fit into the established structure of the Pittsburgh diocese. So, with preliminary arrangements settled, the organizers needed Bishop Phelan's permission to proceed with their plans. After the organizational meeting, the committeemen approached Phelan with their request. The prelate immediately consented and gave his approval for them to continue looking for a suitable church site.[32] The bishop did not hesitate to sanction this national church even though his decision encouraged ethnic pluralism among Catholics in his diocese. For Phelan the vital point was that establishing a Slovak church increased the likelihood that Slovak Catholics would remain faithful to the Catholic church.

Recognizing the bishop's authority did not require any serious adjustment by Slovak Catholics. There was no patriarch in the United States, but the administrative format of the American Catholic church was essentially the same as what these immigrants had known in their homeland. In both countries, bishops exercised authority over Catholics and church affairs in their respective dioceses. To organize a church that was a legitimate part of the universal Catholic church, the founders had to and did accept Bishop Phelan's authority. Indeed, it appears that obtaining the bishop's support was more than obligatory deference. His sanction was viewed as vital to convince wary or hesitant Slovaks to support the effort. In subsequent appeals for funds, the Church Committee listed the various collectors' names and assured their fellow countrymen that these men were collecting money "with the bishop's permission."[33]

While the bishop gave his approval for Slovaks to establish a church and kept watch over their efforts, he did not offer any finan-cial assistance. Catholic parishes in the United States, unlike those in Hungary, had to be completely self-supporting. Hence, even though Bishop Phelan's acquiescence was a prerequisite for founding a na-tional church, it did not guarantee the success nor subsequent survi-val of the proposed church. Slovak immigrants had to rely on their own resources to pay for their church. The selection of lay collectors at the first organizational meeting indicated that church founders realized they had to devise means to solicit funds from the Slovak population. But the Church Committee also knew that the execution of its plans depended upon more than the personal contacts the church collectors could make. Success rested on enlisting widespread support from Slovak Catholic immigrants in the whole area. There-fore, the committee began sponsoring fund-raising events and using the Slovak press to reach area Slovaks.

Fund-raising events became early features of Slovak Catholic par-ish life. The committee scheduled the "first big church ball" for November 1894. In advertising the dance, the committee invited National Slovak Society lodges as well as Slovak Catholic organiza-tions to participate. Hoping to heighten support for the endeavor, the advertisement stressed that the new church would serve Pitts-burgh, Allegheny City, and the surrounding areas.[34] The founders, perhaps almost unconsciously, realized that they had to create a new sense of community among Slovaks from different regions of north-ern Hungary. Successfully creating this new sense of community depended upon nurturing a mutual interest in and a shared obliga-tion toward a national church.

Subsequent appeals for money reiterated the theme that the pro-posed church would serve the entire metropolitan area, not a par-ticular section of the city. At a general meeting held in June 1894, the participants chose an abandoned Polish church on Penn Avenue as the future Slovak church. Several factors made it a desirable choice. First, it was cheaper than the other site submitted to the meeting for consideration. Second, the bishop apparently favored it.[35] Finally, a Penn Avenue location had the advantage of being centrally situated among the city's Slovak settlement areas. One pub-lished appeal for money noted that the site selected was recognized as "the most convenient because it is located in the middle of the city and near to all Slovaks."[36] Actually, the church would be several miles from where some Slovak Catholics were living but, given the dispersed nature of the area's Slovak population, the claim that it was centrally placed had merit. The founders realized, as presumably the city's other Slovak Catholic immigrants did, that Saint Elizabeth Church would not be a neighborhood institution. It was to be a national church that would draw Slovak Catholic immigrants into a parish, but not a neighborhood community.

As the movement to form a Slovak church gained momentum, lay involvement increased. This extended participation went beyond assuming financial responsibilities. Saint Elizabeth's founders knew that, without a Slovak priest, Saint Elizabeth's might fail to become a "Slovak" church, and consequently they became involved in the search for a pastor. A priest could not assume the pastorship without Bishop Phelan's approval, but these lay Catholics did not feel this requirement prevented them from presenting him with a candidate.[37] They wrote to priests in Hungary and to at least one in the United States. By December 1894, their inquiries had netted no positive results. Finally, a committee of lay persons went to nearby Mount Pleasant and on behalf of Pittsburgh's Slovak Catholics asked Father Coloman Gasparik to come to Pittsburgh. Gasparik, who reportedly was experiencing difficulties with his parish, indicated his willingness to become Saint Elizabeth's pastor. The Church Committee then petitioned the bishop to transfer Gasparik to the fledgling Pittsburgh congregation.[38] Phelan complied, and in April 1895 Gasparik moved to Pittsburgh, where he remained pastor of Saint Elizabeth Church until his death in 1939.[39]

Assuredly reflecting the attitudes of Pittsburgh's diocesan officials, the *Pittsburgh Catholic* expressed genuine pleasure with the formation of the Slovak parish. Announcing Gasparik's transfer, the paper exuberantly reported that the "progress" of Catholicism "is conspicuously marked in this diocese by the steady increase of churches to accom[m]odate the faithful."[40] By establishing a church, Slovak Catholic immigrants had demonstrated a strong loyalty to their religion. Pittsburgh's Catholic church hierarchy welcomed such loyalty among the foreign-born.

The lay initiative responsible for establishing Pittsburgh's first Slovak Catholic church revealed the deep religiosity of the city's Slovak Catholic immigrants. But for some articulate Slovaks, a Slovak church had a significance beyond its clearly religious function. Announcements for the church's dedication in October 1895 made blatant appeals to ethnic pride. In a notice published in Pittsburgh's Slovak newspaper, the Church Committee invited "all Slovak organizations" in the Pittsburgh area to participate in the dedication ceremonies. Seeking a display of unity, the committee stated that branches of the secular National Slovak Society as well as the First

Catholic Slovak Union were welcome. The committee pleaded for a large turnout for the parade through the city's major streets. It admonished Slovaks to make the dedication a memorable day in the life of Pittsburgh's Slovak "colony" as well as in the city's history. According to the Church Committee, the church dedication offered an opportunity for Slovaks to demonstrate that "we are an educated people [and] we deserve respect."[41]

Organizing Saint Elizabeth Church was certainly indicative of the development of fellowship among immigrants from different regions of northern Hungary. However, even though the emergence of ethnic consciousness is hard to gauge, the establishment of a church in the mid-1890s did not represent the development of a vocal political or even cultural nationalism among Pittsburgh's Slovak immigrants. They accepted, for example, with no registered complaints, the bishop's decision that the church should be called Saint Elizabeth of Hungary.[42] Naming a Slovak church after a Hungarian saint went directly counter to the sentiments of Slovak nationalists who insisted that Slovaks disassociate themselves from the "Magyar" culture and assert a separate cultural identity as Slovaks.

As its founders had hoped, Saint Elizabeth's did succeed in drawing a large number of Slovak Catholics in the metropolitan area into a parish community. From 1895 to 1902, the church boasted a membership ranging from 2,500 to 3,500 persons, including 230 to 479 families. Not all of Saint Elizabeth's parishioners were Slovak; nevertheless, the majority were, and during the first several years of the church's existence its congregation grew. In 1903, however, the number of families belonging to Saint Elizabeth's plummeted to 189 with the total parish membership reaching only 892.[43] Slovaks were not forsaking their Catholic faith but they were abandoning Saint Elizabeth's for neighborhood churches. The church that had brought a large number of Slovak immigrants together into one congregation was falling victim to geographical divisions created by Slovak chain migrations.

The creation of Saint Elizabeth Church had not altered Slovak settlement patterns. After 1895, Slovak immigrants continued to settle in neighborhoods where their village countrymen and families lived. The growing Slovak population in neighborhoods located some distance from Saint Elizabeth's caused Slovaks in these quarters to view themselves as a separate entity whose religious needs would be more conveniently met by a church in their locale.

The shortcomings of Saint Elizabeth's location soon became apparent. Parishioners who lived south of the Monongahela River or in western Allegheny City had to travel several miles to church; many had to rely on streetcars. These trips posed an inconvenience, particularly for parents with newborn infants to be christened. While in Hungary some Slovaks may have walked to nearby villages to attend church,[44] traveling several miles through Pittsburgh's dirty, hilly streets was a real hardship, especially when forced to pay carfare for themselves and their families. Some Slovaks solved these problems by attending a church near their homes and turning to Saint Elizabeth's only when necessary, for example, to make their yearly confession.

Over time, Saint Elizabeth's was increasingly unable to meet the needs of those who sought the services of a church even on a limited basis. At Easter time parishioners complained that, after having journeyed to the church, they were unable to make their yearly confession because there were too many people ahead of them.[45] In such instances, Saint Elizabeth's was actually hindering rather than facilitating the ability of Slovak immigrants to fulfill their religious duties. Requesting an assistant pastor or enlarging the church building was not the solution. Because it was a central church, Saint Elizabeth's could not adjust effectively to the fact that Slovak immigrants persisted in settling in several Pittsburgh neighborhoods. The inability of Saint Elizabeth's to cope with the increasing population reinforced the perception of some Slovaks that they would be better served by breaking with the mother church and organizing neighborhood parishes.

Within fifteen years after Saint Elizabeth Church was dedicated, three more Slovak Catholic parishes were successfully organized in the area once served by the Penn Avenue church. Two of these churches were created just eight years after Father Gasparik arrived to take care of Pittsburgh's Slovak Catholic immigrants. One parish, Saint Gabriel's, was located in Woods Run in western Allegheny City; the other, Saint Matthew's, was situated in Pittsburgh's South Side. The formation of these churches resembled the organizing efforts for Saint Elizabeth Church. Slovak fraternalists led the endeavors, general meetings were held, and then the bishop was consulted. The creation of these two parishes and of the third, in Frankstown, however, illustrates the different kinds of pressure that immigrants could exert on Pittsburgh's diocesan officials. At times, bishops could not base their decisions regarding whether to approve an ethnic church solely on administrative criteria or on a philosophical position concerning the efficacy of national churches. Bishops had to contend with the forces within an immigrant community that stimulated church formation.

By early autumn 1902, a movement was under way to organize a Slovak parish in the South Side. Because Slovaks lived in different parts of the South Side, this entailed bringing Slovaks together in a way resembling that of earlier efforts to create Saint Elizabeth's. The venture was simply undertaken on a neighborhood instead of a citywide scale. On September 1, 1902, some South Side Slovaks convened to discuss the possibility of establishing a Slovak parish. One reporter claimed over a hundred people attended the meeting. According to this man, these Slovaks specifically cited the distance to Saint Elizabeth's as the reason they wanted a church in their area.[46] While it is not clear exactly who called the meeting, soon after it was held, the South Side's Slovak Catholic lodges took an active role in the endeavor. On October 5, Branch 159 of the First Catholic Slovak Union, whose members lived primarily in the northeastern section of the South Side, approached its fellow lodge, Branch 50, and asked its members to cooperate in plans for a church. Branch 159 had already taken a census of Slovaks in the area where its members resided and requested that Branch 50 do the same for the region inhabited by its members. Branch 50 responded favorably by appointing a committee to determine "whether we can establish a [Slovak] parish in the South Side or not."[47] Branch 50 subsequently chose a permanent committee charged with representing the lodge at future planning meetings for the church.[48]

Clearly, members of branches 159 and 50 of the First Catholic Slovak Union as well as other Slovaks living in the South Side had come to a conclusion similar to that of Branch 2's members in 1894. They decided that enough Slovak Catholics lived in their neighborhood to justify a church. There were at least thirteen Catholic churches in the South Side, but with Saint Elizabeth's as a model, South Side Slovaks definitely preferred a separate national church.[49]

The process of founding the South Side's Slovak church advanced smoothly. Besides setting up committees to supervise the effort, South Side Slovaks reportedly sought the assistance of a Slovak priest in nearby Homestead to act as their intermediary with the bishop. By February 1903, the bishop had approved the plans, a church site had been determined, and a Slovak pastor was appointed to the congregation.[50] A church building was not completed until 1906 and, in the meantime, services were held at various locations in the South Side.[51] Having no permanent building did not deter Slovak Catholic immigrants from joining Saint Matthew's, the name the congregation selected for its future church. In 1903, Saint Matthew's claimed a congregation of 250 families. This estimate was most likely high; the

165 families recorded in 1905 probably more accurately reflected the size of the parish.[52] Even without a church building, Saint Matthew's family membership nearly equaled that of the longer established Saint Elizabeth Church.

The decline of the mother church was further hastened by the reluctance of Slovak Catholic immigrants in Woods Run, in western Allegheny City, to travel to Penn Avenue for religious services. The establishment of a Slovak church in Woods Run, however, was more complicated than in the South Side. As early as 1900, Slovak Catholics residing in Woods Run were attempting to organize a Slovak parish. Their efforts did not enjoy any success until the spring of 1902.[53] After several meetings, Woods Run Slovaks finally believed they had enough support among their countrymen to seek Bishop Phelan's approval for their plans. The bishop did not acquiesce immediately. Instead, he appointed a Slovak priest from nearby Charleroi to conduct a census of the Woods Run area. The prelate ruled he would deny permission for the church unless the census found one hundred Slovak families willing to support a national church.[54]

Although supporters of the church believed that two hundred Slovak families lived in the Woods Run area, the census fell short of the required number. The bishop refused his approval. Supporters blamed the small count on two factors. First, some Slovaks were apparently afraid to register in any census. Second, it was alleged that Saint Elizabeth's trustees had encouraged Slovaks to remain with that church.[55] It is not clear if these trustees acted independently or at the urging of Father Gasparik, who did not want to lose parishioners. It is certainly doubtful that Gasparik supported the Woods Run church. A few years later, he tried to prevent the establishment of a fourth Slovak Roman Catholic church in Pittsburgh, and it is not improbable that he did the same in 1902.[56]

Promoters of a Slovak church in Woods Run were not concerned, however, about the interests of Saint Elizabeth's trustees and perhaps of their pastor. These Slovaks wanted a neighborhood church and were unwilling to let the matter rest with the bishop's negative decision. They respected the bishop's authority but not a ruling that, from their perspective, was detrimental to their interests. Some lay persons visited the bishop to plead their case. Finally, Bishop Phelan relented and gave his consent for a church. It is not clear if he finally acquiesced because of the persistent pleading by Slovaks or if the required number of families was ultimately reached.[57] What is clear is that these lay Catholics had asserted themselves and continued to press Bishop Phelan to approve their plans. The only leverage these immigrants had with the bishop was that their desire for a neighbor-hood church was in basic accordance with the Catholic church's ob-jective of keeping the foreign-born faithful to Catholicism. Phelan could hardly be displeased with the fact that pious immigrants wanted to create a means whereby they could more easily practice their faith and remain within the Catholic church structure in the United States. In fact, just two years later, the acceptance of national churches by Pittsburgh's hierarchy was voiced in a pastoral letter that stated it was a sin for diocesan Catholics to frequent churches where "religious instruction is given in a language which they do not understand."[58]

The church's objective of keeping immigrants within Pittsburgh's diocesan structure acted as a compelling factor in the relations be-tween Bishop Regis Canevin, Phelan's successor, and Pittsburgh's Slovak Catholic immigrants. Indeed, the desire to keep Slovaks loyal to diocesan authority forced Bishop Canevin to capitulate to lay de-mands for a fourth Slovak Catholic church in Pittsburgh.

In 1907, less than a year after the dedication of Saint Matthew Church, a movement started to form yet another Slovak Catholic parish in Pittsburgh. Frankstown Slovaks expressed the same mo-tives for wanting a church in their neighborhood as did their countrymen in Woods Run and in the South Side. As one Franks-town Slovak explained: "Pittsburgh [Saint Elizabeth Church] is too far."[59] This call for a church reflected the course and pace of the Slovak emigration movement and especially of the influence of chain migration. A large number of Slovaks who lived in Frankstown and nearby Hazelwood came from western Slovak counties, an area whose emigration was increasing in the early 1900s. A few Slovaks from western counties had been migrating to the Frankstown area before 1900. Slovaks from these counties who came to Pittsburgh in later years followed the paths of the earlier immigrants and hence helped increase the Slovak population in that part of Pittsburgh.[60]

As with the other Slovak Catholic churches in Pittsburgh, the call for a church grew out of the combined forces of a Slovak religiosity nurtured in the homeland and a belief that enough Slovaks lived in a particular neighborhood to justify a national church. But the Slovak inhabitants of Frankstown did not, at first, follow the same aggres-sive procedures as their countrymen elsewhere in the city. Instead, they displayed more deference to the bishop by seeking his permis-sion even before they chose church committees, collectors, or a site for the proposed church. They seemed determined to obtain the bishop's approval before proceeding with any substantive plans.

For nearly three years, Bishop Canevin ignored petitions for a Slovak church in Frankstown.[61] The bishop did not explicitly state why, but he was most likely influenced by Father Gasparik, who served on the diocesan Building Committee and who was ill disposed to recommend that the bishop approve the request. Gasparik opposed the formation of yet another Slovak church because it would further drain his congregation of members. After Saint Elizabeth's suffered tremendous membership losses in the early 1900s, Gasparik apparently became determined not to lose the Frankstown members. His position became evident in 1907 when the federal government needed the Saint Elizabeth property for a post office and forced the parish to relocate. Gasparik adamantly rejected parishioners' pleas to move the church to Lawrenceville, a few miles from the Penn Avenue site but where a majority of the congregation now lived. Gasparik refused because he did not want to lose Frankstown parishioners. Gasparik got his way. Saint Elizabeth Church was rebuilt a few blocks from its original location.[62] The call for a Slovak church in Frankstown could not have pleased Father Gasparik.

Slovak Catholics living in the Frankstown area were concerned about facilitating their religious worship, not the impact their actions would have on Saint Elizabeth's. As time passed, they grew impatient and increasingly displeased with Bishop Canevin's procrastination and continued to press him to grant their request. In 1909, the bishop finally asked for a list of Slovaks who would be willing to support a national church in the Frankstown neighborhood.[63] After being sent the list, Canevin still failed to act. Frankstown Slovaks became more impatient. In October 1909, Frank Benkovsky conveyed this impatience to the bishop. Benkovsky complained that he and his countrymen had done all that the bishop had "desired," but still he ignored them. Benkovsky forcefully related that Slovaks in Frankstown were "very dissatisfied with this delay and in the name of Slovaks living in the vicinity I ask you to answer our letter."[64] He expressed the hope that Canevin would "attend to this [matter] immediately" and even thanked him "for the favor in advance." Benkovsky adopted a properly deferential tone by closing the letter, "your obedient servant." Benkovsky and other Frankstown Slovaks may have been obedient servants, but they were angry.

Diocesan officials did not ignore Benkovsky's letter. They believed that the movement for a Slovak church in Frankstown, if ignored, posed the threat that these Catholics might establish an independent church. In 1909, the fear of a Slovak independent church loomed large in the minds of diocesan officials. Two years earlier, Bishop

Canevin had refused permission to Slovaks in Masontown, Pennsylvania, to build a church in their town. The bishop wanted the Slovak church erected in nearby Leckrone. Masontown Slovaks were miffed because Irish Catholics were permitted to build a church in the town. Finally, Bishop Canevin reportedly decided that, after the Irish church was free of debt, Slovaks could build a separate church in Masontown. Some Slovak Catholic immigrants rejected this proposal and formed an independent church.[65]

More recent events in Homestead, Pennsylvania, located just a short distance from Frankstown, weighed even heavier on the minds of diocesan officials. In the summer of 1909, Slovak Catholics, unhappy with their new pastor and with the location of their church, formed an independent parish.[66] Thus in 1909 diocesan officials were sensitive to any situation that might give rise to an independent church. As a result, whether justified or not, they viewed the Frankstown Slovak community with eyes centered on Homestead.

The Benkovsky letter brought the issue of a Slovak church in Frankstown to a head. Bishop Canevin was faced with a dissatisfied Slovak laity on the one hand and, on the other, a pastor, Father Gasparik, concerned about the future of his church. Benkovsky's missive pushed the bishop squarely onto the side of the lay Catholics. Just three days after the Benkovsky letter was written, he informed Father Gasparik that the diocesan office had received a "number of communications" from Slovaks in the Frankstown area. He candidly told Saint Elizabeth's pastor that "I feel that the urgent demand of these people cannot be put off any longer and steps must be taken to establish a mission or parish in that locality; otherwise we may have another independent on our hands such as we now have in Homestead."[67]

Frank Benkovsky clearly had not threatened that the Frankstown Slovaks would defy the bishop and form an independent church; yet, Canevin acted on the fear that they might take such action. He would not risk the possibility that these lay Catholics would organize a church outside the diocese's administrative structure. He lost no time in taking action. The same day he wrote to Gasparik, he also responded to Benkovsky. Canevin assured this assertive layman that diocesan officials were currently looking for a priest to "undertake the work of forming a mission or parish" in the Frankstown vicinity. Just three days later, Canevin appointed Father Joseph Vrhunec, a Slovene, to take charge of the Slovak Catholics in Frankstown in addition to his parish in Rankin.[68]

The appointment of Father Vrhunec was a demonstration of the bishop's accedence to lay demands. Even though Vrhunec initially held services in Frankstown only on alternate Sundays, Frankstown Slovaks were mollified. They justifiably believed that Bishop Canevin would give full support to subsequent efforts to establish a permanent Slovak church in their neighborhood. From the bishop's viewpoint, the pastor's appointment had staved off the possibility that these Catholic immigrants would attempt a schism. For the Saint Elizabeth parish, however, the bishop's decision to succumb to lay pressure meant further decline. By 1910, the mother church's congregation had dwindled to 141 families and 882 members. These numbers represented only 21 percent of the total membership of Pittsburgh's Slovak Catholic parishes and approximately 19 percent of the families registered as belonging to a Slovak church.[69] Saint Elizabeth's had completed its steady decline: once a large, urban, ethnic church, it had become a small, neighborhood, but still national, parish.

Slovak Catholics living in Frankstown and Hazelwood expressed relief and pleasure when progress was finally made toward establishing a permanent national church in their neighborhood. As one parishioner gleefully exclaimed, "now we will not have to take a streetcar but can walk to Mass."[70] Some desired this walk to be as short as possible—perhaps as short as it had been in their native villages. Each parishioner apparently wanted the church located within a short distance from where he or she lived. Trying to encourage compromise, one distraught Slovak reminded his fellow countrymen that it was impossible to build the church near every parishioner's home.[71] In the spring of 1910, the congregation finally agreed on a site. With the creation of this church, named Saint Joachim by the bishop, the era of Slovak Catholic church formation in Pittsburgh came to an end.[72]

The development of these Slovak Catholic churches had not stemmed from discrimination by other nationalities. Certainly some national churches may have excluded Catholics of different cultural backgrounds.[73] Still, in general, Slovaks could attend non-Slovak churches. Actually, the existence of Irish, German, Czech, and other ethnic churches only encouraged and then reinforced the conviction among Slovak immigrants that they too should build their own churches. The founding of Saint Elizabeth's, in turn, set a forceful precedent for founding additional Slovak Catholic churches in Pittsburgh.

The movements to organize Pittsburgh's Slovak Catholic churches reveal important characteristics of the founders of national parishes. First, while women may have participated in general meetings, the active leadership roles fell to men. Second, the early church leaders were typically not entrepreneurial businessmen. Less than one-third (31 percent) of the men who served on a planning committee, and for whom an occupation could be determined, were businessmen, while nearly 69 percent were laborers. Furthermore, an analysis of all persons—committeemen and noncommitteemen— who were prominently involved in founding the city's four Slovak Catholic churches reveals that only 18 percent were businessmen.[74] The one characteristic that the men did have in common was membership in a Slovak fraternal society; nearly 76 percent of them were active members of a local Slovak lodge. Most were members of a Catholic organization, but a few held membership in the National Slovak Society or in both a religious and a secular society.[75] Thus, if those who led the church-founding efforts among Slovak Catholic immigrants were "elites," this status was based upon their fraternal activities.

The fraternalists and other Slovak immigrants who mounted pressure for churches in their own neighborhoods were unified in their desire to have a church located closer to where they and a number of their countrymen lived. These Slovaks did, however, have different conceptions of the church's potential role. A few adopted a narrow nationalistic, indeed almost ethnocentric, view, while others stressed the broader religious functions a Slovak church could perform.

The differences between these views were evident in the comments of two Slovaks as they called for a Slovak church in their respective neighborhoods. One position was expressed in 1902 when Bishop Phelan required the census to determine if enough Slovaks resided in western Allegheny City to warrant a Slovak church. Finding a large number of persons willing to support a Slovak church would have strengthened arguments for the endeavor. One Woods Run Slovak, however, did not adopt this logic. Instead, he was pleased that the priest charged with taking the census refused to count Polish Catholics, even though they stated they would support a Slovak church.[76] This layman reveled in the idea that the proposed church would be "purely Slovak." For him, founding a church was a matter of ethnic pride and would set Slovaks apart from other Catholic immigrants in the neighborhood. Another Slovak, who called for a Slovak church in Frankstown, held quite a different view. He pointed out that, because Croatian and Polish Catholics would also attend a Slovak church, there were enough Catholics in his neighborhood to support a Slovak church.[77] For this Slovak, the church's religious function was more important than keeping it ethnically pure. Each of these men shared a common religious objective and wanted a Slovak church in his neighborhood. One man, however, envisioned a church restricted to Slovaks. His countryman adopted a broader view of the church's potential role: it would be a Slovak church that would serve fellow Slavs as well.

Far more than ethnic pride stimulated the emergence of Slovak national parishes in Pittsburgh. The combined forces of premigration religiosity, migration patterns, and a practical assessment of individual religious needs underlay the drives for Slovak Catholic churches in Pittsburgh. Although located in an industrial section of Pittsburgh, Saint Elizabeth Church did not alter the pattern of Slovak settlement in the Pittsburgh metropolitan area. Slovak immigrants continued to chain migrate, and settle in the same sections of Pittsburgh as countrymen from their villages or village region in northern Hungary. One way they adjusted to this urban, ethnically diverse city was by founding national churches, where they could worship regularly and relatively easily, as they had done in their homeland. The strong desire to have national churches in neighborhoods where they lived emboldened Slovak lay Catholics to act aggressively. These lay persons did demonstrate a deference to the bishop's authority over Catholics in his diocese, but it was an assertive deference. For their deference was accompanied by the assumption that the bishop would comply with lay requests, and when he did not, they pressured him into bowing to lay demands. Besides expecting the bishop to support their efforts to found churches, Pittsburgh's Slovak Catholic immigrants came to look upon their prelate as the guardian of sanctioned lay rights. Slovak Catholics took this view of their bishop especially as they turned from organizing churches to financing and governing them.

Maintaining Catholic Churches:
The Transformed Role of the Laity

THE FORMATION of national churches allowed Slovak Catholics to **4** continue practicing their homeland religion. But while many of their religious traditions were preserved, some died and still others were born. Consequently, Pittsburgh's Slovak Catholic churches were not transplants; they were hybrid institutions. These were flexible institutions capable of making adjustments to New World conditions. This became even clearer as immigrants set about financing and governing their newly created churches. The role of the laity underwent changes as lay persons participated more actively than they had in northern Hungary in the administration and maintenance of their churches. The need for churches to be self-supporting meant that these institutions assumed an expanded role in the social lives of Slovak Catholic immigrants.

Organizing churches also represented a conscious choice by Slovak immigrants to remain part of the universal Catholic church but to worship separately from other Catholics in their neighborhoods. The fact that Catholic churches had to be self-sufficient encouraged the separation of Slovak Catholics from other Catholics in Pittsburgh. The Pittsburgh diocese did institute religious and administrative regulations that tied ethnic parishes to the larger diocesan structure, but these rules did not destroy the ethnic identity of Slovak national churches and cause them to mesh indistinguishably into the diocese's larger Catholic world.

National churches served the practical religious needs of Slovak Catholics. In a Slovak church, sermons, confessions, marriages, and religious instructions for children were conducted in the language 47 these immigrants understood. Special feasts such as Christmas, Easter, and Palm Sunday could be observed as they had been in northern Hungary. In some instances, Pittsburgh Slovaks observed religious feasts that in their homeland had been holy days but did not enjoy the same status in the United States. Thus in the prewar years, many Slovak Catholics commemorated the feast of Saint Stephen, the patron saint of Hungary. Observance of some Christian feast days simply entailed attending mass, while others, such as Corpus Christi, were marked by processions. Slovak parishes typically followed the village ritual of having children, carrying wreaths or flowers, solemnly file into the church while the adult laity watched. On Holy Saturday, women kept the tradition of taking food to the church for the pastor's blessing. On Palm Sunday, members decorated their churches with wreaths and fresh boughs as they had done in their homeland villages.[1]

For Slovak Catholics, national churches afforded the chance to combine religious ceremonies with socializing among their countrymen. Sunday mornings offered an opportune time to congregate with family and friends. Those who had received a letter from Hungary shared this prized possession with family and countrymen. After services, it was common for Slovaks from the same villages or regions to assemble in groups outside of the church.[2] Baptisms and marriages also provided opportunities for families and friends to meet and celebrate together. These events adhered to Old World customs. The christening over, Slovaks went to the parents' or sponsors' home for a feast. Marriage ceremonies were usually followed by gala festivities, and if the wedding was large, the celebration was held at a local hall rented for the occasion.[3]

Having their own churches meant Slovak Catholics could continue some homeland customs but certainly not all of them. Slovaks were not always able to convince priests, or perhaps even fellow parishioners, to continue some Old World traditions. For example, according to Joseph Bohacek, numerous ceremonies honoring the Blessed Virgin took place during the fall in his native Bratislava County. Saint Elizabeth and Saint Joachim churches, where Bohacek worshiped, did not hold such celebrations in the fall. However, in October 1911 so many "rare" religious activities, primarily involving fraternal societies and parish lay organizations, had been scheduled at Saint Joachim Church that Bohacek ecstatically proclaimed that the parishioners "felt as if we were in the old country."[4] The events that aroused such nostalgic feelings were not the same ones these immigrants had observed in Hungary. Indeed, one of the religious activities Bohacek mentioned was the Holy Name Society parade of Pittsburgh's Catholic men. This specific parade had no precedent in northern Hungary; nevertheless, for Bohacek and other Slovaks, it and other church-related events evoked memories of their religious and village life in the Old World. Thus, although the Catholic churches Slovaks organized in Pittsburgh did not follow exactly the religious traditions of northern Hungary, these institutions made Slovak immigrants feel more at home.

In the United States, the functions of Slovak Catholic churches went beyond the religious services mandated by church law. Slovak churches provided the means for local fraternalists to fulfill easily the religious requirements for membership in their organizations. For example, lodges often asked a pastor to hear the confessions of their entire membership at times not regularly scheduled for confession. Fraternals also requested special masses to celebrate fraternal anniversaries or feasts honoring a patron.[5]

Pittsburgh's Slovak Catholic churches experienced changes that went beyond the expansion of traditional religious functions. The task of maintaining a Catholic church helped alter the role that the Slovak laity had traditionally had in church affairs. In America, immigrants had to adjust to a country with a system of separation of church and state.

In their native villages, Slovaks had voluntarily contributed but little money toward the upkeep of their churches. The government paid clerical salaries, medical costs, and pensions.[6] The church patron, typically a noble or gentleman in whose region the church stood, funded the major costs of maintaining the church. In a few instances, county governments did authorize a temporary collection among neighboring villages for a church that had burned down or that needed repairs.[7] And in some areas, individual villagers were regularly assessed foodstuffs and other goods for their parish priest. Cotters and landless laborers also performed chores for the pastor or made necessary repairs on the church or rectory. In some churches a collection bag was passed at Sunday services, but donations were not obligatory. Some of these bags did, however, have a bell that the collector jingled in front of those trying to ignore the collection, presumably to embarrass the unwilling into contributing. On special religious occasions, villagers voluntarily presented their parish priest with foods customary to the season. For example, at Easter Slovak women gave their pastor *paska* (Easter bread), usually the loaf they considered their best. At times the priest received so much bread that he was forced to feed some to animals or throw it away.[8]

Still, even though Slovaks contributed goods and labor toward their pastors' upkeep and perhaps contributed some money, they were not accustomed to being the church's chief financial backers. The situation was fundamentally different in the United States, where Slovak Catholics had to bear not only the cost of the construction of their churches but the cost of continued maintenance. Indeed, lay support for Catholic churches was viewed by the American church hierarchy as a grave obligation. In 1904, Pittsburgh's bishop pointedly reminded Catholics in his diocese that neglecting to donate money to one's church constituted a grievous sin.[9]

Although not accustomed to providing extensive financial support for their churches, Slovak immigrants devised several means for raising operating funds. Some parishioners loaned money to their churches. Saint Matthew and Saint Gabriel churches, for example, relied heavily on loans from individuals. In 1906, Saint Gabriel's owed its parishioners and fraternal societies $13,556. Saint Matthew's also accrued a large parishioner debt.[10] Some parish creditors were small businessmen with the financial resources to make loans easily, but a number were laborers. Saint Matthew's records reveal that widows also lent money to the church. These women may well have been temporarily investing part of their beneficiary receipts from fraternal insurance policies. Lending money meant that parishioners could aid their church, especially during its early founding stages, and still have their hard-earned savings.

Loans to Slovak churches were not always selflessly motivated. Both fraternal societies and parishioners occasionally charged the parish interest of 3 to 4 percent.[11] While some Slovaks may have ultimately decided to consider their loans as donations, others felt more strongly about such investments. In December 1909, three Slovaks actually engaged a lawyer to procure the interest owed them on money they had loaned to Saint Matthew's. The issue remained in limbo for two years until two of the men again tried unsuccessfully to secure the interest payments.[12] Over the years, these parishioners had consistently and generously donated money to Saint Matthew Church; however, they clearly made distinctions between loans and donations.[13] The men's position on loans was apparently that they were contracted under specific terms and, as creditors, they should receive a return as they would from other business investments or if they had deposited the money in a bank.

Pittsburgh's Slovak Catholic churches relied on an elaborate contribution system to repay commercial and parishioner loans as well as to acquire operating funds. From their inception, all four Slovak

Catholic churches adopted a monthly collection plan. Church collectors, assigned to specific areas, personally visited parishioners and procured prescribed monthly assessments. When Pittsburgh Slovaks initiated plans to found churches, they typically appealed to countrymen throughout the city as well as in nearby towns for money.[14]

These general appeals and the practice of sending collectors throughout the Pittsburgh area raised the possibility of swindles, since some Slovaks were not above preying on their countrymen's willingness to support a church. In 1904, when Saint Matthew's congregation was asking for financial contributions, unscrupulous Slovaks posed as collectors for Saint Matthew's and began seeking "donations." These "collectors" had reason to believe they could collect enough money to make the effort worthwhile. In February 1903, five church collectors garnered $1,168.80 for the Saint Matthew parish. One man alone collected $411.85.[15]

In March, Andrew Pekar, the Church Committee president, warned his countrymen about swindlers. Fearful that wary Slovaks might refuse all requests for donations lest the solicitor be an impostor, Pekar explained that authentic collectors had collection books bearing the bishop's seal, the parish seal, and the signatures of both the diocesan chancellor and Saint Matthew's pastor.[16] After Pekar's warning, no other incidents of fraudulent collection of monies for Slovak churches were reported. And the possibility of fraud was lessened with the formation of neighborhood churches. Established Slovak parishes restricted their collection routes to areas served by the respective churches. This meant that parishioners were likely to know their collectors.

In addition to paying fees to collectors who knocked at their doors, Slovaks were also asked to give money at Sunday and other religious services.[17] On festive occasions like baptisms or marriages, a zealous church member often took up a collection for the church.[18] These various collections, however, amassed only a portion of the money Slovak churches needed. Furnishing newly created Catholic churches was an expensive undertaking, especially since they needed religious articles for the church interior as well as liturgical items for services. To obtain yet more money, Slovak parishes instituted a series of special collections. A special collection typically meant that an individual or group of parishioners pledged money toward statues, pictures, church bells, the altar, or other specific liturgical items.[19]

Slovak churches benefited doubly from the donation of large furnishings such as an altar, bells, or statues. Once received, these items had to be blessed. Besides being festive religious events, the various "blessing" ceremonies caused Slovaks to reach once again into their pockets and give the church money.[20] For Slovaks, the blessing of statues meant the parish came under the added protection of the Blessed Virgin or a particular saint. Hence, in the view of some immigrants, this was most likely comparable to former village rituals honoring a community or parish's patron saint.

The dedication of the church building typically produced the largest financial proceeds. When Saint Gabriel Church was dedicated in the spring of 1906, it reportedly realized donations totaling $2,500.[21] The dedication of the city's other Slovak Catholic churches did not fare as well but still garnered income from voluntary contributions taken during the ceremonies.[22] Building new churches and adjusting to the support system mandated by the Catholic church in the United States, then, meant that Slovak church ceremonies were often both religious and financial in purpose. Combining religious activities with the goal of paying debts was an adjustment that Slovak lay persons who wanted national churches in their neighborhoods had to make.

Religious ceremonies were not the only aspect of Slovak parish life influenced by the requirement that Catholic churches be self-sufficient. The fact that parishioners needed to work together to support their church enhanced, indeed helped create, parish social life. In order to raise additional monies, congregations or associated lay organizations sponsored social activities. At least three of Pittsburgh's newly formed Slovak parishes sponsored well-advertised dances soon after their early organizational meetings.[23] In the 1890s, Saint Elizabeth's Church Committee arranged numerous church socials and picnics. Since Saint Elizabeth's served the whole metropolitan area, its social events were widely publicized in Slovak newspapers.[24] The Church Committee for the Saint Matthew parish also broadly promoted its early fund-raising events and asked all Slovaks in the region to attend. Save for its first social, Saint Gabriel parish apparently relied only on Slovaks in western Allegheny City to participate in fund-raising events.[25] After their formative stages, Pittsburgh's other Slovak congregations seemingly followed Saint Gabriel's pattern. Indeed, the evidence shows that, with the exception of fraternal events, once organized, Pittsburgh's Slovak parishes typically relied on their own neighborhood parishioners for support and did not look to countrymen elsewhere in the city for money.[26]

In addition to being a lay responsibility, supporting churches also became a fraternal activity. This represented a further step in the steadily expanding functions of Slovak fraternal societies. Saint Matthew's records reveal that, especially before 1910, the church profited handsomely from socials sponsored by the South Side branches of the First Catholic Slovak Union. In addition to the fraternals, youth organizations, the parish choral society, and local female organizations also arranged socials for the church.[27] Because they provided parishioners an opportunity to socialize with fellow countrymen, church and fraternal events acted as more than money-making ventures. Often preparations for festivities required donations of food or time from individual members, especially women who prepared food for picnics. With arrangements made, the parishioners could look forward to an evening of dancing, eating, and drinking. Occasionally, a local organization or children's group performed a play or offered a choral presentation. These church socials were often family affairs.[28] Thus while church events played a vital role in the financial solvency of a church, they also became an integral part of Slovak parish, social, and community life in Pittsburgh during the first decade of the twentieth century.

Many Slovak immigrants took their financial responsibility seriously and contributed regularly to their churches. But parishes could not escape the influence of downturns in the economy, transiency among Slovak immigrants, and a premigration experience that did not require routine lay support for churches. Some immigrants, unaccustomed to contributing money to churches in Hungary, especially for pastors' salaries, balked at equating regular money donations to the occasional assessments of food, labor, or even small monetary contributions they had made to village churches. Some Slovaks placed a limit on the amount of money they would voluntarily contribute to the church and went so far as to ask for change when the collection basket was passed.[29] At times paying church fees proved difficult even for those who wanted to give money on a regular basis. During strikes or recessions, they simply could not afford additional drains on their meager incomes.

Since supporting churches was a lay responsibility, a few Slovaks considered it a lay obligation to admonish lax countrymen to be generous toward their parish. In October 1907, one collector for Saint Matthew's lamented that Slovaks were beginning to neglect their monetary duty to the church. He begged them to be less penurious in their giving.[30] In the same year, a parishioner of Saint Gabriel's also complained about a lack of financial support and offered greater insight into why some Slovaks were not donating. Although this resident of Woods Run said the majority of Slovaks gladly gave money to the church, he grumbled that some failed to realize how expensive it was to operate a national church in the United States. He reminded them that Slovak churches in America did not have patrons nor did priests have income-producing property. He felt his countrymen needed to change their attitudes and adjust to this new situation. For those who remained unconvinced by his simple facts, this Slovak resorted to an emotionally charged argument. He told his countrymen, that by supporting their own national churches, they were not giving to "foreigners" but to themselves alone.[31]

It is revealing that these two parishioners began voicing complaints in 1907 when the city's laborers were facing hard economic times. Some Slovaks abandoned Pittsburgh; some who stayed found themselves unable to pay either church or fraternal dues. The impact of these bad economic times frightened one man as he realized that transients in the city might leave and that potential immigrants would stay in Hungary. He beseeched his countrymen to pray for improved economic conditions so that emigration from Hungary would resume. "As we [Slovaks] know," he said, "without immigrants our societies and parishes will decline."[32] He did not say so, but his call was much the same as calling for prayers for good weather for village crops.

Even in good economic times, Slovaks planning to return to northern Hungary were commonly among those reluctant to donate part of their wages to a local church. These immigrants reasoned that they did not belong to a Pittsburgh church but, rather, to one in their homeland.[33] Some Slovaks went beyond trying to use verbal reasoning to convince their countrymen to donate to the church. One pious Slovak woman who ran a boardinghouse in Woods Run was determined that her boarders would nor shirk their parish duty. She added a fifty-cent monthly church assessment to her boarders' monthly bill. At this Slovak boardinghouse, the fees included room, board, and church.[34]

Because Slovak churches were separate ethnic parishes, the systems used to raise money further perpetuated their isolation within the Pittsburgh diocese. With the exception of dedications, which the diocesan Catholic newspaper described, events sponsored by Slovak parishes were not publicized in the *Pittsburgh Catholic*. But the responsibility for notifying the paper of an event rested with individual parishes. The sponsors of Slovak socials thus did not seek to include the larger Pittsburgh Catholic population in their parish activities. Rather, they aimed to attract Slovaks and perhaps other Slavic immigrants. As a consequence of self-sufficiency, then, Slovak Catholic parishes depended upon an institutional structure comprised of Slovak parishioners and lay organizations. This self-reliance helped isolate Slovak and other national churches in the Pittsburgh diocese and encouraged them to become churches within a church.[35]

The interdependence of Slovak priests as they performed religious duties also encouraged the creation of a Slovak subsystem in the diocese. Slovak pastors were often prevailed upon to assist other Slovak clergymen in conducting special religious ceremonies: church dedications, forty-hour devotions, confirmation of the faithful, the blessing of church furnishings, and other important festivities. Occasionally, Slovak pastors would also invite another Slavic clergyman to participate in special church events.[36] Additionally, Slovak priests were generally asked to serve Pittsburgh's Slovak churches in the absence of a sick or vacationing pastor.[37]

Despite the fact that Slovak churches made up a subsystem, they were also part of the Pittsburgh Catholic church structure and consequently had to follow guidelines set down by the diocesan hierarchy. For instance, diocesan statutes placed restrictions on Catholic social events. Fund-raising socials could not be scheduled for holy days or during specified religious seasons. In addition, diocesan law banned alcoholic beverages at all functions held to raise money for Catholic churches.[38] However, diocesan officials either did not or could not maintain tight control over such activities. Advertisements for various socials sponsored by Slovak fraternal societies reveal that some ignored the regulations regarding alcoholic beverages. Slovaks who traditionally served alcohol at festivities did not easily forgo this custom. In this, as in other ways, Slovak immigrants blended New World and Old World customs. Such blendings helped nurture the hybrid nature of Slovak national churches.

The Pittsburgh diocese did try to supervise closely the financial affairs of individual congregations. Each church had to submit a yearly financial report; failure to do so could result in an audit of parish accounts.[39] Diocesan officials also monitored construction, renovation, and large expenditures by individual congregations. Statutes required that all parishes obtain diocesan approval to spend sums larger than five hundred dollars. All four of Pittsburgh's Slovak Catholic churches complied with these rules.[40]

Slovak parishes did not conform as readily with the diocese's dictates regarding parishioner loans. In 1904, borrowing money from parishioners was explicitly banned in the Pittsburgh diocese because it had become "a cause of trouble, anxiety, and injury to pastor and people." In 1905, the ban against such loans was formally incorporated into the diocese's revised statutes.[41] Yet both the Saint Matthew and Saint Gabriel parishes borrowed money from members after diocesan officials had disallowed the practice. However, after 1909, when Saint Matthew's encountered difficulties over such loans, the practice at that parish nearly stopped. On one occasion, the church sought diocesan permission to accept a loan of one hundred dollars. The request was flatly denied.[42] In a few subsequent instances, Saint Matthew's Church Committee still borrowed small sums from an individual or lodge and did not seek diocesan approval. Apparently the pastor and the church's lay committeemen believed they could safely borrow small amounts.[43] Borrowing by Slovak churches from parishioners, despite diocesan forbiddance, indicates that church officials were not well informed concerning the financial practices of some local churches or chose to ignore violations that did not create problems within a parish.

Slovak lay Catholics enjoyed a large measure of power in part because the Pittsburgh diocese was expanding lay participation in parish administrative affairs at the very time Slovaks began building national churches. In 1893, the Pittsburgh diocese accepted the recommendation of the Third Plenary Council of Baltimore and instituted a trustee system for individual parishes. Under the Pittsburgh system, male parishioners could elect trustees unless the bishop chose to appoint them. The trustee plan did not affect the ownership of church properties. Titles to Catholic churches in the Pittsburgh diocese remained in the name of their respective congregations with the bishop as trustee.[44]

When the 1893 conference of diocesan clergymen, the Pittsburgh Synod, outlined the rules for the selection of church trustees, it was careful not to undermine the pastor's authority. The synod ruled that the pastor, and he alone, could nominate persons for a trustee post. However, the pastors were instructed to submit two or three names for each post. Eligibility requirements both to be nominated and to vote for trustees were the same. One had to be: male; twenty-one years of age or older; a member of the parish for at least one year; a regular contributor to the support of the church who had performed his Easter Duty. In addition, if a father, he had to be sending his children to a Catholic school.[45]

Pittsburgh's Catholic church hierarchy moved cautiously toward establishing a trustee system. In 1893, diocesan statutes limited its discussion of trustees to stating eligibility qualifications and to listing numerous restrictions on their powers. By 1905, diocesan officials seemed more disposed to enumerate the specific duties of trustees. In that year, the statutes stipulated that, "as far as possible," the trustees were "to assume the labor of providing the means to pay the debts and expenses of the parish, so that the pastor may be able to devote himself chiefly to the spiritual care of his flock."[46] The priest, however, remained, as he had been, ex officio president of the Church Committee, and he also continued to hold the post of church treasurer. Trustees were required to meet every three months with the pastor to examine the church's financial records.[47]

It is difficult to discern how carefully Slovak parishes followed diocesan rules regarding trustees. In 1915, some parishioners complained that Father Gasparik did not publish Saint Elizabeth's yearly financial reports.[48] But there was no accompanying complaint that he also refused to allow the trustees to examine that church's financial records. Father Ferdinand Prikazky held regular meetings with Saint Gabriel's Church Committee.[49] Saint Matthew's trustees definitely did routinely examine their church's accounts. Saint Matthew's financial records were also subjected to two diocesan audits.[50] No official reason was given for the first audit in June 1908.[51] In 1911, however, a second audit was ordered because the lay trustees, in a dispute with the pastor, refused to sign the yearly financial report required by the diocesan office.[52] The incident revealed that by their refusal the trustees could, in fact, instigate an investigation of a pastor's handling of a parish's finances.

The trustee system did not, however, give lay trustees administrative control over their church. Indeed, lay trustees had little power in the actual governance of their parishes. Trustees could not appoint or dismiss a pastor; that right rested solely with the bishop. The pastor retained the power to choose all persons employed by the parish.[53] Indeed, despite the establishment of the trustee system, Pittsburgh's Catholic church officials constantly reaffirmed the pastor's authority within his parish. Church officials recognized, however, that relations between pastors and parishioners would not always be harmonious, nor could all differences be settled at the parish level. Accordingly, diocesan statutes specified that disputes between priests and the laity that could not be resolved by them were to be submitted to the bishop for final arbitration.[54]

Incidents at two of Pittsburgh's Slovak churches show that the parishes did experience internal dissension involving the administration of their churches. On these occasions the bishop was called upon to intervene in parish matters. The bishop's actions demonstrated his continued concern over keeping immigrants within the established Catholic church structure. Moreover, the incidents show how Slovak lay persons viewed their bishops and the authority these church officials had. Finally, the incidents reveal that an assertive lay deference continued to be a force in relations between the Slovak laity and the diocesan hierarchy. During the formative stage of churches, Slovak immigrants had expected the Pittsburgh bishops to accede to their wishes; after a church was organized, these lay Catholics expected the bishop to uphold sanctioned lay rights.

In January 1915, Saint Elizabeth's parishioners saw their lay rights coming under attack when their pastor, Father Gasparik, ignored the guidelines for selecting the parish's Church Committee. Instead of holding elections as had been done in the past, Gasparik simply announced to the yearly parish meeting that he considered the incumbent trustees satisfactory and, therefore, they would remain as the Church Committee for another term. Although no one objected at the meeting, "the lack of [an] election," outraged some parishioners.[55] They decided to act. They convinced nearly 150 other members of Saint Elizabeth Church to sign a petition asking Bishop Canevin to force their pastor to hold elections according to procedures outlined in the diocesan statutes.[56] The petitioners took this opportunity to level additional complaints against Father Gasparik. They asked that he be required to publish the annual financial statements as was done in other churches. The petition also demanded that the pastor "should cease fighting at the altar with the sexton during Holy Mass, and should not abuse and call us members different names with profane language but live with us in a peaceful manner and in a[n] intelligent way." The petition further stated that if Gasparik did not want to comply with these lay demands, "then he should not be worthy to serve the church."[57] The petition, however, stopped short of requesting Gasparik's immediate removal.

Despite allegations that diocesan rules had been violated, Bishop Canevin did not act upon the parishioners' complaints. Undeterred, ten parishioners appealed to Gasparik to change his mind. He refused.[58] They again petitioned the bishop. This second petition, signed by the ten laymen, reiterated earlier charges that the selection of church trustees had violated diocesan statutes. These angry laymen did not limit their actions to verbal complaints. They informed Canevin that they had stopped attending Saint Elizabeth Church and had not joined another congregation.[59] In short, they had ceased being practicing Catholics and by logical extension had abandoned the Catholic church.

It seems that the bishop was initially willing to overlook the infraction of diocesan election rules by the pastor. Certainly there is no evidence that Canevin or other church officials investigated the parishioners' claims. Church officials may well have thought—or hoped—that the problem would wither away. But the persistence of several resolute parishioners would not permit the issue to fade. Although these dissidents did not threaten to try to create an independent parish, they had disassociated themselves from their church over an issue only the bishop could resolve. And, according to diocesan law, the laymen were indeed justified in demanding that he resolve it. Given this situation, Bishop Canevin finally took steps to settle the dispute. It is not clear exactly when the second petition was sent to the bishop, but it is clear that the efforts of these laymen spurred him to act. In October 1916, nearly two years after the first petition, the bishop heard testimony from parishioners who had signed the second petition.[60]

Approximately two months after the hearings, Bishop Canevin ruled in favor of the petitioners and informed Father Gasparik that he must hold new elections.[61] The pastor accepted the bishop's ruling but expressed fear over the upcoming election. According to Gasparik, none of the ten petitioners (whom he referred to as "impostors" who had been "scandalizing" parishioners) were eligible to participate in the elections because they had not contributed money to the church during the past year. He predicted that since these men would be excluded, "there will be rioting and bloodshed" on election day. Gasparik lamented that until now all had been "peaceable" at Saint Elizabeth's, but the upcoming "election will start serious trouble."[62] The bishop offered advice on possible election procedures but, despite the pastor's uneasiness, remained adamant. Elections had to be held by December 31. Either Gasparik's fears were unfounded or the methods adopted for the election suited parishioners. A Church Committee was elected and approved by the bishop without further incident.[63]

The election results suggest that complaints concerning election procedures were a matter of principle, not a question of dissatisfaction with the appointed Church Committee. Seven of the eight men elected in December 1916 had been members of the contested committee.[64] Because there was no subsequent public discussion of the incident, there is no way of knowing how the ten petitioners viewed the election results. Nevertheless, the reelection of seven of the eight committee members indicates that the parishioners who signed the first petition were more concerned with Gasparik's arbitrary actions than with ousting the appointed trustees. The parishioners seemed determined to keep their pastor from tampering with lay rights. The complaints expressed by some church members concerning Father Gasparik's handling of financial affairs do suggest that Saint Elizabeth's trustees did not exercise the same degree of oversight of church finances as committees in the city's other Slovak Catholic churches did. Thus Saint Elizabeth's parishioners may have accepted some irregularities in the relationship between trustees and the pastor, but they were nonetheless intent upon electing their Church Committee members. Under pressure from assertive and unyielding lay persons who were angered by their pastor's actions and dismayed by the prelate's inaction, Bishop Canevin finally yielded and reviewed the lay grievance. In this instance, Father Gasparik learned that he could not count on the bishop to uphold his decisions, especially if the laity persisted in pressing legitimate complaints.

Saint Matthew's congregation also experienced internal strife that involved church trustees and ultimately the bishop. In this instance, the bishop supported the pastor. The problem stemmed from large loans some trustees had made to the church. In 1909, three trustees hired a lawyer and tried to use legal means to force the church to pay interest owed them on loans. The lawyer, cognizant that the bishop was trustee of Catholic churches in the diocese, informed him of the parishioners' plans to sue. Bishop Canevin responded by asking Father Uhlyarik, Saint Matthew's pastor, for clarification of the original loan agreement made with the three parishioners.[65]

The issue went unresolved for two years, but it did not die. In 1911, two of the three trustees resumed efforts to obtain the unpaid interest. Father Uhlyarik finally complained to Bishop Canevin about their actions. The pastor contended that the trustees should be dismissed because they were trying to force his resignation and had even sought a replacement for him. In addition, Uhlyarik asserted that the trustees were causing trouble between him and his congregation.[66] In April, the bishop, speaking through the chancellor, agreed that the trustees were violating diocesan regulations. He said that, unless the problem over the loans was settled within five days, the trustees would be expelled from the parish.[67] The five days stretched into months. The two dissidents remained trustees until July 1911. On July 23, at a church meeting, one of them gave a detailed report of his complaints and resigned from the Church Committee.[68] The other trustee remained on the committee until July 29, when the bishop officially dismissed him "in order that affairs of St. Matthew's congregation may be conducted with less trouble to you and to the Pastor."[69] Church files do not reveal if the bishop thoroughly investigated the charges against the trustees or why he ultimately decided to dismiss the trustee. He presumably learned of the parish meeting and also heard reports that these trustees were encouraging parishioners not to support Saint Matthew Church. Although the trustees denied this charge, another parishioner stated categorically that they had indeed encouraged parishioners to stop contributing money to the church.[70]

This controversy demonstrated the limitations of trustee power. The trustee positions allowed parishioners to oversee financial affairs, but they could not control the church treasury even to the extent of obtaining money due themselves. In this case, attempts by aggressive laymen to overextend their power led to the loss of a prized trustee position. Both the trustees and other parishioners acknowledged the bishop's authority to settle the disagreement between pastor and trustees. Once the bishop intervened and dismissed an elected church official, the parish accepted his decision.[71] In the case of Saint Matthew's parish, unlike the later incident at Saint Elizabeth's, the bishop supported the pastor against irate parishioners. In both incidents, however, Bishop Canevin took steps aimed at quelling a potential small-scale rebellion within his diocese.

Despite lay assertiveness, relations between Pittsburgh's bishops and the city's Slovak Catholics were not characterized by hostility or conflicts. Different factors accounted for this general absence of difficulties. Important among these determinants was the fact that many Slovak Catholics brought with them to the United States a well-cultivated respect for a bishop's authority. Even when Slovak lay persons pressured their bishops, their actions reflected a recognition of the bishops' legitimate authority in the diocese. However, lay deference alone did not govern relations between Slovak immigrants and Pittsburgh's bishops. The Catholic church's desire to keep immigrants faithful to Catholicism and within the established American church structure added muscle to lay pressure.[72]

Like lay Catholics, the Slovak clergy who administered national churches also had to accommodate to changed conditions in the New World. They had to cope with more aggressive laities and had to learn to accept extended administrative and religious responsibilities. Some, perhaps many, Slovak clergymen did not realize when they decided to emigrate how their duties would expand in newly formed national parishes in the United States. The priests who opted to leave their homeland did know, however, that they were helping to alleviate the shortage of clergymen to care for their immigrant countrymen.

Obtaining a sufficient number of clergy to serve the foreign-born presented a chronic problem for America's churches at the turn of the century. Trying to lessen the shortage, leaders of some American denominations appealed to church leaders in Europe to send clergymen. Slovak lay persons also tried to increase the supply of pastors by writing directly to clergymen in Hungary and requesting that they come and serve the new national churches.[73] Occasionally, advertisements aimed at enticing Slovak priests to immigrate to the United States were printed in newspapers in Hungary. In 1903, *Katolícke Noviny* (Catholic News) published an ad describing the need for Slovak priests in America and the compensation they would receive for their work.[74] The ad made immigrating to America an attractive proposition for the Slovak clergy: depending upon the diocese, pastors would receive eight hundred to one thousand dollars a year, and rectories were fully equipped by parishioners who paid all utilities. This rather glowing picture, which promised clergymen a reasonable livelihood as well as the opportunity to practice their vocation, did not accurately depict the life that awaited priests in the United States. Many Slovak clergymen, both Catholic and Protestant, quickly discovered that administering a national church in America involved more than caring for the faithful.

Slovak clergymen who immigrated encountered no fundamental changes in their religious duties. Catholic priests heard confessions and conducted mass. They performed routine religious services and officiated at baptisms, marriages, and funerals.[75] While clergymen usually had at least one month's notice before a wedding and could schedule them accordingly, they did not enjoy the same flexibility with baptisms or funerals. Ecclesiastical records for Pittsburgh's Slovak churches reveal that on one day, especially Sundays, priests might perform as many as five baptisms in addition to celebrating mass and giving religious instructions to children. Sundays were not the only hectic days. Throughout the week clergymen performed baptisms, marriages, and funerals, and Catholic priests administered last rites to the dying. The Slovak custom of having children baptized within just a few days of birth kept pastors reasonably busy christening the newborn. During religious seasons, clergymen were required to conduct additional religious ceremonies.

The religious duties of Slovak pastors also took them to the homes of their parishioners. After Christmas, for example, Slovak priests were expected to visit each parishioner's home to bless it, a custom followed in Hungary.[76] Visits by pastors were not always for religious reasons. In 1908, during what one Slovak termed "bad times," Father Ferdinand Prikazky, pastor of Saint Gabriel Church, called upon "destitute" parishioners to help relieve their distress.[77]

While their basic religious duties remained the same as in Hungary, Pittsburgh's clergymen had to adjust to differences wrought by New World conditions. In addition to making special religious demands, Slovak fraternal lodges asked their pastors to speak at various functions. Priests also attended church and fraternal social activities such as picnics, dances, and bazaars. Moreover, they were often prevailed upon to assist other Slovak pastors in conducting religious ceremonies.

Extended religious and social demands constituted only part of the difference between clerical activities in northern Hungary and the United States. The administrative responsibilities in a country where there was separation of church and state were sometimes onerous. Some Catholic priests did become pastors of more well-established parishes where buildings were completed even if heavily mortgaged. But priests who came to Pittsburgh during the formative years of Slovak parishes faced the responsibility of overseeing the construction of a church, a rectory, and later a school. Above all, they encountered large parish debts. In essence, the picture painted by *Katolícke Noviny* did not match reality. The added responsibilities as well as parish squabbles and the larger disagreements among the national leaders of Slovak organizations dismayed some priests.

Through personal observations and letters to a friend in Hungary, Father John Gurecky, the second pastor assigned to Saint Matthew's parish, provided a clerical perspective on immigrant parishes in the United States. In 1903, he described his new parish as "most neglected and most poor."[78] Yet, because of construction loans and operating expenses, by the end of 1905 this "poor" congregation was saddled with a debt of nearly thirty thousand dollars. Father Gurecky did receive a starting salary of $66.66 a month, and it was increased in 1904 to $83.33 a month. This amounted to approximately the $1,000 annually that the *Katolícke Noviny* had reported. In addition, the parishioners provided Gurecky's lodging, and he received stipends for various religious services he performed.[79]

Although his personal financial comfort was not neglected, monetary difficulties compounded the frustrations that Father Gurecky felt as he administered a newly established national church. He remained at Saint Matthew's for two years, but he did so reluctantly. He wanted to go back to Hungary. Gurecky had, in fact, been attempting to return home even before he accepted the assignment to Saint Matthew Church. Writing in 1903 to a fellow priest in his homeland, Gurecky lamented that "here in America a man must suffer much and endure a huge struggle." He declared that "I have tired of this and I want to return to holy peace."[80] He longed to receive a position at a parish in his native Spiš County. In a later letter, he appeared less selective about where he might be stationed in his native land, for "I do not want in any event, to spend my old age in America but rather somewhere in the old country."[81] Father Gurecky's desire to return home was not prompted by a troubled ministry. He encountered no recorded difficulties with his parishioners. In 1905, one parishioner even described him as a "zealous and universally popular priest."[82] He was, nonetheless, unhappy in America and determined to return to his homeland. He got his wish in August 1905.[83]

Clearly Father Gurecky found serving Slovak parishes in the United States a far more difficult task than was the case in northern Hungary. It is impossible to determine how representative he was of the immigrant clergy in charge of Slovak churches. But since Gurecky was not the only Slovak clergyman who voluntarily returned to Hungary, perhaps he reflected the frustrations and the loneliness other Slovak clerics experienced in America.

While their own financial comfort was almost surely not uppermost in their minds, undoubtedly part of the "struggle" that Father Gurecky felt that priests faced in the United States revolved around their own as well as their churchs' financial well-being. Individual congregations had sole responsibility for providing the pastor's livelihood. As a result, besides coping with aggressive laities, Slovak priests could encounter criticism from lay persons unhappy with some methods used for increasing clerical incomes. Indeed, despite the respect typically shown toward priests, many Slovak immigrants did not hesitate to criticize them for what was perceived as exploitation. One of the harshest criticisms leveled against Slovak priests resulted from fees assessed for some religious services, especially for hearing yearly confessions. Priests charged for cards verifying that parishioners had made their Easter Duty. Without such verification, lay persons could not receive a Catholic burial and members of Catholic fraternal societies could be expelled. Consequently, those who wanted to remain active members of a Catholic fraternal had no alternative but to pay the fees or lose their membership and, not incidentally, their insurance benefits.

Over time, resentment toward charging fees for religious services became more widespread. The complaints by Slovak immigrants reached such proportions by the early 1900s that some prominent priests felt compelled to defend their fellow pastors. Slovak lay persons were reminded, as they had been before, that the situation was different in the United States than in northern Hungary and, hence, so were lay obligations. The defenders explained that priests needed more than yearly salaries to survive in America. The fact was, Slovak priests in the United States, unlike in the old country, were responsible for their own medical bills and typically did not receive pensions when they reached old age or became disabled. They had to make provisions for such contingencies, and charging fees was part of their contingency plan.[84]

Regardless of why the fees were assessed, many Slovak immigrants resented the practice. One Slovak recounted that in 1901 he traveled thirty miles to Pittsburgh to make his yearly confession. The priest charged him one dollar for a verification card; parishioners paid only fifty cents. The clergyman explained that since the man only came once a year he should pay more. By 1902, when this same Slovak again went to Pittsburgh, the price for nonparishioners had risen to three dollars. Irate at the cost, the man refused to go to confession and indignantly stated, "I did not want to buy salvation."[85]

Slovak priests were not the only ones who charged fees for hearing confessions, other priests did the same. In 1904, Pittsburgh's bishop decided to end the practice in his diocese and forbade all priests under his jurisdiction to charge for confessions. The ruling did not, however, interfere with the practice of assessing fees for baptisms, marriages, and funerals.[86] Priests were not required to report revenues for such services, and church trustees had no supervisory powers over a pastor's personal financial affairs. As a result, there are no records of how much money Pittsburgh's Slovak Catholic priests actually received for religious services. This issue, as did many other affairs in national churches, remained between the respective pastors and their parishioners.

The national churches administered by Slovak priests and maintained by the Slovak laity clearly underwent changes as immigrants attempted to transplant a cherished institution. The trustee system meant that Pittsburgh's Slovak churches were not exact replicas of their premigration antecedents, the village churches. Slovak lay persons were far more active in parish administrative affairs than had been true in their homeland churches. The stipulation that national churches be self-sufficient further enhanced lay involvement in local churches. Indeed, the need for self-sufficiency helped create a parish social life. Combining fund-raising with social activities became a feature of Slovak Catholic immigrant life; it was not a carry-over of the premigration culture. The development of parish social life was thus dramatically influenced by the need for Slovak immigrants to adjust to new world conditions and to accept their extended lay responsibilities. In order for their churches to thrive, Slovak lay persons had to develop a new sense of community that was based upon obligations toward these religious institutions.

The fact that American Catholic churches had to be self-sufficient also had the practical effect of encouraging Slovak immigrants to remain somewhat aloof from Pittsburgh's larger Catholic world. Slovak immigrants did not totally isolate themselves into a closed ethnic community; for example, several parishes established "American organizations" such as the Holy Name Society. But even as Pittsburgh's Catholics joined hands as coreligionists, ethnic exclusiveness was manifested: in the annual Holy Name Society parades, which began in 1910, Slovaks as well as other ethnic groups marched together by parish.[87] The commitment that Pittsburgh's Slovak Catholics repeatedly demonstrated to having their own national churches insured that, for the time being, ethnic parishes would remain distinct entities within the larger structure of the Pittsburgh diocese.

As religious institutions there was a pronounced continuity between Slovak Catholic churches of the Old World and those of the New World. Pittsburgh's Slovak Catholic immigrants clung to their traditional religion. The system of practices that accompanied holy days in their villages remained essentially the same. Unlike Italian Catholics, for example, the Slovak system of rituals that accompanied religious observances did not include elaborate public ceremonies distasteful to American Catholic church officials.[88] Hence, the liturgical changes that Slovaks had to accept primarily involved observing different holy days in the United States than in Hungary. In private, Slovak immigrants perhaps held to their superstitions and to premigration customs that accompanied various religious feasts, but in public communal worship, they followed their traditional religious practices, which were acceptable to the American Catholic church.

Despite the ongoing adjustments that Slovak Catholics had to make in order to have their own churches, these immigrants did not have to face a real attack on their traditional system of religious practices. Pittsburgh's bishops welcomed the religiosity that led Slovak immigrants to form churches and organize religious fraternal associations aimed at preserving the faith. For Slovak Lutheran immigrants, the situation was different. For them, preservation of faith took on different meanings as their traditional religious practices and their newly founded fraternal societies came under attack by the clergy.

Preserving the Faith:
Slovak Lutherans

Pɪᴛᴛsʙᴜʀɢʜ's Sʟᴏᴠᴀᴋ Lᴜᴛʜᴇʀᴀɴ immigrants also strove to retain their premigration faith by founding a national church. In doing so, these Protestants followed a pattern strikingly similar to that of Slovak Catholics. Lay initiative, for example, constituted the crucial motivating force behind the formation of a church. Pittsburgh's Slovak Lutherans, however, had profoundly different experiences with the leadership of their church. In particular, the formation of Pittsburgh's Holy Emmanuel Slovak Evangelical Lutheran Church seemed to foreshadow a close working relationship between local fraternal lodges and the church. Indeed, as Catholics had done, fraternalists worked to draw the city's Slovak Lutherans together into a church community. However, decisions were being made by lay and religious leaders outside Pittsburgh that would affect the city's lay Lutherans and fracture close relations between them and their first pastor. By resisting changes, Pittsburgh's Slovak Lutherans demonstrated that premigration religious customs were not easily abandoned; nor would immigrants docilely accept attacks upon their fraternal societies. Ultimately calls by clergymen for religious reforms encouraged lay challenges to the clergy's authority in religious matters.

As Slovaks were moving into Pittsburgh in the 1890s and early 1900s, seeds of discord among Slovak Lutheran immigrants were already being sown. The disagreements that divided them and their clergy arose in part from religious conditions in the United States. Slovak Lutherans confronted a religious structure different from that in their homeland. Besides the separation of church and state, these Protestants found no single established Lutheran church. In the United States, ethnic and theological differences had divided Lutherans into separate and often competing bodies, called synods. When Slovak Lutherans began moving into the United States, some church leaders attempted to draw these immigrants to their respective synods. As early as 1882, the General Council of the Evangelical Lutheran Church in North America tried to help Slovak Lutheran immigrants obtain pastors for their churches.[1] The Missouri Synod, whose conservative theological views dominated the Evangelical Lutheran Synodical Conference of America, also demonstrated an interest in its foreign coreligionists. In the 1880s, the Missouri Synod admitted Slovaks to two of its seminaries.[2]

Despite the goodwill shown by the General Council and the Missouri Synod, some Slovak Lutheran lay persons and clergymen preferred to establish an independent Slovak synod to bind scattered congregations together. The Slovak Evangelical Union assumed a catalytic role in stimulating early efforts to organize a synod. Lay members of the Evangelical Union felt that unifying Slovak clergymen into a single body was the necessary prerequisite. The first substantive move toward achieving this goal came in 1894 at the second convention of the Slovak Evangelical Union.[3] While the pastors agreed to form an independent Slovak Lutheran body, the effort was practically stillborn. The undertaking failed in part because of religious differences among clergymen that sprang from their affiliation with different synods.[4]

In 1899, again during a Slovak Evangelical Union convention, several Slovak Lutheran clergymen held another pastoral conference. For the next three years clergymen worked to create a Slovak synod. Their efforts, however, were fraught with disagreements between pastors affiliated with the Missouri Synod and those who were not. Finally, in June 1902, Slovak clergymen agreed to organize an independent Slovak synod. However, they stated that the new synod, which would be officially known as the Slovak Evangelical Lutheran Church but was called the Slovak Synod, agreed with the Missouri Synod in doctrine.[5] While this statement of agreement with Missouri's theological principles did not deny the Slovak Synod's independent status, it smoothed the way for a possible affiliation with the Synodical Conference.

During the first five years of its existence, the Slovak Synod interacted harmoniously with the Slovak Evangelical Union. The relationship between this fraternal society and Lutheran pastors resembled that which existed between Slovak Catholic fraternal societies and their priests. Slovak Lutheran pastors who were members of the Slovak Synod served on various boards of the Evangelical Union. Despite the clergy's declaration that money from dances or picnics would not be accepted by Slovak Lutheran churches, the fraternal did provide financial aid to Slovak theological students.[6] Between 1902 and 1906, before the Slovak Synod had its own newspaper, it had a religious supplement published in the Evangelical Union's *Slovenský Hlásnik*. The Evangelical Union also aided the synod by sending synod materials to lodge presidents along with the fraternal's communications.[7] This amiable relationship would sour when the synod gave up its independent status.

Although some Slovak pastors opposed the close relationship that developed between their synod and the Synodical Conference's Missouri Synod, the Slovak Synod moved quickly toward affiliation with the conference. By 1905, the Slovak Synod was even exploring ways to establish a Slovak chair at the Missouri Synod's Concordia Seminary in Springfield, Illinois.[8] In that year, the Slovak Synod selected as president the Reverend John Pelikan, who favored a closer union between Slovak Lutherans and the Synodical Conference. Finally, in August 1908, the alliance was realized when the Slovak Synod was accepted into the Synodical Conference.[9] The Slovak Synod's decision to affiliate with the conservative Synodical Conference exacerbated already existing differences within Slovak pastoral ranks in the United States. It also caused a break between the Evangelical Union and the Slovak Synod, a rupture that produced fierce battles. Consequently, disputes stemming from synodal affiliations plagued America's Slovak Lutherans throughout the prewar years.

The problems that arose between the Slovak Evangelical Union and the Slovak Synod revolved around religious issues.[10] Fissures between these two bodies became evident in early 1908. In the spring of that year, as the Slovak Synod was moving toward formal affiliation with the Synodical Conference, some Slovak clergymen began attacking fraternal practices. The Slovak Synod took umbrage with the Evangelical Union's rule that only Lutherans could join the fraternal. The synod argued that lay persons were not qualified to determine who was a true Lutheran. Some activities undertaken by Slovak fraternals treaded on what the synod's leadership considered religious domain. For example, it opposed the Evangelical Union's plan to build an orphanage for Lutheran children. Battles over what constituted legitimate fraternal activities intensified in 1909, when the Evangelical Union established a mission fund to support Slovak

Lutheran pastors in America who traveled to remote areas to minister to Slovak Lutherans. The synod also disapproved of aspects of fraternal life that it interpreted as contrary to orthodox Lutheran practices. The clergy frowned on dances and other social events held by religious fraternals on Sundays or at nights. Furthermore, synod spokesmen denounced the wearing of fraternal badges in church, especially during funerals.[11] Attacks by clergymen had a rippling effect felt throughout the Slovak Lutheran population in the United States. Zealous fraternalists were stunned and embittered by the clergy's attack.

Under the influence of the Missouri Synod, the clerical leaders of the Slovak Synod did not attempt, as Catholic church officials of the Pittsburgh diocese did, to utilize religious fraternals to preserve the faith. The synod's pastors called for a clear separation of "purely church matters" from those of the Evangelical Union and demanded that the fraternal abolish its mission fund.[12] The synod virtually declared war on fraternals when it adopted the stand that "faithful pastors" and "sincere Christians" must not join the Evangelical Union.[13]

Besides attacking the Evangelical Union, the synod began calling for and instituting changes in premigration religious practices that touched the lives of the general Slovak Lutheran populace. Influenced by the doctrinal position of the Missouri Synod, the Slovak Synod concluded that the Lutheran Church of Hungary had strayed from correct Lutheranism. The synod aimed to lead Slovak Lutheran immigrants back to orthodox Lutheran doctrine.[14] As early as 1905, the Slovak Synod was adopting procedures that it argued represented a return to orthodox Lutheranism. These changes, nevertheless, attacked some traditional premigration practices and beliefs. Attacks on their Old World religious system produced resentment and conflict within the Slovak Lutheran immigrant population.

The first issue that stirred a long and bitter controversy involved the receiving of communion. In 1905, the Slovak Synod decided that pastors should institute the practice of having anyone who desired to receive communion "announce" their intention to the pastor. Pastors could then, of course, refuse to administer communion to those deemed unworthy of its reception. Announcing for communion had not been done in Hungary, and many Slovak Lutherans objected to the proposed new procedure.[15] Among the chief critics of the change was the Lutheran Church of Hungary. The synod boldly countered that the Lutheran Church of Hungary itself erred in its practices and that the Slovak Synod was attempting to set Slovak Lutherans on the right course.[16]

The synod also asked Slovaks to make changes in their communal worship by advocating replacing the Slovak hymnal, the *Spevník*, with the *Tranoscius*. The latter hymnal, it was argued, adhered to scriptural truth, while the *Spevník* contained false teachings. As with the issue of communion, synod pastors claimed they were merely correcting an error, not advocating changes.[17] No matter how they phrased their defense, the synod's clergymen were calling on Slovak Lutherans to cast aside the hymnals they had used in their native churches and which some immigrants had carried with them to the United States. The synod was, events soon proved, calling for too many changes.[18]

The formation of the Slovak Synod reveals that Slovak Lutherans did want to cultivate and preserve a separate Slovak Lutheran identity in the United States. In order to achieve this aim and preserve "Slovak Lutheranism," it was necessary to draw these Protestants together into a clearly defined religious, ethnic body. Ideally, the Slovak Synod aimed to unite Slovak Lutheran immigrants into such a body; in reality, it further divided Slovak Lutherans in the United States. Still, initially it appeared that the Slovak Lutheran and Catholic experiences would be essentially the same. Fraternalists and the Lutheran clergy would cooperate, it seemed, on both the national and local levels to preserve Slovak Lutheranism. In fact, the clergy quickly divided over what constituted preservation of faith and these divisions ultimately stirred bitter factionalism that reached beyond clerical ranks. That certainly was the case in Pittsburgh.

As Pittsburgh's Slovak immigrants first undertook to found a Lutheran church, they appeared removed from the issues dividing the clergy. They also seemed, in many ways, similar to the city's Slovak Catholic immigrants. Slovak Lutherans who migrated to Pittsburgh at the turn of the century faced the same problems of adjustment that Slovak Catholics did, and they followed settlement patterns similar to their Catholic countrymen. This meant that Slovak Lutherans did not concentrate in one section of the city, but settled in neighborhoods where both Lutherans and Catholics from their home regions resided. The formation and success of a Slovak Lutheran church in Pittsburgh thus rested on convincing Slovak Lutherans from different regions of northern Hungary that they shared a common bond based on religious beliefs and ethnic heritage.

During the early years of the Slovak migration into Pittsburgh, some Lutherans clearly recognized a shared religious and ethnic identity. In March 1893, a few of them organized the Martin Luther branch of the National Slovak Society. Although membership in this fraternal's lodges was not based on religious affiliation, the charter members of the Martin Luther lodge were undoubtedly Slovak Lutherans.[19] While some Lutherans came together in this lodge, uniting Slovaks on the basis of religion was not the aim of the National Slovak Society. It was, however, the objective of the Slovak Evangelical Union. In November 1902, this national Lutheran fraternal claimed one lodge in Pittsburgh and one in Allegheny City; within three years, the Evangelical Union had three additional branches in the two cities.[20] That there were lodges in four different neighborhoods indicated that Slovak Lutheran immigrants were indeed settling in different quarters of the Pittsburgh metropolitan area.[21]

Available sources do not reveal the number of Slovak Lutherans in Pittsburgh at the turn of the century. But since the majority of the city's Lutherans came from Liptov, a county that did not experience a large emigration until the early years of the 1900s, the number was probably small. This small Lutheran population, part of which was transient, hindered the formation of a Slovak Lutheran church in Pittsburgh.[22] Yet, from a pragmatic standpoint, Slovak Lutheran immigrants needed national churches far more than did their Catholic countrymen. Lutheran services were conducted in the vernacular instead of a universal language.[23] Thus in order to participate in religious services as they had in Hungary, Pittsburgh's Slovak Lutherans required their own church.

The move to found a Slovak Lutheran church in Pittsburgh began in July 1901. The impetus came from a speech to Branch 65 of the Slovak Evangelical Union by the Reverend Drahotin Kvacala, pastor of the Slovak Lutheran congregation in nearby Braddock. It is not clear if Kvacala specifically urged these Lutherans to organize a national church or if he simply reminded them not to become lax in their religion. But, inspired by the clergyman, Branch 65 members resolved to form a national church. This lodge meeting was in fact the first organizational meeting for a Slovak Lutheran church in Pittsburgh. Nineteen of the men present gave donations to start a church fund. In order to get more funds as well as to stir broader support, the lodge chose two men to collect money from their countrymen in the area.[24]

Organizing a church quickly became a fraternal activity. And, having initiated the move to form a Slovak Lutheran church, Branch 65 maintained its leadership. After the July 1901 meeting, Branch 65's members were eager to start having religious services. However, without a large congregation, there was little hope that they could convince a clergyman to come to Pittsburgh and then subsequently be able to support him. These lay persons turned to their Lutheran countrymen in nearby Braddock and convinced them to permit their pastor to conduct occasional services in Pittsburgh.[25] In 1902, the lodge chose additional collectors to solicit money for the proposed church and set a monthly assessment of twenty-five cents per person.[26] Branch 65 most assuredly sought the help of Pittsburgh's other Lutheran groups; however, little else, except for the activities of Branch 65, has been recorded concerning the very early history of the Slovak Lutheran congregation.[27] Still, the available information reveals that, as with the Catholic ventures, the effort to found a Slovak Lutheran church was led by Slovak fraternalists. Moreover, the groundwork was seemingly being laid for an ongoing symbiotic relationship between the church and local fraternal lodges.

By the spring of 1903, the members of Branch 65 decided that the time had come to advance from a mission to a full-fledged church. The lodge elected two church trustees and a church inspector from among its membership and instituted a building fund.[28] In April 1904, Branch 65's efforts were rewarded. The small congregation that the fraternal worked to bring together selected an abandoned church on James and Suismon streets in Allegheny City. The site was desirable because it was in an area where some Slovak Lutherans lived and across the river from the section of Pittsburgh where a number of Lutherans from Liptov and Orava counties resided.[29] The church officers, in the name of the congregation, invited all Slovak Lutherans in Pittsburgh and the surrounding area to attend services at the church. The congregation had not yet agreed to buy the building, and the officers requested that their Lutheran country-men visit and examine it.[30] By this time, organizing a Slovak Lutheran church had evolved from a fraternal activity into an action that involved the larger Slovak Lutheran population.

Within a month after this public notice, the church officers applied to the Allegheny County government for a charter. The reason for a charter, the officers explained, was to incorporate the congregation as a church whose goal was to hold services for Lutheran "Slovaks in their mother tongue."[31] The formation of Holy Emmanuel Slovak Evangelical Lutheran Church thus represented a practical response by practical people to an ethnically and religiously diverse society. The effort demonstrated a desire by Slovak Lutheran immigrants to preserve and to continue practicing their traditional faith in a new land. These people would not welcome the Slovak Synod's proposed changes in religious traditions. Nor would they easily brook criticism of their fraternal society.

The responsibility for administering Pittsburgh's newly formed Lutheran church rested with the laity. In governing their church, Slovak Lutheran lay persons enjoyed far more freedom from hierarchal control than did Slovak Catholics, who were subject to bishops. For example, Lutherans were able to select their own pastors. Congregations elected a church council composed of a president, a secretary, a bookkeeper, and a treasurer. The council also included trustees, whose number varied and who, by at least 1913, acted as church collectors.[32] The council handled the congregation's administrative affairs and was responsible for securing monetary support for the church. The congregation agreed on the pastor's salary, and the treasurer paid him. The council, however, could not call or dismiss a pastor unless the congregation directed it to take such action. Church officials were answerable for their actions only to the congregation, not to ecclesiastical officials.

Lutheran lay persons had the same financial responsibility for their churches as did Slovak Catholics. Separation of church and state required Lutheran laities to assume the financial burden of maintaining their churches. Pittsburgh's Slovaks fulfilled these obligations in various ways, and methods of church support changed somewhat over time. During Holy Emmanuel's early years, some local branches of the Slovak Evangelical Union collected church dues at lodge meetings. These contributions were mandatory, but not all the members of Holy Emmanuel Church belonged to the Slovak Evangelical Union.[33] So, following a procedure used by Slovak Catholics, Holy Emmanuel's congregation adopted a collection system whereby designated collectors procured monthly church dues from congregation members. It also took advantage of religious ceremonies to solicit money for the church. At celebrations following a christening or marriage, a guest would sometimes seek donations for the church.[34]

While Lutherans adopted some of the same methods of church maintenance as did Catholics, the Protestant church did not, over time, rely on social activities to draw members together in support of their church. During Holy Emmanuel's formative years, Branch 65 did sponsor some fund-raising socials for the church.[35] However, Slovak clergymen and later the Slovak Synod looked askance at the practice of holding dances or picnics to raise money for churches.

Indeed, Holy Emmanuel's first pastor refused to accept money derived from social events. Bowing to the influence of its clerical members, the Slovak Evangelical Union discouraged its lodges from sponsoring fund-raising affairs for churches.[36] In the years after 1908, the Slovak Evangelical Union was sensitive to criticisms advanced by the Slovak Synod and tried to avoid actions that would give more fuel to charges that the fraternal society was a worldly or irreverent organization. Hence, in prewar Pittsburgh, a conservative religious philosophy meant that fund-raising socials sponsored by fraternal lodges or church members did not become characteristic features of the congregation's social life. Support for the Lutheran church became an individual, not a collective, social activity.

The larger divisions among America's Slovak Lutherans had an impact that went beyond influencing the social activities of Holy Emmanuel's congregation. While a segment of the city's Slovak Lutheran population was trying to encourage a sense of obligation toward Holy Emmanuel Church, the congregation also confronted the anguishing debates that divided the Slovak Lutheran clergy and lay persons in the United States. Controversial issues involving the Slovak Synod and the religious practices of Slovak Lutherans in the United States destroyed an amicable relationship between Holy Emmanuel's first pastor and the congregation.

In 1905, the Reverend Theodore Balent, who had sporadically ministered to the city's Slovaks, became the congregation's first permanent pastor.[37] He had arrived in the United States about a year earlier and was affiliated with the Slovak Synod.[38] Balent was an extremely active clergyman. He was a member of Branch 65 of the Slovak Evangelical Union and in 1906 served on the fraternal's national Literary Committee.[39] In 1906, when the Slovak Synod decided to publish its own paper, Svedok, Balent became its editor.[40] Balent's involvement in nonparish affairs did not interfere with his regular pastoral duties; or, at least church members did not seem openly dissatisfied with him. On the contrary, one parishioner described Balent as a "popular" pastor.[41] Presumably, Pittsburgh's Slovak Lutherans held their pastor in the same high esteem that Slovaks characteristically felt toward the clergy.

The amiable relations between Balent and the Holy Emmanuel congregation did not last. As a member of the Slovak Synod, Balent attempted to introduce the practice of announcing for communion. The congregation refused to accept this practice. Some of the city's Slovak Lutherans were also unhappy with other dictates that Balent reportedly tried to enforce. They were not only clearly willing to question the religious authority of this clergyman, they apparently viewed Balent as an agent of the synod. Instead of firing him, the congregation in 1907 decided to oppose changes by disassociating from the Slovak Synod.[42]

Initially, Balent harbored the hope that the congregation's rejection of the synod would be temporary. But by April 1908, he was convinced that the congregation was adamant in its decision to remain independent. Balent was also unhappy with religious irregularities he claimed the congregation tolerated.[43] He presented the congregation with an ultimatum: Holy Emmanuel's would return to the Slovak Synod and those who were not regular members of Holy Emmanuel Church would have to announce for communion or he would resign. The congregation refused to acquiesce in his demands. Balent carried out his ultimatum; he resigned just two weeks before Easter Sunday. He left Pittsburgh soon after and went to St. Louis. He later returned to Hungary.[44]

Balent's untimely departure just before Easter left Holy Emmanuel Church in a desperate situation, and the church officers, retaliated by publicly rebuking their former pastor.[45] In a letter published in the *Slovenský Hlásnik,* they claimed that Balent had left without properly notifying the congregation. They alleged this inconsiderate action had inflicted an unnecessary inconvenience and even a type of religious deprivation on the city's Slovak Lutherans who wanted to attend services on Easter. They recounted that Holy Emmanuel Church was filled beyond capacity with the devout wanting to observe the holy day. The congregation was, reportedly, astonished and dismayed to learn that its pastor had left and that there would be no religious devotions on Easter.[46] Balent unequivocally denied the allegation that he had not given the congregation and its officers proper notice of his intention to leave.[47] But even if church officers had embellished their account of the Easter Sunday incident, their letter unquestionably revealed the bitterness they felt toward Balent.

Holy Emmanuel's officers cited other complaints against Balent that further illuminated the source of problems between this pastor and his flock. In their public letter, they described Balent as a pastor who, during the early years of his pastorate, had been popular and had enjoyed the respect and obedience of his congregation. However, when Balent began introducing a series of what the officers termed "musts" that the congregation had to adopt, dissatisfaction flared. These "musts" involved religious, not secular or administrative, issues. The officers proclaimed exasperation with Balent's answers when questions concerning changes were posed to him.

They lamented that his responses suggested that "everything we do is a sin."[48] The trustees did not itemize all the "musts" that Balent was trying to introduce; nor did they provide examples of what some of their alleged sins were. Still, the public debate clearly indicated that Balent, who represented the Slovak Synod, was seen as initiating a two-pronged attack on some church members. He was demanding changes in premigration religious practices. He was, at the same time, criticizing the fraternal societies that Slovak immigrants had organized in the New World. In sum, the congregation resented the campaign to alter a system of religious practices and beliefs to conform to the dictates of the Synodical Conference.

Indeed, criticism leveled at the Reverend Balent was an expression of the animosity that some of Pittsburgh's Slovak Lutherans felt toward the Slovak Synod. In publicly reproaching Balent, Holy Emmanuel's officers seized the opportunity to rebuke the synod and to challenge its claim that it adhered to orthodox Lutheran principles. These lay persons exhorted the synod to "recognize that we [the Holy Emmanuel congregation] remain as faithful [to Lutheran doctrine] as our ancestors and it is a great mistake if you think we have distorted ourselves."[49] Expressing the anguish these religious disputes inflicted on older lay persons, the church officers told the synod clergy that "if you think you have the truth, roll up your sleeves and devote yourselves to training the youth so that in ten years we will have the kind of parishioners you desire." But, they pleaded, "give us older people peace." The issue was clear: these immigrants wanted to continue practicing the religion remembered from their homeland, while the Slovak Synod, accepting the strict confessionalism of the Synodical Conference, wanted to introduce changes.

Balent's response to the church officers' letters indicated how strong the differences were between him and his former congregation. He expressed displeasure with the congregation for its failure to adhere to what he considered orthodox Lutheranism, and he contended that the congregation permitted Slovak Calvinists and nonconfirmed Lutherans to receive communion.[50] The implication was that, since the congregation refused to institute announcement for communion, he was unable to prevent such violations from happening. Balent also feared that the church's decision to reject the Slovak Synod raised the possibility that it would evolve into a separate sect. He wanted his congregation loyal to Lutheranism, but he wanted their loyalty to be to the Lutheranism he now accepted, that of the Synodical Conference.

Squabbles between the synod and the Holy Emmanuel congregation did not end with Balent's resignation and the published attack and counterattack, nor did the disagreement remain a local matter. Immediately after Balent's departure, Pittsburgh's Slovak Lutherans began searching for another pastor. However, the Slovak Synod reportedly warned Lutheran clergymen against accepting a call from the Holy Emmanuel congregation. Indeed, synod spokesmen strongly disapproved when the Reverend Ladislav Boor, pastor of the Slovak church in Braddock and a member of the Slovak Synod, conducted occasional services at Holy Emmanuel Church.[51] Holy Emmanuel's officers defended Boor. In an "open letter" to the Reverend John Pelikan, the synod's president, the officers lambasted the synod for reprimanding Boor. An ecclesiastical body should not, the laymen stated, criticize a clergyman for providing religious services for the faithful. Expressing an antagonism for the Slovak Synod that had become disdain, they indignantly queried, "do you and your synod alone have a patent on salvation? Do you and your synod alone have some sort of special mandate from God?"[52] These articulate laymen, who claimed they were writing on behalf of the Holy Emmanuel congregation, made it clear that they and fellow church members did not accept the teachings of the Slovak Synod as the only correct interpretation of Lutheran theology. They were challenging clerical authority in religious matters.

The Balent affair caused other pent-up indignations to boil to the surface. Some Slovak Lutherans in Pittsburgh were directly affected by the synod's stand in 1908 against fraternal societies. For example, the Slovak Evangelical Union's headquarters and printery were located in Pittsburgh's North Side and members of the Holy Emmanuel Church worked there. In 1908, Holy Emmanuel's president was a national officer in the Evangelical Union, and the church's secretary, the bookkeeper, and one trustee were officers in the fraternal's lodges. The second national president of the Evangelical Union, a charter member of Branch 65, had been active in the founding of Holy Emmanuel Church.[53] Thus the synod's denunciation of the fraternal society was an affront to members of Branch 65 who had been instrumental in creating a Slovak Lutheran church in Pittsburgh.

It is difficult to discern how Pittsburgh's ordinary Slovak Lutherans felt about the Balent affair and the synod's attacks on the Slovak Evangelical Union. Some of Holy Emmanuel's fraternalists did, however, go on the offensive against the synod's opposition to the fraternal, and their views represented those of at least a segment of the city's Slovak Lutheran population. In 1908, in the midst of altercations with the synod that had grown out of the Balent resignation,

George Teraj, a layman who had been active in Holy Emmanuel Church since its inception and who also belonged to Branch 65, denounced the synod for its opposition to fraternal organizations.[54] He pointed to the "Christian" deeds performed by the fraternal, especially its aid to widows and orphans. He rejected the synod's description of the Evangelical Union as a "secret society" and countered by claiming that the synod's pastoral meetings were secret. When pastors had met in Allegheny City, he was, said Teraj, barred from the meeting even though he was a church officer. The complaint that a Holy Emmanuel lay officer could not attend a meeting of the Slovak clergy may well have been frivolous, but it reflected the ill feeling created by the synod's criticism of the Evangelical Union.

Certainly with the Balent affair fresh in mind, George Teraj also offered revealing insight into the lay perspective on the thorny issues that ordinary Slovak Lutheran immigrants were grappling with. He lamented that America's Slovak Lutherans were dividing into two hostile camps—"the orthodox and the nonorthodox." "Never," he agonized, had similar divisions occurred "in the old country" because "there we recognized that we were all Lutherans, but suddenly here [in the United States] there is a division between the orthodox and the false believers."[55] As a layman who felt a shared religious heritage with other Slovak Lutherans and who wanted to remain loyal to his homeland faith, this man was distraught by the issues that separated his fellow Lutheran immigrants.

Some members of Holy Emmanuel Church certainly disagreed with the positions stated by these articulate Slovaks. However, at least a majority of the congregation rejected the synod and refused to accept announcement for communion. Those who supported Balent may have announced for communion as he requested. Nevertheless, those who may have supported the pastor and opposed the congregation's decisions did not become separatists. There is no recorded evidence, for example, of a move to organize a church to oppose positions adopted at Holy Emmanuel's. Nor did Balent's resignation create divisions within the congregation sharp enough to cause a segment to form an opposition church. Equally important, in all of the printed railings engendered by the Balent affair, not one member of the Holy Emmanuel congregation took up a pen in public defense of either the pastor or the Slovak Synod. Besides agreement with articulate members, this silence and inaction probably reflected, in part, an ambivalence toward church affairs that existed among some Slovak lay persons.[56]

Although Slovak fraternalists continued to smart under attacks by the Slovak Synod, after the flurry surrounding Balent's resignation subsided, the heated relations between the synod and Holy Emmanuel congregation cooled down. In July 1908, the church finally acquired another pastor, the Reverend Karol Molnar, a former minister of the Hungarian Reformed Church. Because Molnar was not a member of the Slovak Synod, his appointment insured that the Holy Emmanuel congregation had no immediate intention of affiliating with the Synodical Conference.[57]

Despite the adamant position taken by the Holy Emmanuel congregation in 1908, members demonstrated flexibility in their attitudes toward clergy affiliated with the Slovak Synod. This flexibility developed in 1913 when the congregation faced a critical situation. In that year, after the Reverend Molnar resigned to accept a call by another congregation, Holy Emmanuel's members found themselves confronted with what some perceived as a crisis. For nearly eight months, church officials searched feverishly for a new pastor. They wrote to clergymen in both the United States and in Hungary. They even appealed to persons affiliated with the Slovak Synod. Holy Emmanuel's minutes during the search period convey a real sense of desperation, as one contingent of the city's Slovak Lutherans honestly feared the church would die if a pastor was not found quickly.[58]

Finally, in March 1914, the congregation received a somewhat positive response from the Reverend John Marcis, a pastor affiliated with the Slovak Synod who was currently stationed in Detroit. Marcis asked Holy Emmanuel's members to clarify what had happened between Balent and the congregation; he would not accept the call without an explanation. A meeting of church members composed the response to Marcis. These lay persons, who desperately wanted a pastor, tried to reassure Marcis of their respect for the clergy. Nevertheless, they were not willing to assume any responsibility for the disagreement between them and their former pastor. The secretary was told to inform Marcis that the Reverend Theodore Balent had violated the terms of his appointment by abandoning Holy Emmanuel Church. It was his actions, they explained, and not the congregation's that had sparked the controversy. The congregation also directed the secretary to tell Marcis that Holy Emmanuel's members no longer wished to discuss the matter. From their viewpoint, it was over. Indeed, the secretary was to convey to the pastor that the congregation desired "peace to govern" Holy Emmanuel Church. The "crown" of this peace was an "authentic faith." In this way, church members tried to convince Marcis that they were devout Lutherans. Despite their disagreements with the Slovak Synod and

Balent, they believed that they were loyal to the principles of the Lutheran faith. They wanted Marcis to know this. They pleaded with him to take over the pastorship of their church as soon as possible.[59] The tone of the message revealed the congregation's position: Holy Emmanuel's was a church without a pastor, and its members apparently stood willing to acknowledge the spiritual leadership of the pastor who accepted their call.

At least one person at the meeting expressed some concern about the selection of Marcis. He wanted to call clergymen on a trial basis, a practice he described as being in force in Hungary. Others at the meeting reminded him—as the Reverend Joseph Kolarik, a Lutheran clergyman, had explained to them—that such a procedure was impossible. "Conditions and customs in America do not permit" the calling of several pastors on a trial basis, they told the wary member. This exchange demonstrated a recognition by several Slovak Lutherans, indeed obviously a majority at the meeting, that they had to adjust to the realities of the New World.[60] A shortage of clergymen was one such reality. In the search for a pastor, these lay persons had to be pragmatic and pliant. They were, and the Reverend John Marcis responded positively to the call by Holy Emmanuel's members.

Several factors accounted for the selection of a pastor affiliated with the Slovak Synod. The church's new officers were openly fearful that the church might not survive unless they found a pastor quickly.[61] Also, Slovak Lutherans looked to their clergy for spiritual guidance. The difficulties with Balent had not been an outright unprovoked rejection of him as the church's spiritual leader but, rather, part of the congregation's opposition to broader stands being taken by the Slovak Synod. Even during the height of the furor with Balent, it was clear that several of the city's Slovak Lutherans realized that a Slovak Lutheran church could not continue to exist without a Slovak pastor. The congregation may have resented calls for reforms, but members knew they needed the services that only a pastor could provide. Desperate for a pastor, the congregation had to be flexible in its choice.

The selection of Marcis represented an improvement in relations, but not a reconciliation, between Holy Emmanuel Church and the Slovak Synod.[62] The congregation was flexible and so was Marcis. The pastor did not make his acceptance of the Pittsburgh call contingent upon Holy Emmanuel's affiliation with the synod. And the congregation accepted Marcis despite his association with the synod. Once in office, Marcis did not initiate an overall attack on the religious and social lives of his congregation. His judicious actions prompted two of Holy Emmanuel's laymen to counter public criticisms of the Slovak Synod. Responding to a letter published in *Slovenský Hlásnik* in 1915 that chastized the synod and especially its opposition to the Slovak Evangelical Union, these men reminded critics that not all of the synod's pastors merited such rebuke. For instance, they wrote, the Reverend John Marcis did not deserve the kind of reproaches being leveled at synod pastors. In short, they called for a more balanced approach when evaluating Slovak clergymen.[63]

The relations between Marcis and his congregation continued to be amicable. Despite the synod's position, Marcis displayed a seemingly tolerant attitude toward fraternal societies. In November 1915, when relations between the Slovak Evangelical Union and the Slovak Synod remained bitter, he attended Branch 65's anniversary celebration.[64] The pleasant experience with their pastor did not, however, cause the Holy Emmanuel congregation to forgo its independent status and join the Slovak Synod. In the early 1920s, when Marcis did finally try to persuade the Pittsburgh congregation to affiliate with the synod, a majority of members declined. Rebuffed, Marcis resigned and accepted a call from another congregation.[65] Holy Emmanuel Church never associated with the Slovak Synod or the Synodical Conference. The animosity ran too deep.

As a comparison of the Slovak Lutheran experience with that of Catholics demonstrates, the actions of church leaders in America influenced the lives of ordinary immigrants, but in varying ways. Differing attitudes regarding what constituted preserving the faith helped make the Slovak Catholic and Lutheran experiences different. In the view of Pittsburgh's Catholic church officials, preserving the faith meant keeping Slovak immigrants loyal members of the Catholic church. This objective of preserving the faith worked to the advantage of Slovak lay persons in dealings with their ordinaries. For Slovak Lutheran immigrants, the contrary was true.

Influenced by the strict confessionalism of the Synodical Conference, some Slovak Lutheran clergymen tried to reform Slovak Lutheran immigrants. For these clerics, preserving the faith meant changing the way Slovak Lutherans practiced their religion. This reform attempt affected both traditional religious procedures and the relations between churches and fraternal societies. A strident contingent of Pittsburgh's Slovak Lutherans resented what they interpreted as arrogant self-righteousness on the part of synod pastors. It was after all, some felt, Slovak fraternalists who had founded Holy Emmanuel Church. Indeed, they had established a church because they wanted to remain faithful to their homeland faith. They did not expect that the outcome of their actions would be a demand to change some of their religious practices. Equally important, fraternalists were undoubtedly bewildered and angered when Lutheran pastors of the Slovak Synod rejected the Slovak Evangelical Union as an undesirable meddler in religious issues. Not only did synod pastors view fraternals as trespassers treading on religious domain, they also saw fraternal activities as a hindrance to the objective of guiding Slovak Lutheran immigrants to orthodox Lutheranism. Slovak Catholics did not experience similar rebuffs. Instead, the Pittsburgh diocese opted to accept Catholic fraternal organizations in its endeavor to keep Slovak immigrants loyal to Catholicism.

Under the Catholic system, religious fraternals became closely attached to Slovak national churches. These organizations assumed an active role in church maintenance. In fact, fraternal activities became one part of the social life of Catholic parish communities. Pittsburgh's Slovak Lutheran lodges did sponsor public social events, but they did not arrange fund-raising socials for the church. The fact that fund-raising events did not form an intrinsic part of the social life of the Holy Emmanuel congregation, together with the fact that Holy Emmanuel's was not a neighborhood church, ultimately created problems for its laity. These problems emerged as the lay members of Holy Emmanuel Church wrestled, as did their Catholic countrymen, with issues growing out of extended lay responsibilities. The remainder of this study focuses upon such issues and delves into the social relations among the members of Pittsburgh's Slovak congregations.

Taking Charge:
Lay Perceptions in Action

6 Pɪᴛᴛsʙᴜʀɢʜ's Sʟᴏᴠᴀᴋ Lᴜᴛʜᴇʀᴀɴ and Catholic congregations were more than ethnic branches of America's Catholic and Protestant churches. As church communities, the city's Slovak congregations took on a life of their own, separate from their dealings with clerical hierarchies. In this separate world, beyond the purview of church leaders, immigrants developed their own perceptions of what constituted the role of the laity in the church. Lay persons realized that the continued existence of their churches rested on laities committed to national churches and willing to take the steps and make the sacrifices needed to insure their survival.

The discussion of parish governance has already described the impact that enhanced lay responsibilities had on the development of social life within immigrant congregations. A significant aspect of the internal life of Slovak congregations was the right of lay persons to choose their lay church leaders. As Slovak Catholic and Protestant immigrants looked into their communities for persons to manage secular affairs, they often selected persons with ability and a record of involvement in fraternal activities.

A close examination of Holy Emmanuel Church shows even more clearly how lay persons viewed their elected leaders. On the eve of World War I, the church's lay leaders faced challenges that the combined forces of Catholic church law and the neighborhood location of churches had in large measure spared their Catholic countrymen. Despite differences between Catholic and Lutheran churches there were, nonetheless, vital similarities between the experiences of immigrants of both religious groups. The clergy of both denominations

84

had in some way to adjust to active laities. And, only a determined, energetic laity could insure the survival of national churches, Catholic and Protestant.

The perceptions that lay persons had regarding their responsibilities became dramatically evident in Holy Emmanuel Church in 1913 when a contingent of Slovak Lutherans, acting without clerical leadership, undertook to revive the church. The problems that the congregation faced did not suddenly appear in 1913; they had complex, far-reaching roots.

The problems that the Holy Emmanuel congregation faced were partially rooted in settlement patterns. Some Slovak Lutherans lived in the North Side near the church, but others dwelled across the river in Pittsburgh's Sixth Ward, as well as in Frankstown, Manchester, and nearby Etna and McKees Rocks.[1] Pittsburgh's Slovak Lutheran church, then, differed from the city's Slovak Catholic churches: Holy Emmanuel's was not a neighborhood institution. It was not easy for all Slovak Lutherans to attend regular Sunday services. Recognizing this fact, Holy Emmanuel's pastors and church officials used the Slovak Evangelical Union's newspaper to notify infrequent worshipers of scheduled services, especially during the Christmas and Easter seasons.[2]

The church did provide a means to draw Pittsburgh's Slovak Lutherans together for communal worship. At least during the Reverend Karol Molnar's pastorate (1908–1913), Pittsburgh's Slovak Lutherans had the opportunity to observe their traditional holy days, particularly during the yuletide. Molnar conducted services on the feast of Saint Stephen (December 26), a holy day in Hungary. He also held vespers on December 31, referred to in public announcements as Sylvester, the saint whose feast day it was. Holy Emmanuel's pastor was apparently responding to his congregation's desire to celebrate feasts that had been part of their religious lives in the homeland. After the vespers, a supper was provided for those in the congregation who wanted to await the arrival of the new year at their church and with fellow Lutherans. On January 1, the devout could again participate in communal prayers for a prosperous year for themselves, their family, and their coworshipers.[3]

The need for Holy Emmanuel's pastor to rely on newspapers to announce religious services and activities is revealing. It testifies to the fact that Holy Emmanuel's congregation was scattered about the city and that a number of these Protestants did not habitually participate in Sunday services. The pastor and church officers knew, however, that even those Slovak Lutherans who did not routinely attend Sunday worship would want to observe the holy seasons of Easter and Christmas and occasionally receive communion.[4]

The dispersed nature of Holy Emmanuel's congregation and the irregular participation in religious services ultimately created serious concerns for the congregation's more zealous lay persons. These concerns centered on the extent of lay involvement in Holy Emmanuel Church. Although the existence of a national church meant that religious services were available to all Slovak Lutherans who desired them, apparently only a small segment of this Protestant population became actively engaged in church affairs.

Concerns began surfacing in 1910. In February, Molnar called for a general meeting of all Slovak Lutherans residing in the Pittsburgh area. His published appeal called on Slovak Lutherans to attend this "friendly" gathering, which would launch plans "to inspire better interest not only in our dear church but also in our Slovak Evangelical Union." Specifically, the meeting was to focus on the "easiest and quickest" ways "to increase the number of members" in both the church and in the Slovak Evangelical Union and its female counterpart.[5]

The pastor's February appeal only hinted at the type of problems that the Holy Emmanuel congregation faced. A few months later, a lay member echoed Molnar's call but was more explicit about the issues at hand. In the spring of 1910, George Teraj, a lay member who had been active in the formation of Holy Emmanuel Church and had subsequently served as a church officer, boldly declared that Holy Emmanuel had ceased to exist. He called for the formation of another Slovak Lutheran church in Pittsburgh. Teraj's allegations were, it turned out, more figurative than real. By pointing to what he called the decline of the church, Teraj was expressing concern over what he saw as a lack of interest in the church and its financial welfare. He was also insinuating that the city's Slovak Lutheran immigrants were lax in their attendance at religious services. In Teraj's view, these issues were not relevant only to the clergy. He revealed his beliefs concerning the responsibility of lay officers when he specifically blamed them for the congregation's lack of spirit.[6] He obviously felt that, besides devising methods to insure the church's financial stability, lay officers should work to keep religious enthusiasm alive. In a letter published in *Slovenský Hlásnik*, Holy Emmanuel's officers responded to Teraj's allegations by simply denying them.[7] They offered no comment on their responsibilities as lay leaders.

If Teraj was serious about founding another Slovak church in Pittsburgh, he did not rouse a following. No movement got under way in 1910 or in subsequent years to start another Slovak Lutheran congregation in Pittsburgh. But, although Holy Emmanuel Church and its officers successfully weathered Teraj's criticisms, his complaints and Molnar's call for a meeting of the city's Slovak Lutherans presaged difficulties the church would confront within a few years. As time passed, other Lutherans besides Teraj became increasingly disillusioned with their church officers and with what they saw as a growing "indifference" by their Protestant countrymen toward Holy Emmanuel Church. Matters reached a head when Molnar decided to accept a call by the Slovak church in Charleroi, Pennsylvania.

In June 1913, Molnar informed the Holy Emmanuel congregation that he was resigning.[8] He had been sick during the latter part of his pastorate and cited frail health as the reason for his imminent departure. But some church members clearly felt that other factors had helped prompt Molnar's resignation. When the pastor announced his decision at a meeting of approximately one hundred people, those present pleaded with him to reconsider. To demonstrate their sincerity, they took up a collection that grossed three hundred dollars. It is revealing that the collection was held up as proof that parishioners were not "indifferent" to the church's needs.

Despite the congregation's pleas and resolve to support the church, Molnar did resign.[9] The congregation did not secure another pastor until late spring 1914. During the interim, some lay persons feared that Holy Emmanuel Church would cease to exist if drastic preventive measures were not quickly undertaken. This concern led to a flurry of lay activities aimed not only at keeping the church from dying but also directed toward revitalizing it.

In August 1913, 35 church members, including some church officers, met to discuss Holy Emmanuel's situation and the issues they believed had prodded their pastor to leave.[10] One constant theme of the meeting was the church's financial situation. These lay persons expressed apprehension that the congregation could not meet an upcoming debt payment. A second theme, and one inextricably tied to monetary questions, was that of the church's membership. In 1913, the congregation claimed only 114 "active" members.[11] This total excluded Slovaks who irregularly or even regularly attended religious services at the church but did not pay their assessed monthly church fees. Thus these 114 persons did not represent the Slovak Lutheran population served by Holy Emmanuel Church. At the same time, Pittsburgh's Slovak female and male Lutheran lodges had a total membership of 230 persons. Not all of these lodge members necessarily lived in the Pittsburgh area; yet, not all of the city's Slovak Lutherans belonged to a fraternal society.[12]

The fact that the area's Slovak Lutheran population was significantly larger than Holy Emmanuel's active membership bothered lay persons who gathered for the August meeting. They also expressed strong displeasure with the church president, who did not attend the meeting. The minutes do not provide explicit reasons why those present were unhappy with the man who had served as their president since 1904. But, voicing allegations couched in general terms, the participants blamed him for the fact that the church was not "growing." Convinced that Holy Emmanuel Church had been undergoing a gradual and potentially destructive decline in membership, financial support, and "spirit," the lay persons at the meeting were determined to reverse the trend. They set out to create or rekindle a sense of obligation toward the church. They took it upon themselves to call a general meeting for August 31 of Slovak Lutherans living in the Pittsburgh area. So that the pressing issues would definitely be covered, they set a detailed agenda. Officers advertised the meeting and pleaded for all Slovak Lutherans interested in the future and "the good" of Holy Emmanuel Church to come.[13]

The secretary did not record or even estimate the number present at the August 31 meeting, but at least forty persons attended.[14] Again, the church president failed to participate and perhaps for good reason: a move was decidedly underway to oust him from office. Several articulate lay persons expressed a strong general displeasure with him and, after some deliberation, elections were held for new officers and trustees. Although the meeting voted to remove the church's long-time president, it prepared a letter to inform him of the decision and asked him to continue to work for "the good of the church." Perhaps fearful that some church members might be unhappy with the coup, the new president made an emotional appeal for unity. He told those present they had to work to inject "new life" into the church and proclaimed that "the church must unite not divide us into cliques."

The decision to remove the church's president was not a veiled attempt to get rid of officers associated with the Slovak Evangelical Union and perhaps move toward compliance with the Slovak Synod's position against fraternal societies. Although the ousted president was active in the Evangelical Union, at least eight of the thirteen men elected at the August 31 meeting were also fraternalists.[15] Indeed, the minutes make no reference to the congregation's earlier battle with the Slovak Synod. Published letters discussing Holy Emmanuel's problems in 1913 are equally devoid of any such references. This was a local matter involving lay support for the church and, in the opinion of some of the city's Slovak Lutherans, involving the preservation of the faith among their fellow countrymen.

With elections completed, the meeting turned its attention to the prearranged agenda. The first concern centered on calling a new pastor, and during the following months this remained a primary concern as the congregation appealed to Slovak clergymen in the United States and Hungary as well as to the Synodical Conference and the General Council for help. Church officers also busily worked to get Slovak pastors to hold services during the Christmas and Easter seasons.[16]

Increasing financial support for Holy Emmanuel Church was another primary issue of the August meeting. It is evident that part of what lay persons considered as "indifference" was the reluctance of Slovak Lutheran immigrants to contribute money to their church. Without fund-raising socials, the small congregation relied solely on the generosity of its members. But some Slovaks refused to pay regular assessments to the church because they were not members of the congregation. Faced with these problems, the meeting took two steps. First, it increased the monthly assessment and established a "ceremony fund" to which nonmembers were expected to donate when they attended services.[17] Second, in order to expedite and improve the collection of fees, persons were elected to canvass every area of Pittsburgh and its immediate environs where Slovak Lutherans lived. The collection routes established at the meeting illustrate that Holy Emmanuel's was a national but definitely not a neighborhood church, as Pittsburgh's Slovak Catholic churches had become. The collectors were also to act as recruiters, seeking out Slovak Lutherans and convincing them to become active church members.[18] The stress on monetary concerns indicates that lay persons considered contributing financial support a vital part of being "active" in the church.

The minutes of the meeting do not include an explanation or even speculations why some of the city's Slovak Lutherans did not routinely attend church. It seems highly unlikely, however, that Slovak Lutherans in large numbers were abandoning their faith for another or joining a non-Slovak church. Neither the minutes nor published discussions about the church's situation mentioned loss of faith or conversion as issues. In addition, attendance at religious services was reportedly high on important feast and holy days.[19] Moreover, the church's records do not show an unexplainable drop in the number of baptisms, marriage, or burials. Finally, although not proof positive that Lutherans were not converting, the membership in Pittsburgh's Slovak lodges remained basically consistent throughout the prewar era. Those who joined and remained members of these lodges certainly were offering some indication that they were remaining loyal to their religion. It is not unreasonable, then, to speculate that distance from the church was one factor discouraging regular church attendance by faithful Lutherans who lived in different parts of the city. The task of church officers and other energetic lay persons was clear: they needed to instill a sense of obligation in Slovak Lutherans so that they would take an active part in the church community and, consequently, would be more concerned about the church's well-being.

Knowing that their efforts to revitalize the church would fail if additional funds were not found, church members and officers continued the search for ways to raise money. They went so far as to set fees for baptisms, weddings, and funerals, as was the practice in some Catholic churches. The fees were to be divided, with half going to the pastor and half to the church treasury.[20] Despite the good intentions behind instituting these fees, Martin Luther certainly would not have approved. Neither did Holy Emmanuel's pastor when the congregation finally obtained one. The Reverend John Marcis refused to charge fees for administering sacraments.[21]

Some anxious lay persons were not willing to let the future of their church rest on the intensified efforts of church collectors and other officers. Matthew Blistan, for example, turned to the ethnic press, which had long been a source of communication among Slovaks.[22] He used reasoned arguments, pointed criticisms, and emotional appeals to try to persuade his countrymen to become more active in Holy Emmanuel Church and its community. Blistan condemned the failure of some Slovak Lutherans to support their church or to frequent religious services. He lamented that this "indifference" toward Holy Emmanuel Church wounded his heart. The problem, as he perceived it, was not that Slovak Lutheran immigrants were converting to other religions or even attending non-Slovak churches. Instead, he implied that some immigrants attended Holy Emmanuel Church only on special religious occasions and otherwise avoided the church. He called on these Slovak Lutherans to be more habitual in performing their religious duties and trenchantly appealed to parental responsibility by reminding parents of their obligation to act as role models for their children. He also interjected arguments tinged with nationalistic and emotional overtones by asserting that youths would be lost to Slovak Lutheranism if parents were not diligent in setting a good example.

Blistan's admonishments touched on more than trying to shame or perhaps frighten Slovak Lutherans into being regular in their church attendance. He chided persons who were lax in providing financial support for the church. This layman dismissed as "weak" the claim by some immigrants that they had no obligation to donate money to Holy Emmanuel Church because they belonged to a church "at home, in the old country." "God is everywhere," he told them.

In essence, Matthew Blistan was asking Slovak Lutheran immigrants to realize that their religious life was both similar to and yet different from what they had known in their homeland. Just as in northern Hungary, these Slovaks were part of a "community" whose unifying bonds were religion and language. But in the United States, the unifying bond of religion could not be taken for granted; one had to accept a communal obligation to keep the national church alive, and that obligation included both the duty to attend religious services and the duty to support the church financially. In short, Slovak Lutheran immigrants had to accept their lay responsibilities— the survival of their church and their children's faith depended upon it.

In his public criticisms, Matthew Blistan was analyzing a few of the real obstacles that immigrant churches, both Protestant and Catholic, confronted. Sojourners of whatever religious persuasion were not inclined to donate voluntarily the hard-earned money they planned to use to pay off debts or perhaps to buy land in northern Hungary. Some permanent immigrants, too, were unwilling to accept the responsibility for maintaining their churches. A dispersed congregation made matters worse for Holy Emmanuel Church, as persons who did not regularly go to church apparently did not feel a strong sense of obligation for its financial condition.

The failure to attend regular religious services, was not, however, a complaint that Slovak Catholic immigrants voiced against their countrymen. One reason for this difference was that Catholics, unlike Lutherans, were required by strict church laws, under pain of grievous sin, to attend Sunday services. Hence, for some Slovak Lutherans, such worship was reserved for the traditional holy seasons and religious feasts. For them, regular attendance at Sunday services simply was not an inviolable tradition, and voluntarily supporting a church was a difficult transition. Those persons who were so consciously committed to the survival of a national church that they volunteered time as well as money to insure its continued existence felt threatened by the ambivalence some of their country-men displayed. These committed lay persons sought to replace ambivalence with enthusiasm.

The lay revitalization efforts that got under way at Holy Emmanuel Church in 1913 included an attempt to make the church a social and cultural center. Activists hoped to use a shared language as well as a shared religious and cultural heritage to bring Slovak Lutherans together into a more cohesive church community. In November 1913, a few of Holy Emmanuel's zealous members organized an Educational Group. Its purpose was "to become acquainted with our famous churchmen, to strengthen the faith for which our fathers suffered, [and] to perfect our mother tongue." The group planned to sponsor public lectures and plays to help the city's Slovak Lutherans "become acquainted with the pearls of Slovak Lutheran literature and many things necessary for the good and advancement of [our] religion and nationality."[23] Throughout the next two years, the group arranged dinners, picnics, and other social activities. None of them were advertised as church fund-raisers.[24]

Not all of Pittsburgh's Slovak Lutherans, or even of Holy Emmanuel's "active" members, joined the Educational Group. In 1914, it had only about fifty members. Still, although some Slovaks complained that this was a small membership, they nevertheless proclaimed the group a success because its activities supposedly drew large numbers.[25] Regardless of the extent and nature of its success, the formation of the Educational Group by lay persons attests to the fact that geographic boundaries were secondary to the shared interest, obligations, religion, language, and culture that, for these immigrants, defined Pittsburgh's Slovak Lutheran community.[26]

There is no precise way to assess how influential the Educational Group was in helping to spark and maintain lay interest in Holy Emmanuel Church. Moreover, it is difficult to determine the effect that the other lay efforts initiated in 1913 had on the church. But this much is evident: Holy Emmanuel Church did face serious problems in the period 1910–1914; concerned lay persons, who defined these problems as lay issues, did adopt vigorous measures to overcome them; and Holy Emmanuel Church survived as a Slovak Lutheran institution.[27] Active lay persons, willing to take charge, kept the church alive.

Coping with lay activism and, at times, assertive laities was an adjustment that both Lutheran and Catholic Slovak clergymen had to make in the New World. The early history of Holy Emmanuel Church shows that Slovak lay persons were not willing to be deferential when they felt their religious traditions were under attack. Members of Saint Elizabeth Church refused to act in a docile manner when their pastor challenged legitimate lay rights. Nevertheless, Pittsburgh's Slovak lay persons did maintain a deference toward pastors, although, at times, this was an assertive deference that had limits. In Catholic churches, lay members typically respected the pastor as chief administrator of church affairs. But even the typical must suffer exceptions. On at least one occasion, some members of Saint Matthew Church did try, by interfering with their pastor's administrative authority, to extend their influence in church affairs beyond what diocesan regulations allowed. Besides challenging the pastor's authority, this instance offers another example of how congregations took on a life of their own, separate from their relations with clerical hierarchies.

The attempt by some of Saint Matthew's parishioners to tread on their pastor's authority took place in late 1911, just a few months after Bishop Regis Canevin had settled the dispute between Father John Uhlyarik and two church trustees. This time, however, the issue, which involved Uhlyarik's power as church administrator, remained a purely parish affair between pastor and congregation.

The controversy began in December 1911 at a parish meeting that illness prevented Father Uhlyarik from attending. A majority of parishioners voted to dismiss the church organist, Rudolf Loskot.[28] Since the power to hire or fire church employees rested solely with a pastor, this action violated diocesan statutes. The illegal vote, which was not unanimous, reflected internal parish divisions. According to one reporter, the divisions resulted from competition between Slovaks who lived in different sections of the South Side.[29] Unfortunately, the reporter did not elaborate on the root causes of these splits, but it is most likely that they stemmed from regional rivalries. Chain migration patterns meant that Slovaks from the same region of northern Hungary had settled in the same section of the South Side, separate from Slovaks from other parts of their homeland. Apparently, this spatial separation encouraged factional antagonisms among South Side Slovaks.[30] For unrecorded reasons, a "majority" of persons at the meeting, most of whom resided in the "higher" sections of the South Side, wanted to fire Loskot. A minority steadfastly supported the organist. Father Uhlyarik chose to side with the minority.[31]

On New Year's Day, a few parishioners expressed their displeasure with the organist by refusing to sing at services. They tried to convince others to do the same and, as a result, a few persons began bickering in the back of the church. Some worshipers, interpreting the disturbance as a fight, began leaving the church. In order to quiet the squabble and stop the exodus, Father Uhlyarik went to the back of the church and stood by the door. Parishioners still pressed to leave the building and, in the rush, Father Uhlyarik either fell or was pushed to the ground. Someone called the police, who arrived to find only a few pious women in the church.[32]

One newspaper reporter in describing the "riot," denounced the incident but also criticized Father Uhlyarik. The writer stated that, even though church law allowed the pastor to choose the church organist, the pastor would do well not to ignore the wishes of a majority of his parishioners.[33] Loskot left his position after the New Year's Day "riot" and was replaced within a month. Unfortunately, there is no record of how the new organist was selected. The replacement was apparently acceptable to the various factions, because no subsequent controversy developed over the organist.[34]

The trouble that the Saint Matthew congregation experienced over the church organist demonstrated that Catholic pastors could not always expect to exercise even their legitimate authority in parish affairs. Perhaps because lay persons provided the financial support for the church, they believed they had a right to a more extensive say in church affairs than diocesan law allowed.[35] Moreover, at times, a pastor could not avoid being caught up in the internal disagreements or rivalries within his church community. In this instance, these rivalries ultimately created a challenge to the pastor's authority. The parishioners who demanded Loskot's removal went beyond the assertive deference that generally characterized the attitude of Pittsburgh's Slovak Catholic immigrants toward their pastors. In this case, a determined segment of Saint Matthew's laity was able to enforce its will and extend its influence beyond sanctioned lay rights.

The various "crises" and confrontations between pastors and congregations of Pittsburgh's Slovak churches raise questions regarding the proportion of lay persons who actually became involved in church affairs. The number of participants is impossible to gauge, but the evidence suggests that active participation in such affairs was limited to a vocal minority. For example, it was a concerned minority that instituted efforts to revitalize Holy Emmanuel Church. The number of Saint Matthew's parishioners interested in the organist issue cannot be definitely determined. And in 1915, while 150 members of Saint Elizabeth's signed the petition against Father Coloman Gasparik, only 10 worked actively to keep the issue alive. Overall, the evidence supports the seemingly obvious: some persons were extensively involved; others varied their involvement according to the issue; others were, if not ambivalent, not actively concerned about such affairs.

Whether Lutheran or Roman Catholic, however, fraternalists were among the most active immigrants in each of the national churches. This was the case even though Lutheran lodges did not develop the symbiotic relationship with their church that Slovak Catholics did with theirs. Over the years, Slovak Catholic fraternals supported their churches in a variety of ways and especially by sponsoring fund-raising events. In turn, Catholic churches provided the means for lodge members, both male and female, to fulfill easily the religious requirements attached to fraternal membership.

The Catholic lodges and their churches publicly displayed their mutually supportive roles in various ways. The members of Branch 2 of the First Catholic Slovak Union expressed their feelings about the importance of a Slovak church when, in 1894, they voted to postpone the celebration of their five-year anniversary until the following year, when they would have their "own [Slovak] church."[36] The commemoration could have been carried out with religious services at Saint Wenceslaus Church; the pastor had accommodated Slovak fraternalists before. But this was no longer an acceptable arrangement for Branch 2 members, who were prime movers behind the effort to give Pittsburgh's Slovak Catholics their own church. They clearly wanted to celebrate fraternal events in the church they nurtured. The intertwining relationship between Pittsburgh's Slovak Roman Catholic churches and parish fraternal societies continued to thrive over time. The strict stance adopted by Lutheran pastors hindered a similar continued cooperation between Pittsburgh's Slovak Lutheran lodges and Holy Emmanuel Church.[37]

Despite the different levels of cooperation that Lutheran and Catholic lodges had with their churches, the leadership roles that Slovak fraternalists assumed in their respective churches did not stop with the successful founding efforts. As Slovak lay persons continued to acquire a more enhanced role in church affairs, the correlation between fraternal activities and church leadership remained pronounced. Indeed, in Pittsburgh, election to a fraternal office opened one possible avenue to prominence in Slovak communities.

The trustee system that operated in the Pittsburgh diocese provided a means for some Slovak Catholic immigrants to achieve distinction in their parish. Under the guidelines established by diocesan statutes, pastors could nominate any eligible male parishioner they desired.[38] Individual pastors, of course, may have felt some pressure to put forth the name of a particular parishioner, especially a popular lay person. Those Slovaks who did gain their pastors' attention and were elected to committee posts in the prewar era, however, could not be described as the business elite of Pittsburgh's Slovak communities. In fact, an examination of Slovak Catholic parishes shows that the selection of church committeemen was not based on occupation.[39]

Slovak laborers far outnumbered the businessmen who served on church committees for Saint Elizabeth, Saint Gabriel, and Saint Joachim churches. Information could be garnered for twenty-nine of the fifty-one men who served at one time or another on these church committees to 1915. Twenty-one were laborers; only eight were businessmen or professional persons. Overall, of the committeemen for whom an occupation can be discerned, 73 percent belonged to the laboring class.[40]

In its early years, Saint Matthew Church deviated from this trend. The committeemen for this South Side church did tend to be owners of small businesses, not laborers. In 1905, the six trustees of the church consisted of two grocers, a butcher, a liquor distributor, and two laborers. Only one man, an ironworker, served less than a year. The remaining five continually served as church trustees until 1911.[41] However, by 1909, a change was definitely taking place, as laborers began moving into leadership positions in the Saint Matthew parish. Between 1909 and 1912, seven men were added, at various times, to Saint Matthew's Church Committee. This new group definitely included four laborers.[42] In 1912, after two long-time trustees ceased serving, the committee consisted of two grocers, four laborers, and two men whose occupations cannot be determined.[43] There is no evidence that Saint Matthew's parishioners consciously decided around 1909 that they no longer wanted businessmen as church officers. Rather, the change reveals that the parishioners, like those in other Slovak churches, did not assume a natural correlation between socioeconomic position and community leadership.[44]

The pattern of Church Committee membership suggests that if Slovak immigrants did see a natural correlation between community leadership and an acquired status, it was based on a prominence in

fraternal activities. From 1895 to 1915, a large portion of the committee members for Slovak Catholic churches belonged to the First
Catholic Slovak Union. Also, a few committeemen were affiliated
with the National Slovak Society. At least forty of the sixty-four
committeemen were members of a local Slovak lodge; thirty of these
fraternalists had previously been or were fraternal officers at the
time they were elected to a Church Committee.[45]

An examination of the fraternal posts held by laborers before
their election to a Church Committee suggests an even more refined
relationship existed between fraternal activities and obtaining a committee position. Nine of the eighteen committeemen definitely identified as laborers had formerly been secretary, bookkeeper, or treasurer of their respective lodges.[46] Two laborers had been lodge
presidents, and a third became president after being elected a
church trustee. One laborer became a treasurer and another became
a secretary after they assumed a Church Committee position. Several
of the Church Committee members for whom no occupation could
be discovered had also been lodge officers. Six of the fifteen men in
this category had served as treasurer, bookkeeper, or secretary of
their lodges; another two had been lodge presidents.[47] The link
between fraternal offices and committee membership was not limited to laborers. Seven of the eleven businessmen elected to a committee post were fraternalists, and four of them had previously held
a position as secretary, treasurer, or bookkeeper.

Only scant information, especially regarding occupations, is available for the men who served on Holy Emmanuel's church council.
Anton Miller, who acted as church president from 1904 to 1913, was
a businessman. He had been a saloonkeeper until 1902, when a
Pittsburgh judge refused to renew his license; he subsequently entered into a partnership in a steamship ticket business. Miller was
also active in the Slovak Evangelical Union and, from at least 1908
until 1910, served as a national officer in that organization.[48] There
is no complete extant list of persons who served as officers for Holy
Emmanuel Church during the Miller tenure, but some of the names
appeared sporadically in *Slovenský Hlásnik*. Of the eight men reported as serving as officers in 1908 and 1909, only two were included in city directories. One of the men was listed as a laborer; the
other was described as a blacksmith in 1907 and as a "helper" in
1909.

In 1913, the Holy Emmanuel congregation replaced its long-time
president with a man employed by the Slovak Evangelical Union as
its bookkeeper. At least eight of the other thirteen men elected to

church posts were members of a Slovak fraternal; one was active in the National Slovak Society, and the remaining seven belonged to the Slovak Evangelical Union. Similar to Slovak Catholic committee-men, at least six of these church officers had been officers in their respective lodges. In addition to the church president, who was an employee of the Slovak Evangelical Union, only one other officer was included in Pittsburgh's city directories. John Karcis, church treasurer, was listed as a "driver" in 1912, but in 1913 he opened a saloon. Hence there is not enough evidence to determine if the men chosen as Holy Emmanuel's lay leaders in 1913 were businessmen, professionals, or laborers. The evidence, however, does show that there was a strong correlation between being active in a Slovak fraternal and being elected to a lay office in the church.

Several factors can account for the large representation of Slovak fraternalists in church leadership roles. The fact that a number of church officers had been a fraternal treasurer, bookkeeper, or secretary suggests that these men were at least minimally literate. They were, therefore, especially qualified to act as overseers of church affairs. Additionally, belonging to a local lodge made a person familiar to at least a segment of the congregation. This familiarity almost surely aided his rise to a Church Committee position. Persons willing to devote time to fraternal societies were also apparently more inclined to contribute time to their churches.

Donating time to one's church and fraternal society produced intangible benefits for Slovak immigrants, especially for ordinary laborers. Slovaks who perhaps had not been prominent in their native villages could assume new leadership roles and achieve prominence through church and fraternal activities. As a result, immigrants who remained locked in the lower ranks of the socioeconomic scale in American society could achieve recognition and some power within the parameters of their own ethnic community.

Slovak national churches, composed of lay persons and clergymen, then, made up a community that operated as a subsystem within Pittsburgh's and even America's broader urban society. In this subsystem, Slovak Catholic and Lutheran immigrants concentrated on issues that were relevant to them and essentially to them alone. Pittsburgh's bishops wanted Slovaks to remain faithful to Catholicism, but the hierarchy had no real stake in who served as organist for Saint Matthew Church. Whether or not Holy Emmanuel Church survived as an ethnic institution was probably of interest only to the city's Slovak Lutheran immigrants. At a time when American church leaders, especially Catholics, were grappling with questions of the proper role of the laity in the church, lay immigrants were developing their own conceptions of lay responsibility.[49] These conceptions grew in part out of a determination to have their own national churches.

Events at Holy Emmanuel Church show that immigrants were willing to work to counter the destabilizing effects of mobility and change, which some historians allege affected American society in general and ethnic communities in particular.[50] Those Slovak Lutherans who worked to keep Holy Emmanuel Church alive showed that these immigrants had developed a sense of community based on religion and culture. Those Slovak Catholics who established neighborhood churches also proved that ethnic communities based on a shared interest could develop amid the change and flux that accompanied the immigration process.

The juxtaposition of the Slovak Lutheran and Catholic examples shows that ethnic communities were not defined solely by religion or territory. Pittsburgh's Slovak Lutheran community transcended neighborhood boundaries. And, in an area where Slovak Lutherans and Catholics lived together, the Slovak community could not be equated with a neighborhood Slovak parish.

Besides adjusting to American society, immigrants had to adjust to their own complex ethnic communities. Within these church and neighborhood communities, former strangers from different parts of northern Hungary worshiped together and assumed the responsibility for maintaining their churches. Although Slovak immigrants shared a common language and background, Slovak communities, nevertheless, harbored internal and persistent differences based on regional identities. During the years before World War I, premigration ties and localisms influenced social relationships among Slovak immigrants, even among those who worked together as a parish community in support of their church. The following chapters consider further the types of diversity and divisions that underlay the picture of unity ethnic churches could convey.

Diversity Within Unity:
Regionalism and Social Relationships

7 NATIONAL CHURCHES brought together Slovaks who shared a common language and religion but who had emigrated from different regions of northern Hungary. On occasions such as the dedication of Saint Joachim Church in 1910, Slovaks from the Pittsburgh area came together to celebrate their countrymen's achievement and to share in their satisfaction. In addition to Saint Joachim's congregation, fifteen Slovak lodges from Pittsburgh and nearby towns marched in the parade. Five bands engaged by various Slovak societies added pomp to the day's festivities.[1] Describing the dedication, one Slovak boasted that "other nationalities could not help but be overwhelmed with how Slovaks stick together so nicely and publicly demonstrate their solidarity."[2] This Slovak celebration probably did impress passersby and non-Slovak residents of the area.

During the two decades prior to World War I, Pittsburgh's non-Slovak residents saw repeated examples of such activities. Marriages and funerals, as well as the dedication of churches, provided opportunities for joint public observances worthy of the occasions. To onlookers, Pittsburgh's Slovaks probably did appear as a unified community whose members were cognizant of a unique ethnic identity. These immigrants certainly attached themselves to clearly ethnic parishes. A shared commitment to their churches' survival had helped coalesce strangers as well as family and Old World friends into church communities.

A view from within Pittsburgh's Slovak communities, however, reveals that they harbored significant diversity. Despite the ethnic 100 awareness that joining a Slovak church seemed to exemplify, paro-

chial ties and identities cultivated in northern Hungary often persisted. These ties affected social relationships among Slovaks as they
decided which fraternal society to join, whom to marry, and whom
to choose as godparents for their children. Regional diversity was
one of the divisions within unity that Pittsburgh's Slovak communities tolerated as they grew.

The persistence of regionalisms was evident in Slovak marriages.
During the prewar years, the majority of marriages were between
immigrants from the same region of northern Hungary. Table 2
provides a summary of these marriage patterns. It includes only
marriages in which at least one partner came from one of Hungary's
sixteen northern counties and lived in Pittsburgh when the marriage
took place.[3] In 65 percent of these marriages, the partners came
from the same Old World county. Equally important, the high percentage of marriages between Slovaks from the same county was due
in no small part to the fact that immigrants often married someone
who had lived close to them in the old country. A total of 84 percent
of the people who married a person from their own county married
someone from the same or neighboring Slovak village or town (see
table 3).
    Even when Slovaks did not marry someone who had lived in a
neighboring village, they often wed an immigrant from the same
section of the county who had dwelled perhaps no more than twenty
miles away (table 3). For example, Saint Matthew's parishioners from
Spišská Magura, in the northern tip of Spiš County, who did not
marry immigrants from the same or nearby villages, generally married persons from villages in northern Spiš just east or south of the
Magura region. Slovaks from Spišská Magura rarely married members of Saint Matthew Church from southern or central Spiš County.
Similarly, Slovaks from eastern and central regions of Zemplín
County who migrated to the Manchester–Woods Run section of
western Allegheny City displayed a decided preference to wed persons from their own section of the county.
    There is, of course, no way of knowing where Slovaks who were
married in Pittsburgh's churches first met. Surely many knew their
prospective spouses before they emigrated, while others became acquainted in the United States. Moreover, the tendency for Slovaks to
chain migrate and settle in the same sections of Pittsburgh no doubt
accounts in part for the high rate of marriage between immigrants
from the same regions of northern Hungary. Nevertheless, the
marked preference displayed by Slovaks to wed men or women from

Table 2

Geographic Origins of Partners in Prewar Pittsburgh Slovak Marriages

Church	No. of Marriages	Both Partners from Same Slovak County	Each Partner from Different Slovak County	One Partner Non-Slovak or from Non-Slovak County[a]	One Partner American-Born Slav	One Partner American-Born Non-Slav
St. Elizabeth	726	464	174	63	24	1
St. Gabriel	223	138	63	19	2	1
St. Matthew	185	135	42	3	5	0
St. Joachim	72	38	31	3	0	0
Holy Emmanuel	110	84	18	7	0	1
Total	1,316	859	328	95	31	3
% of total[b]		65	25	7	2.4	0.2

Sources: Marriage records from St. Elizabeth Church, 1895–1910; St. Gabriel Church, 1903–1910; St. Matthew Church, 1904–1910; St. Joachim Church, 1909–1913; Holy Emmanuel Lutheran Church, 1904–1910.

a. Non-Slovak counties lay outside of Hungary's sixteen northern counties.

b. Because of rounding these percentages do not total one hundred.

Table 3
Regional and Village Origins of Partners from Same County, Prewar Pittsburgh Slovak Marriages

Church	Total Partners from Same County	Partners from Same Village	Partners from Villages Less than 10 Miles Apart	Partners from Villages More than 10 Miles Apart
St. Elizabeth	464	161	213	90
St. Gabriel	138	53	58	17
St. Matthew	135	62	68	15
St. Joachim	38	15	19	4
Holy Emmanuel	84	38	37	9
Total	859	329	395	135

Sources: See table 2.

the same area or county offers an illustration of the persistence of regional identities among the city's Slovak immigrants.

In instances when Pittsburgh Slovaks did marry Slovaks who emigrated from different counties, as 25 percent did, there is evidence that more broadly based regional identities, resting on geography or dialect, still could influence the choice of a partner. The three Slovak dialects (eastern, central, and western) corresponded with specific geographic regions and counties in northern Hungary. Nearly 76 percent of the Slovaks who married someone from a different county still chose a partner from the same geographic region who, hence, spoke the same dialect (see table 4).[4] Only 17 percent of Slovaks from the eastern counties married persons from a central or western county.

The low incidence of marriage between Slovaks from different regions of northern Hungary apparently did not result solely from the migration and settlement patterns that brought Slovaks from the same regions together in Pittsburgh. Even when Slovaks from different regions lived in the same neighborhood and attended the same church, marriage between them rarely took place. For example, Saint Joachim Church in Frankstown claimed a number of Slovaks from Zemplín, an eastern county, and from Bratislava and Nitra, two western counties. But marriages at Saint Joachim's between Slovaks from Zemplín and the western counties were uncommon. From 1909 to 1914, the church's marriage register recorded seventy-two marriages in which at least one partner was Slovak; only one of these united a Slovak from Zemplín with an immigrant from a western county.[5] Frankstown Slovaks from the two western counties of Bratislava and Nitra, however, did frequently intermarry. Since part of the emigration from Nitra and Bratislava was in fact a chain migration from the central border regions of these two adjoining counties, some of the county intermarriages were actually between persons from neighboring villages. A significant portion of Nitra's emigrants, however, came from the northwestern tip of that county, which was a far distance from central Bratislava County. When immigrants from this northern region married persons from central Bratislava County, as they often did, they broke out of the tightly limited geographical marriage pattern. But they still adhered to a regional pattern, for they did not marry people from such distant counties as Zemplín.

Saint Gabriel Church in Woods Run also claimed Slovaks from different areas of northern Hungary, primarily the central county of Liptov and Zemplín, in the east. Again, these immigrants did not

Table 4
Dialects of Prewar Pittsburgh Slovak Marriage Partners

Church	Total Intercounty Marriages	Both Eastern	Eastern and Central	Eastern and Western	Both Central	Central and Western	Both Western
St. Elizabeth	174	121	20	8	6	7	12
St. Gabriel	63	42	7	4	4	3	3
St. Matthew	42	14	11	3	3	6	5
St. Joachim	31	5	0	1	0	2	23
Holy Emmanuel	18	2	2[a]	1	9	4	0
Total	328	184	40	17	22	22	43

Sources: See table 2.
a. One of the couples came from neighboring villages that lay across county boundaries from one another.

usually intermarry, only seven of the sixty-three intercounty marriages were between immigrants from an eastern and central county.

The influence of regional ties among Slovak immigrants is also evident in the choice of godparents for children born in Pittsburgh. Moreover, the available evidence suggests that such ties and regionalisms persisted among Slovaks who remained in the city long enough to have more than one child.

The information on godparents' origins is not as complete as that for marriage partners. Only one Slovak pastor, the Reverend Theodore Balent, routinely listed origins for godparents, and after his resignation in April 1908, such information was no longer recorded in Holy Emmanuel's registers. The village backgrounds for godparents were gleaned primarily from marriage and baptismal registers, and consequently data on origins could not be obtained for all sponsors. Still, Slovak church records yield background information on the persons that 1,004 Slovak families chose as godparents for their children. Of these families, 452 had two or more children.[6] This sample of 1,004 families represents 57 percent of the Slovak families who had children baptized at Saint Elizabeth's, 1895–1910, Saint Matthew's 1903–1906, Saint Joachim's, 1909–1913, and Holy Emmanuel Lutheran Church, 1904–1910.[7]

Before data summarizing the relationship between the parents' origins and that of the godparents is presented, some explanatory observations are necessary. It is impractical to chart all of the various combinations of parent-godparent origins, especially in those cases where the mother and father came from different villages or counties. Therefore, for this discussion, parents are considered as a single unit. Hence, unless otherwise specified, the totals provided in all subsequent tables and analyses represent instances in which the children's sponsor or sponsors came from the village area or county of at least one of the parents.[8] Correspondingly, godparents who were married to each other and sponsored the same child are also treated as a unit. In the few cases where these married godparents came from different Slovak counties, they are counted as being from the parents' home area if at least one sponsor came from the same area or county as either parent. Treating married parents and godparents as a unit is based on the rationale that the choice of a godparent, even if from the same village or county as only one parent, still represents the preference of at least one parent for sponsors from his or her home region. Moreover, it must be noted that there were only a few instances when marriage partners, either the parents or the godparents, came from different counties.[9]

Finally, as has been pointed out, it was impossible to determine the origin of all who served as godparents. In order to present the most accurate picture possible of the available information on the relationship between parent and godparent origins, statistics on sponsors are divided into categories: married and unmarried. The unmarried category covers those instances when the two sponsors were not married to each other. The unmarried category is further subdivided and indicates when the information for a baptismal entry is for only one or both godparents. However, because of the small number of cases involved, no attempt has been made to provide the marital status of godparents labeled in tables 5 through 8 as "godparents from same region as parents" and "godparents from different region than parents."

Fifty-five percent of the Slovak families for whom some information on the godparents could be found had only one child recorded in church registers (see table 5). Ninety-one percent of these children had at least one godparent who came from the same village area or county as the parents. Sixty-two families (11.2 percent) did choose at least one godparent who was not from their own home county, but in forty-nine of these cases, the sponsor or sponsors came from the same dialectal region as the parents.[10]

While the choice of godparents by families who had but one child baptized demonstrates the existence of familial, friendship, or regional ties among Pittsburgh Slovaks, it does not prove their persistence over time. It was natural for Slovak immigrants who had recently arrived in Pittsburgh or, perhaps, had been in the city only one or two years to ask countrymen from their own villages or from a nearby area to sponsor their children. The persistence of regional and kinship ties over time among Pittsburgh Slovaks becomes evident by analyzing the 452 families who had more than one child.

Church records reveal information on the origin of godparents for the first child of 237 Slovak families who later had a second child. An analysis of these families shows that in the case of the first born, 88.6 percent chose sponsors from the parents' village area or county. And, when it came time to select godparents for their second child, these parents still preferred countrymen from their home regions in northern Hungary. Origins could be learned for the godparents of 164 of these families, and 149—nearly 91 percent—were from the parents' village areas or counties (see table 6). No information could be learned regarding the first child's godparents of an

Table 5

Origins of Slovak Godparents and Parents, One Child Baptized, Prewar Pittsburgh

Church	Total	Parents and Godparents from Same Village[a]	Godparents Married; from Parents' County	Godparents Unmarried				
				One from Parents' County[b]	Both from Parents' County	One from Parents' County, One Not	Godparents from Same Region as Parents	Godparents from Different Region than Parents
St. Elizabeth	349	—	99	152	52	4	30[c]	12
St. Matthew	67	—	5	35	24	0	3	0
St. Joachim	40	—	17	17	1	2	3	0
Holy Emmanuel	96	32	37	5	14	6	1	1
Total	552	32	158	209	91	12	37	13

Sources: Baptismal records from St. Elizabeth Church, 1895–1910; St. Matthew Church, 1903–1906 (see note 7); St. Joachim Church, 1909–1913; Holy Emmanuel Lutheran Church, 1904–1910.

a. The totals derived are limited to Holy Emmanuel Church, because it was the only church whose baptismal records provided sufficient information for this category. The totals included in this category are not repeated in any other category.

b. Origins could be determined for only one godparent.

c. For the vast majority, origins could be determined for only one godparent.

Table 6
Origins of Slovak Godparents and Parents, Two Children Baptized, Prewar Pittsburgh

Church	Total	Parents and Godparents from Same Village[a]	Godparents Married; from Parents' County	Godparents Unmarried					No Information
				One from Parents' County[b]	Both from Parents' County	One from Parents' County, One Not	Godparents from Same Region as Parents	Godparents from Different Region than Parents	
St. Elizabeth	127								
First child		—	30	52	23	1	9	12	0
Second child		—	31	42	12	1	8	3	30
St. Joachim	23								
First child		—	8	6	4	0	5	0	0
Second child		—	11	5	2	0	4	0	1
St. Matthew	51								
First child		—	3	25	20	2	1	0	0
Second child		—	1	5	5	0	0	0	40
Holy Emmanuel	36								
First child		12	10	1	9	4	0	0	0
Second child		9	11	2	12	0	0	0	2
No information for first child									
Second child	44	—	15	25	3	0	0	1	0

Sources: See table 5.
a. See note a, table 5.
b. See note b, table 5.

additional 44 Slovak families with two children. However, the persistence of regional ties was evident in the selection of sponsors for the second child: 43 of the 44 families chose sponsors from one of the parents' home areas.

Slovaks who remained in Pittsburgh long enough to have more than two children did not deviate from the practice of seeking godparents from their own village areas or counties. The evidence demonstrates there was little difference in the origin of sponsors chosen for the first, second, and third child (see table 7). Families with four or more children followed the same pattern (see table 8). Saint Elizabeth Church recorded the largest number of families with four or more children baptized before 1910. (The cities' remaining Slovak churches listed a combined total of just nine families with four children and one family with five children.) Saint Elizabeth's baptismal records reveal that Slovaks who lived in Pittsburgh for long periods typically continued to ask countrymen from their home areas to serve as their children's godparents.

The high percentage of families who chose sponsors from their village areas was due in part, but only in part, to the same persons serving as godparents more than once. Baptismal records show that, of 527 families who had two or more children, only 178, approximately 35 percent, chose the same two godparents for their first and second child; another 138 families chose one of the first child's godparents to stand for the second child.[11] A survey of Slovak church records does reveal that families, especially of Slovak Lutherans, commonly chose different godparents for the third, fourth, or fifth child. In some instances, however, the same godparents would sponsor the first or second and then perhaps the fourth child. Regardless of whether parents chose the same or different godparents for their children, the tendency was to choose persons from their own village areas or counties.[12]

The examination presented here does not, of course, include all the families who had children baptized in Pittsburgh's Slovak churches. Nevertheless, the evidence is strongly suggestive: it was unquestionably common for parents to choose persons—either family or fellow Slovaks—from their own village area, county, or region to be their children's godparents. Residing in Pittsburgh for longer periods and belonging to a Slovak church with countrymen from various parts of northern Hungary did not significantly alter the parochialisms and kinship-friendship ties that Slovaks had developed in their homeland and that chain migration assuredly encouraged. During the years prior to World War I, then, Pittsburgh Slovaks continued to identify with persons from their own counties or

| | | | | Godparents Unmarried | | | | | |
Church	Total	Parents and Godparents from Same Village[a]	Godparents Married; from Parents' County	One from Parents' County[b]	Both from Parents' County	One from Parents' County, One Not	Godparents from Same Region as Parents	Godparents from Different Region than Parents	No Information
St. Elizabeth	67								
First child		—	22	27	13	1	4	0	
Second child		—	21	25	13	1	1	0	6
Third child		—	20	19	10	0	1	0	17
St. Joachim	6								
First child		—	3	2	0	0	1	0	
Second child		—	4	0	1	0	1	0	
Third child		—	4	1	0	1	0	0	
St. Matthew	19								
First child		—	3	6	9	0	0	1	
Second child		—	2	2	2	0	0	0	13
Third child		—	0	1	1	0	0	0	17
Holy Emmanuel	10								
First child		2	4	0	1	3	0	0	
Second child		1	6	0	2	1	0	0	
Third child		1	3	1	1	3	0	0	1
No information for first child									
Second child	11	0	5	3	1	0	1	1	
Third child[c]	13	0	7	2	1	1	0	2	

Sources: See table 5.
a. See note a, table 5.
b. See note b, table 5.
c. The totals for the second and third child differ because the totals for the third child include the eleven families for whom information was available for the second child and also for two additional families for whom information was available for only the third child.

Table 8
Origins of Saint Elizabeth's Godparents and Parents, Four to Six Children Baptized, 1895–1910

Number of Children Baptized	Total	Godparents Married; from Parents' County	Godparents Unmarried						No Information
			One from Parents' County[a]	Both from Parents' County	One from Parents' County, One Not	Godparents from Same Region as Parents	Godparents from Different Region than Parents	
Four children	33							
First child		6	21	6	0	0	0	5
Second child		13	10	4	1	0	0	6
Third child		10	12	4	1	0	0	9
Fourth child		10	9	5	0	0	0	
Five children	17							
First child		5	6	6	0	0	0	
Second child		5	5	6	0	1	0	
Third child		7	5	2	1	0	0	2
Fourth child		6	5	4	1	0	0	1
Fifth child		7	2	4	0	1	0	3
Six children	6							
First child		3	2	1	0	0	0	
Second child		1	2	3	0	0	0	
Third child		2	1	3	0	0	0	
Fourth child		1	0	5	0	0	0	
Fifth child		2	0	4	0	0	0	
Sixth child		2	0	3	0	0	0	1

Source: St. Elizabeth Church, baptismal records, 1895–1910.
Note: No information could be found on the origins of godparents for the two families who had seven children.
a. See note b, table 5.

local regions, and such identifications helped preserve their Old World parochial identities.[13]

Regional ties could cut even across religious lines. The registers of Holy Emmanuel, Saint Gabriel, and Saint Elizabeth churches contain records of thirty marriages between Slovak Catholics and Protestants. Nearly 64 percent of these interfaith marriages were between Slovaks from the same or neighboring villages; the partners in 30 percent of the mixed marriages came from different counties.

Some Pittsburgh Slovaks also chose countrymen of a different faith as godparents for their children. Between 1904 and 1910, Holy Emmanuel's records listed eighteen baptisms in which one or both godparents were Roman Catholic. In one other baptismal entry, the godfather was Greek Catholic while the godmother was a Calvinist. For at least eleven of these baptisms, the godparents came from the same village area as the child's parents.[14] In 1906, two Slovak Catholics also served as witnesses for a wedding between two Lutherans; all four had emigrated from the same village. This marriage as well as the choice of non-Lutheran godparents offer examples of instances where friendship ties rooted in Old World villages superseded religious affiliations.

Even the fraternal societies responsible for bringing Slovak immigrants together to found churches could not escape the influence of regional ties. When Slovaks united in Pittsburgh to create these societies, they typically were associating with countrymen from their village or region. Furthermore, over time, Slovaks continued to join the same lodge as persons from their village or region. A brief analysis of representative samples reveals the strength of premigration ties on fraternal membership.[15]

At first glance, the First Catholic Slovak Union lodges associated with Saint Matthew Church in the South Side seem to offer only partial support for the claim that regionalism influenced fraternal membership. Branch 159 did draw its members from only a few village areas, but Branch 50 attracted Slovaks from a number of counties. Yet, despite its cosmopolitan nature, a breakdown of Branch 50 membership shows that village and regional ties influenced the make-up of this fraternal lodge. For example, between 1902 and 1912, forty-eight of the lodge's fifty-five members from Trenčin County came from sixteen villages and towns in the northern part of that county.[16] Moreover, thirty-one of these men came from just three settlements in that region. Seven other members came from neighboring communes in southern Trenčin County. During the same period, fifteen of the lodge's nineteen members from Orava County hailed from just two of that county's villages. Similar patterns held true for lodge members from the nine other counties represented in Branch 50.

A comparison of Branch 50's members with those who belonged to Branch 159 for the period that comparable data is available indicates that these two fraternal lodges attracted Slovaks from different counties and districts of northern Hungary. Between 1908 and 1911, Branch 159 accepted fifty-four new members.[17] Thirty-six were from Spiš County. Twenty-three of these men came from the single village of Nedeca, ten others came from three of its neighboring villages, and the remaining three came from villages south of Nedeca. In contrast, during that period, Branch 50 did not record any members from Nedeca. And despite the fact that 19 percent of the families listed in Saint Matthew's baptismal records were from Nedeca, and 28 percent came from Nedeca plus neighboring villages, only one man from Nedeca and one from a nearby village joined Branch 50 from 1902 to 1912. Thus, if Slovaks from the Nedeca area joined a branch of the First Catholic Slovak Union, they joined Branch 159. This was the continuation of a long-standing practice; at least three of Branch 159's charter members had emigrated from Nedeca. Obviously, from its inception in December 1894 and continuing to at least 1912, Slovaks from the Nedeca area chose to join Branch 159 instead of Branch 50.[18]

Geographic origins clearly continued to have an impact upon lodge membership for certainly a decade after branches 50 and 159 had cooperated to establish Saint Matthew Church. Slovaks from various regions of northern Hungary worshiped together in this church, but their choice of fraternal lodges reflected the ongoing influence of regionalisms on their social relationships. The persistence of similar membership patterns was evident in other Slovak congregations where more than one branch of the First Catholic Slovak Union existed before a church was founded.[19]

At times, Slovaks from the same village opted to start another lodge instead of joining an already existing lodge whose members belonged to their church. For instance, in 1904, although Saint Elizabeth's parish had two branches of the First Catholic Slovak Union, its parishioners from the village of Teplá decided to form Branch 460.[20] In the period 1908 to 1911, natives of Teplá and its neighboring villages continued to choose this branch over the parish's other two lodges. At the same time, Branch 460 did not attract persons from counties evident in the membership of Branch 4 or Branch 21, Saint Elizabeth's other Catholic fraternals.[21]

Thus Slovak Catholic fraternal societies had several, almost contradictory, affects on Pittsburgh's Slovak communities. They helped tie Slovaks to a larger Slovak religious organization and they helped bring Slovak immigrants from different regions together to establish churches. Yet, they also reflected and encouraged the persistence of regional differences and premigration family and friendship ties. These regional differences fostered diversity within individual parish communities.

Articulate Slovak nationalists decried the persistence of county identities among Slovak immigrants in the United States. Throughout the latter part of the nineteenth and early twentieth centuries, these nationalists attempted to raise a Slovak ethnic consciousness among immigrants from northern Hungary who spoke Slovak. They pleaded with Slovaks to cast aside parochial identities and embrace a more encompassing identity as Slovaks.[22] In the prewar period, this did not happen among Pittsburgh's Slovak immigrants. Regionalism remained strong among these immigrants well after they began settling in the city.

Some Pittsburgh Slovaks inveighed against these regionalisms.[23] Urging his countrymen to abandon regional loyalties, in 1902, one Pittsburgh man scolded his "narrowminded" countrymen—"ignoramuses" in his opinion—who continued to judge fellow Slovaks on the basis of their local origins. He implored Slovaks to adopt a more nationalistic stance and asked, "Are we not all sons of one Slovak mother?"[24] In 1907, an Allegheny City man complained that divisions stemming from both class and regional differences were creating antagonisms among area Slovaks. But while pleading for unity, he actually made appeals that, if followed, would have fostered more regional division. He reminded Allegheny City Slovaks from northeastern Hungary that they outnumbered Slovaks from the country's northwestern region who lived in Allegheny City. He maintained that, if eastern Slovaks worked together, they could become a "powerful voice" in the Slovak nationalist movement and in local issues affecting Slovak immigrants. In this case, even one who spoke for Slovak unity could not fully escape the influence of regional identities.[25]

Regional rivalries flared in a variety of ways. Even children were aware of—and influenced by—the prejudices of their elders: one child tried to insult a playmate by making an unflattering reference to her parents' county origin.[26] Regionalisms also complicated the 1912 election of officers for a Pittsburgh branch of the First Catholic

Slovak Union. Much to the dismay of some members, the elections created infighting among lodge brothers.[27] According to one reporter, the minority was unwilling to accept the choices of the majority. He beseeched his fellow fraternalists to "give more respect to one another and disregard whether this one or that one is from a certain village or county."[28]

The existence of regional identities did not seriously disrupt Pittsburgh's Slovak communities. Instead, the persistence of regionalisms among Slovaks suggests that the immigrants maintained two cultural identities—one based on a shared language and another on geographic origin. This two-tiered identity structure, with the concomitant persistence of parochialisms, is an example of the internal, often unseen, diversity that characterized Slovak, and perhaps other, immigrant communities during the prewar era. This diversity meant that, for immigrants, adjusting to American society included adjusting to their own new ethnic community as well. For Slovaks, this new ethnic community differed from their homeland villages in part because it comprised Slovaks from various regions of northern Hungary. In the face of this diversity, many Pittsburgh Slovaks apparently hoped to maintain the unity they had had with countrymen in their native villages.

In the prewar years, enduring regionalisms hindered Slovaks from developing a sense of belonging to a unique nation or people. Some immigrants did develop a strong ethnic identity and became Slovak nationalists. They urged the preservation of the Slovak language and culture, both in Hungary and in the United States. But in a city like Pittsburgh, Slovaks differed in the degree of their ethnic consciousness and in their willingness to embrace Slovak nationalism.

Slovak churches tolerated the range of political and regional differences that existed among these immigrants. This tolerance somewhat obscures the complexity of the city's Slovak communities. Actually, the image of unity that Pittsburgh Slovaks conveyed as they developed their communal institutions distorts the divisions that characterized the internal dynamics of this ethnic community. A further glimpse into the inner life of Slovak communities reveals that coping with divisions became part of the process of adjusting to newly emerging ethnic communities.

The Slovak Church and Community: Divisions Within Unity

PERSISTENT REGIONALISMS represented but one of the factors that spawned diversity within Pittsburgh's Slovak communities. Pittsburgh's Slovak immigrants also differed in their response to Slovak nationalism as the movement took root in the United States toward the end of the nineteenth century. After national churches were founded, the differences between Slovak nationalists and their less nationalistic and often more religiously oriented countrymen became more pronounced. These differences influenced attitudes regarding the role Slovak churches should play in the ethnic communities. Nonnationalists viewed Slovak churches primarily as institutions dedicated to performing traditional functions. Nationalists saw churches as vehicles for promoting political or cultural nationalism and ethnic consciousness among Slovak immigrants.

In Pittsburgh's Slovak churches, the divisions between nationalists and their less ethnically conscious countrymen were manifest in the selection process for parish priests and in subsequent pastor-parishioner relations. In addition, nationalists were more likely to agitate for schools. While Slovak nationalists stressed the religious functions of Slovak parochial schools, they saw them also as a means of preserving the Slovak language and inculcating Slovak culture in their children. Such differences could produce fractures but did not split the city's Slovak churches. Nevertheless, the differing responses to Slovak nationalism again illustrate that neither Slovak churches nor Slovak communities were unified entities.

The mixed reactions by parishioners toward Saint Joachim's pastor reveal how a Slovak congregation could live with a wide range of 117 differences based upon varying degrees of nationalist sentiment. In 1909, when Bishop Regis Canevin initially appointed Father Joseph Vrhunec to the newly established Saint Joachim parish, Vrhunec served the congregation only part time. The following year, the bishop made Vrhunec the parish's full-time pastor. Soon after Vrhunec's permanent appointment, a group of parishioners, including some church trustees, complained to the bishop because Vrhunec did not understand Hungarian. They were reportedly disturbed because they did not know how to confess their sins in Slovak.[1] Clearly, these immigrants had not become nationalists. For these Slovaks, a "Slovak" church was apparently one where both the Hungarian and Slovak languages could be used. Slovak nationalists would not have welcomed this dual language use in a "Slovak" church.

The criticism that Vrhunec could not speak Hungarian evoked an angry response from at least one of Saint Joachim's Slovak nationalists. Outraged by his countrymen's actions, Joseph Bohacek indignantly asked: "What kind of Slovaks are these?" He queried why they should even "pretend" to be Slovaks.[2] To Bohacek, a Slovak who spoke Hungarian was a traitor to the Slovak people.

Other parishioners were unhappy because Vrhunec was not a Slovak.[3] The fact that he had mastered the Slovak language and could minister to his Slovak parishioners in their native tongue did not satisfy them.[4] They wanted a Slovak pastor. For these Slovaks, nationality was more important than a priest's ability to serve them in their native tongue.

Again Joseph Bohacek came to Father Vrhunec's defense.[5] He stated that at least Vrhunec was a Slav and hence far better than a "Magyarone," who would oppose Slovak nationalism and support Hungary's efforts to Magyarize its subject nationalities. Bohacek was a nationalist, but he was also a devout Catholic who was fearful lest Slovak Catholic churches "vanish."[6] He pointedly reminded his disgruntled countrymen of Bishop Canevin's claim, voiced when they had petitioned for a church, that it was difficult to find Slovak priests. Bohacek feared that if these parishioners insisted upon a Slovak priest, "then never in all our life will there be a [Slovak] parish here [in Frankstown]." Father Vrhunec's appointment meant that Frankstown could have a Slovak church without the immediate threat that a Magyarone Slovak priest would be assigned to it. Certainly to Bohacek's relief, the bishop did not transfer Vrhunec, who remained at Saint Joachim's until 1924.[7]

Bohacek insisted that only a few parishioners, whom he termed "the cockle among the wheat," complained about the pastor.[8] Apparently, the majority of Saint Joachim's members were content to have a priest who could speak Slovak and serve their religious needs. His nationality was of secondary importance. Nevertheless, the complaints voiced about Father Vrhunec, together with Bohacek's responses, illustrate the type of important divisions that a single Slovak congregation could experience.

In his defense of Father Vrhunec, Joseph Bohacek raised the issue of Magyarone priests, those Slovak clergymen who opposed Slovak nationalism and supported Hungary's efforts to Magyarize its subject nationalities. Slovak nationalists did hold Magyarone priests in disdain.[9] But Pittsburgh's articulate Catholic nationalists, including Bohacek, did not typically allow their nationalism to take precedence over their religiosity. Nor were Pittsburgh's Slovak Catholic immigrants unified in their concern regarding Magyarone priests.

The issue of Magyarone clergymen was raised in 1904 as Saint Gabriel's parishioners sought a replacement for their recently transferred pastor. At the meeting called to discuss obtaining another pastor, there was an apparent lack of interest regarding any future pastor's nationalist views. Alarmed by this disinterest, one parishioner lobbied the congregation to restrict its choices to non-Magyarones. A self-described Slovak nationalist, he opposed suggestions that the parish appeal to the Bishop of Košice for a priest. The bishop, he argued, would send "some sort of Magyarone."[10] He claimed that he left the meeting relieved because the list of possible pastors was suitable. Still, when writing a letter to a Slovak newspaper, he took the opportunity to appeal to Slovaks to oppose Magyarone priests.[11] Apparently he was fearful that, in their zeal to obtain a pastor, Saint Gabriel's parishioners, as well as members of other Slovak churches, would overlook the candidates' cultural commitment.

Two of Pittsburgh's Slovak pastors were Magyarones. Father Coloman Gasparik, a former chaplain in the Hungarian army, felt a reverence for the Hungarian culture.[12] Father John Uhlyarik, Saint Gabriel's first pastor and later pastor to Saint Matthew's, also had Magyar sympathies.[13] If Slovak nationalism had taken strong root among Pittsburgh Slovaks in the prewar era, one would expect these two priests to have come under attack for their Magyarone attitudes.

Father Gasparik did, as already noted, experience serious difficulties with his Saint Elizabeth congregation over the issue of holding annual parish elections. Although a petition signed by 150 church members angrily denounced the pastor for not holding the elections, it is significant that the petition made no mention of his Magyarone sympathies. More important, there is no evidence that any lay persons tried to turn their legitimate complaints about lay rights into an opportunity to get rid of Gasparik. Indeed, the petitioners stopped well short of requesting his removal. They suggested that he should be dismissed only if he failed to recognize their established lay rights. As long as Gasparik honored lay rights, he had peace in his parish.

Father Uhlyarik found that his Magyarone sentiments could create ill feelings but not strong opposition to him as pastor. His appointment to Saint Gabriel's certainly must have given some nationalists cause for concern. Indeed, Peter Rovnianek had earlier refused to loan the Saint Gabriel congregation money because he believed it was going to build a Magyar church.[14] But in 1903, when Saint Gabriel's newly founded parish reportedly asked the bishop to remove Uhlyarik, the reason given was that he was too old to shoulder the responsibility of serving a new church.[15] When Uhlyarik was transferred, it is not clear why or even if parishioners had requested it. Moreover, the parishioner who had opposed appealing to the Bishop of Košice for a priest because he feared he would send "some sort of Magyarone" expressed surprise at Uhlyarik's departure. More important, this man went so far as to lament the fact that Uhlyarik had left the parish at an inopportune time.[16] If Uhlyarik's political position had been the cause for his transfer, this nationalist would not have been so concerned about the parish's future selection, because the congregation would already have demonstrated a dislike for Magyarones. Again, as was the case with Saint Elizabeth's parish, it appears that the Saint Gabriel congregation was not deeply concerned about having a Magyarone for its pastor.

In 1908, Father Uhlyarik was assigned to Saint Matthew Church in the South Side. Some of the neighborhood's Slovaks reportedly did refuse to join branches of the First Catholic Slovak Union associated with the church because of its Magyarone priest.[17] However, there was no concerted effort by nationalists to take advantage of the parish's troubled times between 1910 and 1912 and seek Uhlyarik's dismissal. Uhlyarik remained pastor of Saint Matthew's until his death in 1918.[18]

Some of Father Gasparik's and Father Uhlyarik's parishioners did harbor hostile attitudes toward them because they were Magyarones. This hostility could have made some parishioners prone to criticize them, if given the opportunity. And there is no doubt that Pittsburgh's Slovak immigrants held differing views concerning their pastors. Nevertheless, there is little evidence that a pastor's nationalist sentiments were important to a majority of a church's members. With the notable exception of the non-Slovak Father Vrhunec, the recorded complaints against Pittsburgh's Slovak pastors stemmed from: management of church affairs; charging fees for religious services; or, in the case of the city's Lutherans, trying to institute unacceptable changes. Therefore, it appears that, unless lay rights were involved, once a Catholic priest was appointed by the bishop, Pittsburgh's Slovak nationalists and nonnationalists displayed deference toward him as their spiritual leader.[19]

Slovaks were not as unified in their positions regarding parochial schools. Pittsburgh's Slovak clergymen, both Protestant and Catholic, did provide religious instructions for Slovak children. The primary purpose of the religious classes was to prepare youths to receive the sacraments necessary to make them full-fledged communicants of their respective faiths. These sessions were usually held on Saturdays or Sundays in church basements. Beginning in 1910, the pastor of the Saint Gabriel Church offered daily instruction in religion as well as in Slovak reading and grammar.[20]

Some Slovak immigrants felt that Sunday school or short daily instructions were insufficient education for Slovak children. They wanted a system that would preserve both their children's ethnic identity and their faith. Such a system was not developed in the prewar years because a complex interplay of forces was at work influencing Slovak attitudes regarding schools. These forces caused some Slovak immigrants to accept and some to reject the idea of attaching schools to their church's institutional framework.

During the early years of the twentieth century, Slovak Catholics were urged to establish parochial schools. The First Catholic Slovak Union required its members to send their children to a Catholic school. The fraternal preferred "Slovak" schools and encouraged all Slovak Catholics to support Slovak parochial schools.[21] Slovak clerical leaders viewed schools and the preservation of the Slovak language as crucial to the preservation of Catholicism among their immigrant countrymen. These religious leaders, such as Father Stephen Furdek, founder of the First Catholic Slovak Union, feared that if Slovak children became Americanized they might shed their parents' Catholicism along with their mother tongue.[22] The Pittsburgh diocese also supported parish schools. Diocesan regulations required that Catholic churches, including the national parishes, establish parochial schools if possible.[23]

Despite these pressures, most of Pittsburgh's Slovak Catholics demonstrated little interest in establishing schools for their children.

In 1902, some South Side Slovaks included a school in the initial plans for a church in their neighborhood. But building a school was only a passing consideration and church organizers quickly dropped the proposal.[24] In 1907, an advocate of a Slovak church in Frankstown simply assumed that organizing a parish would include establishing a Slovak parochial school in the area.[25] However, plans for a school were not subsequently pursued as part of the effort to found a Slovak church. Once Saint Joachim's was organized, it proved difficult to arouse enthusiasm for a school. The situation in Frankstown was hardly unique. Although Pittsburgh Slovaks had established their first church in 1895, by 1914 only one parish, Saint Gabriel's, had an elementary school. This school was, moreover, the result of intense efforts by the parish priest, not an outgrowth of lay initiative.

The clear hesitancy of Slovak immigrants to establish schools in Pittsburgh, as well as in the United States, sprang from interrelated cultural and economic factors. Slovaks did not have a premigration tradition of educating their children and, therefore, hesitated to donate money for schools. In addition, economic necessity often caused Slovak immigrant families to send their children to work instead of to school.[26] But not all Pittsburgh Slovaks were ambivalent about providing a Slovak education for their children, and they argued vigorously for founding Slovak schools. The different positions regarding parish schools again reflected divisions between a congregation's nationalists and their less nationalistic countrymen. Some Slovaks did worry about preserving a Slovak ethnic identity and perhaps combatting Americanization, while others lacked such concerns.

The differences between nationalists and nonnationalists over the issue of schools emerged in the Saint Joachim parish within a year of the church's dedication.[27] In 1911, the nationalist, Joseph Bohacek, pleaded with Saint Joachim's parishioners to build a school. He was not satisfied with the fact that parish children were receiving religious instructions in the church basement. He wanted a regular Slovak parochial school. In trying to convince fellow parishioners to support his idea, Bohacek succinctly summarized the views of a Slovak Catholic nationalist on education when he reasoned that "without a school our offspring will be raised for foreigners and not us, and our churches will vanish."[28] Bohacek insisted that a mutually reinforcing link existed between ethnic survival and the preservation of religion.

Bohacek's views did not hold sway with the majority of his fellow parishioners. In 1913, the parish did purchase a lot adjoining the church, but the application to the diocese for permission to obtain land merely noted that "the property will be needed if the Parish ever builds a school."[29] Building a school simply was not an immediate imperative, and buying the property was not even a definite commitment to build a school. Indeed, five years elapsed before serious efforts were finally undertaken to erect a Slovak school in Frankstown.[30]

Parishioners in Pittsburgh's other Slovak Catholic parishes also differed about the necessity of building Slovak schools. Letters by two Slovak youths in 1911 reveal some of the divisions within the Saint Elizabeth and the Saint Matthew congregations. Saint Elizabeth's youthful member categorically stated that her parents wanted and would support a Slovak school but that other members of the parish were not amenable to the proposal.[31] Saint Matthew's young critic asserted that his church did not have a school because Father Uhlyarik refused to listen to parishioners' pleas for one.[32] However, a year later, an adult member of Saint Matthew's offered a quite different assessment of why the parish had failed to build a school. He suggested that only a minority of parishioners really cared about a school. The sad fact was, he said, that while these members were "agitating" for a school, their efforts were "going poorly." He criticized the majority of his fellow parishioners for being unwilling to donate "a few cents for a school." This Slovak tried to emphasize the importance of schools by stressing that although he himself was an "uneducated person," he wanted parish children to receive a "Slovak education."[33] He clearly hoped to preserve a Slovak ethnic identity.

While several years would pass before the South Side or Frankstown churches built schools, by 1913, the Saint Gabriel parish was providing an elementary education for its children. Even though Saint Gabriel's parish was the only Slovak church in the city to establish a regular school before World War I, the congregation as a whole did not express a strong interest in founding one; but the parish priest did. Father Ferdinand Prikazky was determined that Saint Gabriel Church would have an elementary school where parish youths would also receive regular religious instructions. Besides parishioner indifference, Father Prikazky faced a shortage of religious teachers. After at least one unsuccessful attempt to obtain teachers from the Sisters of Saints Cyril and Methodius, a Slovak teaching order in Danville, Pennsylvania, Father Prikazky turned elsewhere for help. In 1913, he asked the Order of Saint Francis, a teaching order whose mother house was in Prague, to send teachers for his parish. Prikazky made arrangements, with Bishop Canevin's approval, to provide the order with a mother house in Pittsburgh, where young women could be trained for the religious life. In 1913 the Franciscans sent women who began teaching children in Saint Gabriel's church basement.[34]

Now that the church had an actual elementary school, parents seemed more inclined to send their children. In 1913, 148 pupils were enrolled in the Saint Gabriel parochial school.[35] As already described, Slovak parents were under pressure from several sources to send their children to a parochial school. This pressure intensified once a regular elementary school existed. Father Prikazky warned parents from the pulpit that it was their religious duty to provide their offspring with a Catholic education.[36]

Still, even when a Slovak education was available, nationalists were disappointed by their countrymen's ambivalent response. When Father Prikazky began providing daily lessons in religion and Slovak reading and grammar for parish youth in 1910, not all of Saint Gabriel's parents sent their children to the classes. In 1911, one dismayed member of the church accused parish families of ignoring their children's "Slovak education." He complained that, while youths were going to public schools, only seventy-four children routinely attended religious and language instructions at Saint Gabriel Church.[37] After the parish elementary school was opened, another parishioner voiced similar complaints. He related that one Slovak family was sending its children to a parochial school other than Saint Gabriel's, because, according to the father, he could in that way avoid paying tuition. Hence, the children were receiving a Catholic but not a "Slovak" education. The parent argued that, since their prayers were in English, there was no need for them to learn to read and write Slovak.[38] His more nationalistic countryman obviously did not agree.

There is no evidence that Pittsburgh's Slovak Lutherans wanted to establish a Slovak school. Neither at Holy Emmanuel's inception nor in later years was there a public call to found a school. Moreover, the issue of a parochial school was not raised in any of the controversies that plagued the Holy Emmanuel congregation during the first decade of the church's existence. Part of the reason that the city's Slovak Lutheran immigrants failed even to consider establishing a school was certainly due to the scattered residences of the Holy Emmanuel members and to the numerically small size of the congregation. The Educational Group formed in 1913 did, however, propose to teach both adults and children Slovak Lutheran history and to preserve the Slovak language among Pittsburgh's Slovak Lutheran population.[39] This attempt to make the church more of a social center also reflected the belief that the church could be used to advance Slovak ethnic consciousness. Given the objectives of the group, its advocates assuredly saw preservation of religion and cultural identity as mutually reinforcing. While more people reportedly attended some of the group's functions, only approximately fifty persons chose to join it. These lay activists demonstrated a concern about advancing Slovak nationalism, especially a kind of Slovak Lutheran nationalism. Not all of Holy Emmanuel's congregation shared their concern.

The divergent attitudes toward establishing Slovak schools or providing a Slovak education for children offer insight into the precedence of religion over ethnic nationalism in the lives of Pittsburgh's immigrants. These attitudes illustrate how extensively—or, perhaps more accurately, how inextensively—the city's Slovaks embraced the Slovak nationalism that was gaining force in the United States, particularly in the Slovak press.[40] The lay initiative responsible for the formation of Slovak national churches in Pittsburgh had demonstrated the religious tenacity of Slovak immigrants. The subsequent weak and divided lay support for parochial schools, despite pressure from Slovak Catholic organizations and the Pittsburgh diocese, suggests that many of the city's Slovak immigrants ignored the arguments advanced by Slovak nationalists as well as by clergymen who stressed that a crucial link existed between the preservation of language and religion. On the issue of Slovak schools, in pre-World War I Pittsburgh, there was definitely a gap between the rhetoric of articulate nationalist and Catholic leaders and the actions of most lay persons.

The various positions regarding non-Slovak pastors, Magyarone priests, and Slovak schools indicate the range of divisions that a congregation could both experience and tolerate as immigrants wrestled with questions involving the function and character of their churches. Although the differences between nationalists and non-nationalists were significant, these differences did not create serious internal conflict within Pittsburgh's Slovak congregations, as they did among some Polish parishes in the United States.[41] Slovak nationalists and nonnationalists agreed in their support of Slovak churches; however, Slovak nationalists wanted these churches to go beyond their prescribed religious functions. By creating and supporting ethnic churches, immigrants typically shared a unity of religion but not a total unity of purpose.

During at least the decades before World War I broke out in Europe, it seems that most of Pittsburgh's Slovak nationalists did not allow their nationalism to supersede their religiosity. For Slovak Catholic nationalists, having a Magyarone pastor or failing to convince fellow parishioners to support a school were reasons for distress, not causes for rebellion. Had they tried to instigate rebellions over such issues, they probably would have been leaders without a following. The majority of Pittsburgh's Slovak immigrants who founded and subsequently supported churches seemed to be demonstrating religious fidelity, not ethnic nationalism.[42]

Many Slovak nationalists were frustrated by the fact that Slovak nationalism or a strong ethnic awareness was seemingly not taking hold among Pittsburgh Slovaks. "I am a Slovak in body and soul; I am not ashamed of my own language," J. Spilka cried out in 1907. Because he felt so strongly, it "grieved" him to admit that, although there were a large number of Slovaks in Allegheny City where he lived, they did not support "national causes."[43] Spilka was especially distraught over Slovaks singing Hungarian songs at a recent dance sponsored by a National Slovak Society lodge. Angered by this spectacle at a function arranged by a local branch of a nationalist society, Spilka left the hall and vowed not to attend any more Slovak dances in Allegheny City. Spilka's account of the dance again demonstrates that the actions of some local Slovak immigrants did not always match the rhetoric of their nationalist leaders. The Slovaks singing Hungarian songs most decidedly were not following the admonitions of their National Slovak Society leaders, who were calling for members to reject all manifestations of Hungarian culture.

Spilka's letter prompted a quick response from another local Slovak. Signing merely as "Prítomný" (one present), this writer sadly concurred with his countryman's account.[44] However, Prítomný added that Spilka had failed to mention instances when these Slovaks had sacrificed money for "national causes," especially to aid Slovak nationalists in Hungary. To illustrate his point, Prítomný noted that only recently a collection had grossed $3.10 to aid Slovaks in Hungary. He did not indicate how the collection was taken, but such a paltry amount is hardly persuasive evidence that the city's Slovak immigrants were really supporting nationalist causes. Moreover, while defending the efforts of some of his countrymen, this man, too, called on Slovaks to do more to support the Slovak "people." A few months later, yet another immigrant scolded his fellow Pittsburgh Slovaks for their failure to support their "people." He went so far as to accuse some of his countrymen of being ignorant of what a "Magyarone" was.[45]

The sudden surge in 1907 of complaints about nonnationalist sentiment among Pittsburgh's Slovaks was most likely spurred by events in Hungary. In December 1906, the Hungarian government arrested Andrew Hlinka, a Catholic priest and Slovak nationalist, and sentenced him to two years in prison.[46] These actions prompted strong denunciations by officials of Slovak organizations in the United States and ultimately led to the formation of the Slovak League of America. The league's goal was to send monetary assistance to Slovak nationalists and to newspapers being persecuted by the Hungarian government.[47]

On February 10, 1907, Slovaks from Pittsburgh and nearby towns met to protest the Hungarian government's actions. The display at the meeting of numerous lodge banners from various Slovak organizations indicated that members of area fraternals attended in groups. According to the description published in the First Catholic Slovak Union's newspaper, Slovak Lutherans were active, vocal participants in the rally. John Feriencik, one of Pittsburgh's prominent Slovak Lutheran fraternalists and a member of the National Slovak Society as well, opened the meeting. A Lutheran clergyman gave the welcoming address, while a local Catholic priest presided over subsequent proceedings.[48] In this case, Slovaks of different faiths were brought together by a shared interest in a political issue that transcended religious or regional identities.

In October 1907, the Hungarian government offered even more apparent proof that it was treacherously persecuting Slovaks. In that month, a confrontation between Hungarian police and Slovaks in Černová, in Liptov County, ultimately left fifteen Slovaks dead. The battle occurred when parishioners of Černová's newly established Catholic church protested the installation of their new pastor. They wanted Father Hlinka, a native of Černová and the nationalist recently imprisoned by the government.[49] Subsequently known as the Černová Massacre, this incident evoked strong denunciations and helped stir Slovak nationalism in the United States.[50]

Once the furor over Hlinka's imprisonment and the Černová Massacre diminished, however, the Slovak nationalist movement in America subsided. By December 1911, the Slovak League, which had received a great deal of vocal support in 1907, was barely surviving. It had but 515 members and a treasury of a meager $1,259.33.[51] In Pittsburgh, Slovaks turned once again to more immediate matters involving their churches, their communities, and their own survival in a fluctuating economy. Unified outbursts, as occurred in 1907, needed a catalyst such as the imprisonment of a priest or the massacre of civilians. No similar flash points took place in prewar Hungary. By 1910, in the opinion of one Pittsburgh Slovak, the enthusiasm for nationalist causes among the city's rank-and-file Slovaks had reached a nadir. He complained that not only was there discord among Pittsburgh's fraternal lodges but that some Slovaks were "ridiculing" and "scorning" those who worked for Slovak "causes."[52]

The interplay of nationalist and religious issues did, on at least one occasion, create acrimonious internal strife in a Pittsburgh branch of the First Catholic Slovak Union. Such dissension developed after the fraternal's leadership and also clergymen began criticizing the Slovak League of America.[53] In August 1912, a member of a South Side lodge castigated his local officers for failing to take the necessary steps to affiliate the lodge with the Slovak League, as members had mandated. He reported that the officers asserted that the league's work did not coincide with the religious goals of their society. This angry member seized the opportunity to accuse lodge officers of being Magyarones.[54] In response, the lodge president explained, seemingly with a yawn, that this was a typical accusation by a lodge member unhappy with anything an officer did.[55] But the president did not explain why officers had failed to affiliate with the league; nor did he challenge the statement that the officers had argued that the league's work did not coincide with the religious goals of the lodge. Obviously, this Catholic society was divided between members influenced by religious leaders critical of the Slovak League and members unwilling to permit religious issues to interfere with their backing of a nationalist organization.

At times, as in the case of the Hlinka incident, "nationalist causes" did provide opportunities for Pittsburgh's Slovak Catholics and Protestants to work together. But, simultaneously, the divided support for some of these causes reveals divisions within Pittsburgh's larger Slovak community.

A 1912 visit to the United States by Pavel Blaho, a Slovak nationalist from Hungary, for example, helped stimulate a small-scale Slovak nationalist movement in Pittsburgh. As Blaho traveled to various cities where Slovaks lived, he was welcomed by gatherings of Slovaks. Not to be surpassed, some Pittsburgh Slovaks began making preparations in October for Blaho's late December visit. The first organizational meeting was initially scheduled to be held at Saint Gabriel Church in Woods Run, but for unexplained reasons it was changed to the Slovak Evangelical Union headquarters in nearby Manchester.[56]

Although Pittsburgh's Slovak Lutheran lodges were far more active in formulating plans for the Blaho visit than were local branches of the First Catholic Slovak Union, the undertaking was an interreligious one.[57] Representatives of three of Pittsburgh's five male Lutheran lodges attended planning meetings. Only one local branch of the First Catholic Slovak Union sent representatives, but persons from two branches of the Pennsylvania Slovak Catholic Union came.[58] And there were, of course, Catholic members of the National Slovak Society, several of whose lodges participated in the arrangements. The *Slovenský Hlásnik* even expressed pleasure that the plans were being undertaken by both Catholics and Protestants.[59] Still, the absence of most of the city's First Catholic Slovak Union lodges suggests that criticism of Blaho by both local and nationally prominent priests caused some Catholic lodges not to participate in plans for his visit.[60] This absence further suggests a lack of a strong nationalist sentiment among Pittsburgh Slovaks. Throughout the first decade of the twentieth century, the city's Slovak nationalists had bemoaned this indifference. It was far easier to convince Slovak lodge members to protest the imprisonment of a priest than to participate in arrangements for a Slovak nationalist to speak.

A large contingent of those helping to prepare for the Blaho visit came from the North Side. It was not the only time that North Side Slovaks joined forces to support Slovak causes. Just a few weeks before meetings were getting under way for the Blaho visit, seven local lodges and a Slovak singing group, all located in the North Side, had agreed to form the "Association of Slovak Societies in the North Side." The association's goals were purely nationalistic. It aimed to bolster support among Pittsburgh Slovaks for the Slovak League and for Slovak nationalists in Hungary.[61] When news of Pavel Blaho's proposed visit reached Pittsburgh, spokesmen for the association called on all Slovak organizations in the city to participate.[62] Although only a minority of Slovak lodges in the Pittsburgh area aided with preparations, organizers of the event said they were gratified by the turnout for Blaho.[63]

After Blaho's visit, the association focused its energies on other local projects. By March 1913, the group was working to establish a Slovak "national house," meaning a national hall or center, in Pittsburgh.[64] According to its proponents, the hall would serve Slovak adults as well as their children. It was to have a library and classrooms, a restaurant, sleeping rooms, meeting places for lodges, and a hall for social functions.[65]

To achieve their objectives, advocates of the hall adopted the same plans the founders of national churches had followed. They turned to the fraternal network and to the Slovak press. Besides publishing requests for money and support, the association sent representatives to Slovak lodges to plead their case. In March 1913, twelve members of the First Catholic Slovak Union's Branch 2 responded to such appeals by each loaning ten dollars to the national hall fund.[66] Other Pittsburgh Slovaks were not as enthusiastic over the project. The association continued to press for support for the hall, but it never stirred enough enthusiasm to achieve its goal and, by the end of 1914, the project was abandoned.

The forces that had combined to create Slovak ethnic churches were either absent or actually worked against the creation of a Slovak center in Pittsburgh. The move to found a national hall lacked the kind of magnetic pole that had drawn Slovak immigrants together to organize their churches. Religion was that pole. Religion served further as the catalyst that animated the forces of a shared language and culture and led to the creation of national churches. Without a strong activating factor like religion, proponents of the national hall could not energize the forces of a shared language, culture, and origin to draw Slovak immigrants together in the way that the founders of churches had done. The national hall failed in part because its purpose lacked the same force of tradition that had stimulated the founding of national churches.

The failure of the plans for a Slovak cultural center in Pittsburgh was actually indicative of the type of community development that had been and still was taking place among the city's Slovaks. In essence, the venture represented the antithesis of what had been happening as these immigrants established their national churches in neighborhoods. As Slovaks gravitated to different sections of the city, they became neighborhood oriented. This narrower orientation was manifested in the organizing of fraternal lodges and, more importantly, in the founding of neighborhood churches. By 1914, Slovaks had already established meeting places for fraternal lodges and halls for social gatherings. A central hall located somewhere outside their neighborhood posed more of an inconvenience than a benefit to these immigrants, now used to socializing in their own neighborhood facilities. In short, the dispersed nature of the city's Slovak population and yet the convergence of these immigrants into specific neighborhoods made a national center unappealing and impractical. Obviously, the idea of a national hall was not impractical or undesirable to a segment of the city's Slovak population, but this was a small segment and one unable to rouse support from the majority of immigrants.

On the eve of World War I, as it had for nearly three and a half decades, Pittsburgh's Slovak church and neighborhood communities harbored internal differences. Some differences had roots in premigration religious and regional identities. Other divisions, especially those developing between nationalists and nonnationalists, were a partial outgrowth of immigration. Slovak churches tolerated the regionalisms and other differences among these immigrants because the significance of these churches lay in their functions as religious institutions. Slovak churches did not represent strong expressions of ethnic nationalism. Despite the ethnic pride and even chauvinism voiced by a few supporters of national churches, ethnocentrism or cultural nationalism had not been major forces behind their formation. In the early twentieth century, the majority of Pittsburgh's Slovak immigrants did not view their churches as instruments to advance cultural nationalism. Nevertheless, Slovak national churches and fraternal societies did tie Slovaks to larger religious and ethnic institutions. Hence, they encouraged Slovak immigrants to develop a more encompassing ethnic identity. But, on the eve of World War I, this broader ethnic identity was not yet fully developed among Pittsburgh's Slovak immigrants.

Conclusion

9 SCHOLARS HAVE LONG tried to assess the significance of religion and of national churches in the lives of America's immigrants. Such investigations, however, have not been limited to scholars. The experience of Slovak Catholics and Lutherans in Pittsburgh shows that immigrants themselves had to make similar assessments about the relevance of religion and the role of national churches in their lives. While the importance of these churches rests in the inner thoughts of immigrants, the process of church formation and maintenance can help illuminate the meaning and nature of the ethnic church and "ethnic community" in the urban America of the past.

The immigrant church was a transplanted institution but not an exact replica of its Old World antecedent, the village church. It could not be. In minute and also significant ways, their Pittsburgh churches differed from those the immigrants had left in Europe. In bustling Pittsburgh, the familiar peal of church bells no longer beckoned Slovaks to services. Nor were these churches the places where generations of the immigrants' ancestors had worshiped, been christened, married, or laid to rest. Unlike the situation in Europe, in early twentieth-century Pittsburgh, immigrants most likely had participated in founding their church or knew some of the founders. The historian can reconstruct the administrative history of the national churches that immigrants organized in the United States, but he or she cannot fully expose what these churches and religion meant to the immigrants themselves. Their determination to build churches and to support them does offer revealing insight into the 132 importance of religion in their lives. Still, we cannot know the feelings of the foreign-born as they prepared to go to church for regular communal worship with fellow countrymen. One can speculate that the church must have had a deeply personal and traditional significance for individual immigrants as they went to marry their betrothed, christen their newborn, or bury their dead. Moreover, the church surely had special meaning to the laymen elected to trustee positions by fellow church members. The churches whose administrative affairs these lay trustees oversaw were indeed different from their village counterparts in Europe. Nevertheless, as one immigrant implied, national churches did help immigrants, in some way, feel more at home.

The formation of ethnic churches is perforce the story of immigrants coming together and recognizing their shared goals and interests as well as their common language, religion, and culture. Establishing national churches did not represent a defensive response to a hostile environment or even a conscious attempt to keep "alive the national group identity."[1] Rather, Slovak churches grew out of a deeply rooted religiosity. Simultaneously, they were products of Slovak migration patterns and of Slovak adjustment to an ethnically diverse society. Pittsburgh's Slovak churches developed as the immigrant population changed and grew larger and more permanent. Slovaks themselves became aware of these changes and acted.

Desiring to preserve and practice their homeland faith, Slovak Catholics organized a central church in 1895. The neighborhood churches that Catholics subsequently founded represented a pragmatic response to the scattered and yet directed nature of the Slovak migration into the Pittsburgh area. The small number of Slovak Lutherans prevented them from establishing neighborhood churches. The strong tradition of chain migration, coupled with the economic realities of gainful employment and practical concerns of living near their jobs, kept Slovak Lutherans from clustering together as a group. They wanted a church but the realities of life in the urban, industrial Pittsburgh of the early twentieth century helped prevent Holy Emmanuel Church from becoming a neighborhood institution as the city's Slovak Catholic churches did. The formation of Slovak churches was thus the result of a blend of pragmatism and traditional piety.

Once organized, Pittsburgh's national churches helped Slovaks adjust to their new environment. At the same time, the very act of founding ethnic churches represented part of the adjustment process taking place among these former denizens of northern Hungary. Besides adapting to the realities of an urban, industrial, and culturally diverse society, Slovak immigrants had to adjust to a country where there was separation of church and state. Without state aid, individual congregations had to be self-supporting, a requirement that compelled Slovaks to develop a new sense of community. In northern Hungary, "communities" were territorially based, by village, town, or village clusters, and community obligations grew out of the circumstances of shared residence. But Pittsburgh's Slovak immigrants had come from different regions of northern Hungary. If their churches were to survive, these immigrants *had* to cultivate a notion of "community" based on a shared interest in an institution, the church.[2] This interest went beyond joining together in communal worship; it required a financial and an emotional commitment. For Slovak Catholics, over time, this shared obligation typically became one they had with persons in the same general neighborhood. For Slovak Lutherans, this commitment was one that drew Slovaks who lived in various parts of the Pittsburgh metropolitan area together into a church community.

Although Slovak Lutherans did disperse into different sections of Pittsburgh, they still embodied a kind of ethnic community. Regardless of where they lived, those Slovak Lutherans who wanted to continue practicing their homeland religion in the traditional manner had a shared interest and responsibility toward their church located in Pittsburgh's North Side. The Slovak Lutherans who joined in communal worship and cooperated to support Holy Emmanuel Church composed the city's Slovak Lutheran community. This community was defined by a shared religion and language and an interest in the welfare of their church rather than being based on an ethnic population in a neighborhood. For Catholics, the church combined with fraternals to provide needed religious and social services and activities for neighborhood residents. For Lutherans, the church was limited primarily to providing religious services for the city's scattered Lutheran population.

The successful formation of churches and their continued existence bear witness to the sense of mutual obligation and interest that developed among immigrants who had come together from various parts of northern Hungary. The prewar history of Pittsburgh's Slovaks, and perhaps that of other immigrant groups, is, then, not one of community disintegration. On the contrary, the successful establishment of national churches reflected the emergence of communities and an ongoing community and institutional development. Coming together, not disintegration, was a theme of the immigrant experience.

Immigrants came together in a variety of ways, and the process was a cumulative one. Kinship and friendship ties often brought Slovaks to the same section of Pittsburgh. Slovak newspapers and fraternal societies were part of an ethnic communications network that further drew immigrants together. Although Pittsburgh's Slovaks established and joined fraternals primarily for pragmatic reasons, their conception of fraternal activities changed as the city's Slovak population changed. As a result, fraternal lodges gradually expanded their activities once Slovaks decided a church was needed in their city or neighborhood. Of course, religious restrictions limited the importance that some lodges had in their churches.

Churches and fraternal societies became vital parts of the institutional and social structure of Slovak communities. While these organizations served transient as well as permanent immigrants, Slovak fraternals and churches provided avenues for the latter to become prominent members of their respective communities. However, Pittsburgh's Slovak communities were not headed by merely a business elite. Indeed, evidence suggests that, except for Saint Matthew's in the South Side, fraternalists, who were also typically laborers, initiated the efforts to establish ethnic parishes. Many of the men who subsequently held lay positions in the city's Slovak churches had previously been fraternal officers. The skills required for fraternal offices, together with the recognition gained from holding such offices, helped pave the way for rank-and-file immigrants to achieve prominence within their community. These Slovaks may have remained at the bottom of America's social scale, but they achieved an important status within their own ethnic community.

The importance of fraternal lodges within Slovak communities varied. Pittsburgh's Catholic lodges became closely affiliated with their respective churches and were actively involved in parish activities. The Lutheran experience was different. After initiating the formation of the church, Lutheran lodges were forced to limit their involvement in church affairs. Thus these lodges, like the city's secular lodges, were part of the Slovak communities' institutional structures but not closely tied to churches. Some Slovak immigrants, of course, never joined any fraternal organization, religious or secular, and hence remained outside that part of the social and institutional life of Slovak communities.

The existence of Catholic, Protestant, and secular fraternal societies attests to the religious diversity among Pittsburgh's Slovak immigrants. In some parts of the city, Slovaks of different religious persuasions lived together. Pittsburgh's Slovak communities were, then, complex and multidimensional but could be defined by either religion or loosely by geography. While neighborhood communities were religiously diverse, church communities transcended territorial boundaries. The religious diversity of Slovak neighborhoods precludes equating ethnic communities with neighborhood churches and their memberships.[3] Additionally, some Slovak immigrants, especially those committed to stirring Slovak ethnic consciousness, defined Pittsburgh's Slovak community without regard to religious or territorial boundaries.[4]

Besides offering insight into the nature of ethnic communities and churches at the turn of the century, a comparison of the Pittsburgh Slovak Catholic and Lutheran experiences sheds light on the ongoing relations between immigrants and their church leaders. By establishing national churches, Slovaks unavoidably became involved with church hierarchies in the United States. Catholics and Lutherans experienced decidedly different relations with their respective hierarchies. Confrontation between Slovak Catholics and Pittsburgh's diocesan officials was the exception, not the rule. Slovak lay Catholics displayed a deference toward their bishops, but it was an assertive deference. They recognized and accepted the bishop's authority, but at the same time, they expected bishops to acquiesce in lay demands for churches and to resolve fairly lay grievances, especially those against pastors. To Slovak Catholic lay persons, bishops became guardians of sanctioned lay rights in the Pittsburgh diocese—rights conferred by diocesan statutes. In Pittsburgh, the ongoing relations between Slovak Catholics and the diocesan hierarchy were characterized by mutual, if not always willing, accommodation.[5]

The relations between Pittsburgh's Slovak Lutherans and their Slovak Synod were marked by a mixture of accommodation and conflict. The problems that Slovak Lutherans encountered reveal the importance of religious traditions as factors influencing relations between immigrants and church hierarchies. As did Catholics, Lutherans wanted to maintain their religious practices and traditions. A contingent of Slovak clergymen, however, under the influence of a conservative Lutheran body in the United States, did try to institute changes. These clergymen also attacked the newly established rituals of Slovak fraternal societies. Pittsburgh's Slovak Lutherans balked at making changes, and conflict ensued. Some Slovaks may have hesitated at accepting their new responsibilities as the church's financial supporters, but this hesitation was minor in comparison to their reluctance to accept significant alterations in their religious traditions. Giving up hard-earned money may have been difficult for immigrants, but relinquishing religious traditions or shunning fraternals seemed impossible. Churches had been organized to preserve their communal religious practices, not change them.

A comparison of the Slovak Lutheran and Catholic experiences in Pittsburgh suggests that when conflict occurred between immigrants and church hierarchies it had complex and different roots. As some scholars have shown, lay initiative, control of church property, or the ethnicity of a pastor could well spur conflict. The case of Pittsburgh's Slovak Lutherans demonstrates that challenges to religious traditions or practices, too, could create volatile, potentially explosive situations.

Preservation of faith, then, was a constant theme in the history of Pittsburgh's Slovak Catholic and Lutheran immigrants. But the Catholic and Lutheran experiences also show that preservation of faith could have different meanings. For the diocesan hierarchy, it meant keeping Slovak Catholic immigrants faithful to Rome and subject to diocesan authority. Hence, this hierarchy responded favorably to fraternal societies. In addition, the Catholic church did not seek to make fundamental changes in the religious practices of Slovak Catholics. In general, the traditions of Slovak communal worship were not repugnant to the Catholic hierarchy. For the Synodical Conference and the Slovak Lutherans who supported it, preservation of faith required changes. For Slovak Lutheran lay persons, preservation of faith meant maintaining traditional religious practices and incorporating fraternal rituals into some religious ceremonies, such as funerals. Given these determined and differing positions, conflict became inevitable. Ultimately, challenges to religious traditions caused some lay persons to question the religious authority of their pastors.

Transplanting churches can be described as a basically conservative move by immigrants to preserve their premigration faith. Nevertheless, national churches proved to be flexible institutions as they adapted to New World conditions. For example, in the course of trying to transplant their church, Slovak laities generally did adjust to the demands of self-sufficiency. In addition, Slovak Catholics recognized the bishop's authority and at times even invited his intervention in parish affairs. Relations between Pittsburgh's Slovak Lutherans and their synod were marked by varying degrees of flexibility. Lay persons were initially rigid in their attitudes regarding the Slovak Synod and its theological principles. Faced with a crisis of having no pastor, their attitudes softened. The congregation did, however, remain adamant in its decision to reject affiliation with the Synodical Conference.

This examination of the internal workings of Slovak church communities reveals that Pittsburgh's Slovak congregations took on a life of their own, separate from church hierarchies. In this way, immigrant churches were subsystems within the city's established religious structure. Self-supporting and separated by language and culture, Slovak congregations became somewhat interdependent. This interdependence was encouraged through social functions and by cooperation among pastors. Hence, Slovak churches, perhaps like those of other ethnic groups, remained distinct entities within larger church bodies. This encouraged cultural pluralism not only within America's denominations but within early twentieth-century Pittsburgh. The establishment of Protestant immigrant churches serves as a reminder that the Catholic church was not the only denomination in the United States that harbored and, indeed, encouraged cultural pluralism within its ranks.

The success of their national churches is evidence of a unity among Slovak immigrants who settled in Pittsburgh. There was, however, a complex diversity within the unity symbolized by a national church. This diversity within unity was evident in a number of ways. For instance, national churches did encourage Slovaks to identify and recognize themselves as separate from other nationalities who shared their religion. Consequently, these institutions did encourage the development of a "consciousness of kind" among Pittsburgh Slovaks. Nevertheless, regional and parochial identities cultivated in Hungary clearly persisted, even though Slovaks from different regions belonged to the same church and lived in the same neighborhood. The durability of regional identities was encouraged and, indeed, reinforced by chain migrations into Pittsburgh. Slovak marriage patterns also encouraged the persistence of regionalism, as Slovaks for the most part married someone from their own village or region. Regionalism was again evident in the choice of godparents for their children. Thus regional identities formed one basis for social relationships within Pittsburgh's Slovak communities.

The establishment of Slovak fraternal lodges was both a manifestation as well as a reinforcement of regionalism. While these organizations served a practical function for Slovak immigrants, there is evidence that at least those who joined Pittsburgh branches of the First Catholic Slovak Union often chose the same lodge as family or countrymen from their home regions in northern Hungary. Nevertheless, by linking their members to national Slovak organizations, these lodges helped encourage unity within the diversity that existed among Slovaks. Therefore, Pittsburgh's Slovak Catholic and perhaps Lutheran lodges played a dual role of encouraging regionalisms while providing a foundation for the development of a stronger ethnic identity among these immigrants.

The persistence of regionalisms among Slovaks suggests that these immigrants often maintained two identities—one based on a shared language and culture, another on Old World geographic origins. Hence, a two-tiered identity structure existed within Pittsburgh's Slovak communities and congregations. Once in the United States, contact with Slovaks from other regions of northern Hungary could sharpen regional differences among Slovaks instead of eradicating them. The intensity of these differences, however, varied and their importance was often relative.

It seems clear that not all, and perhaps only a minority, of Pittsburgh's Slovaks developed a strong ethnic awareness or identity as members of a unique "people" by the eve of World War I. National churches did encourage ethnic pride and laid a basis for a stronger more consciously felt ethnic identity. Nevertheless, churches by themselves did not spur the rise of ethnic consciousness among Pittsburgh Slovaks. Indeed, the existence of these churches belies the diversity that persisted within Pittsburgh's Slovak congregations and within the larger Slovak community. Significantly, besides regional divisions, Slovaks were divided in their nationalist convictions. And they differed over whether churches should become forces to counter Americanization by transmitting Slovak culture and preserving it among their children. The issue of schools suggests further that, while Slovak churches were flexible institutions, in the early twentieth century, the laities were not yet sure how flexible they should be.

Still, during the prewar years, divisions among Slovaks did not erupt into open conflicts. Churches did not become battlegrounds between Slovak nationalists and their countrymen who did not share their nationalist enthusiasm. In general, Pittsburgh's nationalist Slovaks did not permit their nationalist sentiments to override their religiosity. Religious and ethnic differences did not clash in these years and lead to fierce battles, as was the case with Polish immigrants in the United States.

Slovaks were but one immigrant group that migrated to Pittsburgh. Their adjustment may well have differed from that of other immigrant groups. Furthermore, Pittsburgh was but one of several American cities that attracted Slovaks, and their experience may not have been the same as that of Slovaks migrating to other cities or perhaps to small industrial towns.[6] Only additional studies can show whether the experiences of Pittsburgh's Slovak Catholics and Lutherans were representative or atypical. Still, this study does have implications that reach beyond the Slovaks of Pittsburgh. Their experiences indicate that the "immigration experience" was not characterized by social disorganization. Old World familial and friendship ties could persist and help give direction to migration and settlement patterns. Shared religions and practical assessments of perceived needs allied immigrants from different parts of northern Hungary into a quest for national churches. There was continuity between the Old World and these New World churches, but continuity accompanied by change and characterized by accommodation, an adjustment of differences. National churches were flexible institutions, capable of making adjustments to conditions in America. Moreover, there was a dynamic relationship between the durability of cultural and religious heritages and the flexibility of both immigrants and America's religious bodies.

On Sunday, June 28, 1914, as Europe would be shaken by news of the assassination of Archduke Ferdinand of Austria, Pittsburgh's Slovaks were going about their daily lives. Except for those who had to work, Slovaks went to church as usual. Catholics placed money in the collection basket as usual; some may have even asked for change from the collector. After services, these churchgoers probably congregated with family and friends from their native villages. Surely someone had a letter from the old country to share with those eager for news from home. Fraternals that regularly held meetings on the fourth Sunday of the month did so. At Holy Emmanuel Church, the Reverend John Marcis was holding services for the fourth time. The congregation sang from the *Spevník*, not the hymnal the Slovak Synod approved, but the one the congregation preferred. The congregation had come through a trying ordeal and, for the time being, it could heave a collective sigh of relief as it looked forward to the autumn and the ceremony formally installing Marcis as its pastor. The Educational Group had not advertised any events recently, but its members were still actively working to draw the city's Slovak Lutherans together. The city's Slovak Catholic parishes were, as a group, enjoying relative peace. At Saint Gabriel's the children enrolled in that church's parochial school were on summer vacation. Across the city, at Saint Matthew's, the parish had resolved the problems that had stirred controversy in that church. Some parishioners were surely grumbling about the fact that the church did not have a school, and some of their compatriots at Saint Joachim's were doing the same. In addition, some of Saint Joachim's members may have, for one reason or another, still been hoping for a different pastor. If Father Gasparik was correct in his description of his parish, Saint Elizabeth's was also enjoying relative peace. In less than six months, this pastor and his parish would be embroiled in a dispute over trustee elections. On June 28, however, a number of parishioners were probably preoccupied with preparations for a marriage scheduled for the following day in the church.[7] Members of the Association of Slovak Societies in the North Side were still trying to arouse enthusiasm for a Slovak hall. The movement had been under way for more than a year, but by this late June Sunday had experienced little success.

For the more than five thousand immigrants and their children who made up Pittsburgh's Slovak population, this fourth Sunday of June 1914 was similar to other Sundays. The events taking place in Europe, however, would ultimately have an impact on the city's Slovak communities. Similar to other immigrant groups, after war broke out in Europe, Slovaks could not avoid feeling concern about friends and relatives left behind in a country now at war. For Slovak immigrants, the war raised yet another issue: the creation of a homeland. Once this issue surfaced during the war, Slovak Protestants and Catholics would confront the question of determining the relationship between the religious identities they had long nurtured and the ethnic identity they were discovering.

As war engulfed Europe in 1914, many of America's immigrants did turn their attention to events in their homelands. This interest made Americans realize that the country's foreign-born had not abandoned a sentimental attachment and perhaps a loyalty to their native lands. The concern displayed by immigrants regarding events in Europe bothered Americans and, consequently, a new emphasis was laid on "Americanizing" the foreign-born, on turning them into "Americans." This transformation, many Americans concluded, had not been occurring during the recent decades, despite Israel Zangwill's optimistic and graphic depictions to the contrary.[8] Instead, immigrants had been forming ethnic communities and developing their own ethnic institutions.

For Pittsburgh's Slovaks, institutions such as their national churches had worked to preserve their traditional language, culture, and religion. At the same time, founding and supporting these institutions had constituted part of their adjustment to American society. Churches did remind the foreign-born of their homeland. One Slovak perhaps spoke for many of America's immigrants when he revealed that church-related activities had evoked fond memories and that, consequently, he and others "felt as if we were in the old country."[9] Ironically, by stirring such nostalgic emotions, national churches encouraged immigrants to feel more at home in America.

APPENDIX

ABBREVIATIONS

NOTES

BIBLIOGRAPHICAL ESSAY

INDEX

Appendix: Methodology for Deriving Data from Church Records

T HE BAPTISMAL, marriage, and burial records of Slovak churches contain a variety of useful information. For this study, primarily baptismal and marriage records were used. It is from these records that data on the village origins of Pittsburgh and Allegheny City Slovaks were derived.

Baptismal records are the most reliable sources for village origins and, hence, the regional composition of a parish. With the exception of Saint Gabriel Roman Catholic Church in Allegheny City, the baptismal records of Slovak churches usually listed the parents' village and county origins. This information was extracted from the records and tabulated. So that the total number of families from different villages and counties would not be skewed by multiple births, those families having more than one child were counted only once. Also excluded from the totals were single-parent entries and non-Slovak families. Since this study focuses on Slovak immigration to Pittsburgh and Allegheny City, all Slovak families listed as living outside of these two cities were also excluded.

The origins of "families" in this study are usually based on the husbands' origins. This procedure was followed for several reasons. First, often, especially in Saint Matthew's records, no village origin was listed for the mother, and it was not clear if this was an oversight or if the woman came from the same village as her husband. In several of the families with multiple births, I discovered that the mother's origin was different in the various entries: usually in one entry she was listed as being from the same village as her husband and in another entry she had a village origin different than her 145 husband's. But I found only one instance where the father's village origin was listed differently in separate entries. In short, information concerning the fathers' origins was more reliable. Because the pastors of Saint Gabriel Church did not list the parents' origins in baptismal records, that church's marriage and burial records were used to derive information on the composition of that parish.

Marriage records are not as reliable as baptismal records for determining the background of persons living within a particular neighborhood or belonging to a specific church. This is the case because it is not always clear if a couple was married at the bride or the groom's church. Although the custom in Catholic churches was to be married in the woman's church, this practice was not always followed. Hence, while it is safe to assume that, unless the pastor noted otherwise, the families listed in baptismal records lived in the area served by the church where the baptism was performed, the same is not true for persons included in marriage records. Therefore, when marriage records were used to determine the origins of persons, only individuals listed as living in the neighborhood served by the church were included. For example, in determining the origins of Slovaks living in western Allegheny City, only persons listed in Saint Gabriel's records as living in "Allegheny" were counted. The pastor of Saint Joachim Church (Frankstown) usually listed persons as living in "Pittsburgh," a designation that probably meant the Frankstown-Hazelwood area and sections of the city contiguous to Frankstown. This assumption is made because this church's registers do include entries that clearly designate that the individuals or families came from towns or boroughs outside Pittsburgh.

In a few instances, totals include Slovaks who did not reside in Pittsburgh or Allegheny City. One instance is in the analysis of the origins of godparents (chapter 7). The principle concern of that analysis was to assess the persistence of regional ties over time, and hence the village origins of the godparents is more relevant than where he or she lived in America. The data on marriage patterns of Slovaks include some persons who did not live in Pittsburgh (chapter 7). Non-Pittsburgh Slovaks were included in those instances when one partner did live in Pittsburgh or Allegheny City. Marriages in which both partners lived outside of Pittsburgh or Allegheny City were excluded from the data.

It should be noted that persons and families listed in church records do not include all of the Slovaks who lived in Pittsburgh and Allegheny City or even in a particular neighborhood. Slovaks who were married in Hungary or somewhere besides Pittsburgh are obviously not included in the marriage records. Slovaks who had completed their families before coming to Pittsburgh or who did not have any children born while living in the city are excluded from baptismal records. In addition, Slovaks who did not belong to a church or who may have attended other nationality churches in Pittsburgh or Allegheny City would not be recorded in Slovak church records. However, the number of Slovak Catholics or Lutherans who would have relied on non-Slovak churches for baptisms, marriages, or funerals was probably extremely small.

Abbreviations

Newspapers

ASN	*Amerikánsko-Slovenské Noviny*
	[American Slovak News]
NN	*Národné Noviny*
	[National News]
PC	*Pittsburgh Catholic*
SvA	*Slovák v Amerike*
	[Slovak in America]
SH	*Slovenský Hlásnik*
	[Slovak Herald]

Slovak Organizations

FCSU	First Catholic Slovak Union
	[Prvá Katolícka Slovenská Jednota]
NSS	National Slovak Society
	[Národný Slovenský Spolok]
SCPU	Slovak Calvinistic Presbyterian Union
	[Slovenská Kalvínska Presbyteriánska Jednota]
SELC	Slovak Evangelical Lutheran Church
SEU	Slovak Evangelical Union
	[Slovenská Evanjelická Jednota]

Pittsburgh Slovak Churches

HEC	Holy Emmanuel Slovak Evangelical Lutheran Church
SEC	Saint Elizabeth of Hungary Slovak Roman Catholic Church
SGC	Saint Gabriel Slovak Roman Catholic Church
SJC	Saint Joachim Slovak Roman Catholic Church
SMC	Saint Matthew Slovak Roman Catholic Church

149

Archives or Record Locations

DA   Archives of the Diocese of Pittsburgh
HSWP   Historical Society of Western Pennsylvania, Pittsburgh
IHRC   Immigration History Research Center, St. Paul, MN.
NSSH   National Slovak Society Headquarters, Pittsburgh
OVGC   Office of the Vicar-General Chancellor, Pittsburgh Diocese (Pittsburgh)
SMA   Slovak Museum and Archives, Middletown, PA.

Office of the Vicar-General Chancellor, Church Files

CC   Church Committee
EB   Erection and Boundary
FB   Finance and Building

Notes

Introduction

1. Interviews with Ferdinand Dvorsky, Pittsburgh, 12 Apr. 1977, 28 Nov. 1978; Helen Dvorsky to June Alexander, 26 June 1984.

2. Interview with John and Mary Ciganik, Pittsburgh, 17 May 1977; Mary Ciganik to June Alexander, 9 June 1984.

3. Stephan Thernstrom, *Poverty and Progress: Social Mobility in a Nineteenth Century City* (Cambridge: Harvard University Press, 1964).

4. National churches served particular ethnic groups and were based on language instead of strict geographic boundaries. Over time, individual churches did have recognized boundaries, but they remained national churches because each church served a particular ethnic group residing within its boundaries. As used in this study, the terms "national," "ethnic," or "immigrant" are interchangeable when used with "church" or "parish." For a further explanation of national churches, see Jay P. Dolan, *The Immigrant Church: New York's Irish and German Catholics, 1815–1865* (Baltimore: Johns Hopkins University Press, 1975), pp. 4–5.

5. U.S. Congress, Senate, Immigration Commission, *Reports of the Immigration Commission*, vol. 3, *Statistical Review of Immigration, 1820–1910—Distribution of Immigrants, 1850–1900*, S. Doc. 756, 61st Cong., 3d sess., 1911, pp. 450–51 (hereafter, Immigration Commission, *Statistical Review*); U.S. Department of Interior, Census Office, *Compendium of the Eleventh Census: 1890*, pt. 3, *Population*, p. 54 (hereafter, Census Office, *Compendium of Eleventh Census*); U.S. Department of the Interior, Census Office, *Twelfth Census of the United States Taken in the Year 1900*, vol. 1, *Population*, pt. 1, pp. clxxvi, clxxvii (hereafter, Census Office, *Twelfth Census*); U.S. Department of Commerce and Labor, Bureau of the Census, *Thirteenth Census of the United States Taken in the Year 1910*, vol. 1, *Population 1910: General Report and Analysis*, p. 824, and vol. 3, *Population: Reports by States, with Statistics for Counties, Cities and Other Civil Divisions: Nebraska–Wyoming, Alaska, Hawaii, and Porto Rico*, p. 609 (hereafter, Bureau of Census, *Thirteenth Census*); Peter Roberts, "Immigrant Wage-Earners," in *Wage-Earning Pittsburgh*, ed. Paul Underwood Kellogg (New York: Russell Sage, 1914), pp. 34–35.

6. Because Allegheny City was annexed by Pittsburgh in 1907 and became known

as the North Side, Slovak immigration to Allegheny City is considered in this study as part of the general Slovak immigration into Pittsburgh. For discussion purposes, unless otherwise indicated, the term *Pittsburgh* includes both Allegheny City and Pittsburgh.

7. For an incisive discussion of ethnicity as a "neglected dimension" of American history, see Rudolph J. Vecoli, "Ethnicity: A Neglected Dimension of American History," in *The State of American History*, ed. Herbert J. Bass (Chicago: Quadrangle, 1970), pp. 70–88.

8. See, e.g., John W. Briggs, *An Italian Passage: Immigrants to Three American Cities, 1890–1930* (New Haven: Yale University Press, 1978); Thomas Kessner, *The Golden Door: Italian and Jewish Immigrant Mobility in New York City 1880–1915* (New York: Oxford University Press, 1977); Humbert S. Nelli, *The Italians in Chicago, 1880–1930: A Study in Ethnic Mobility* (New York: Oxford University Press, 1970); Howard P. Chudacoff, *Mobile Americans: Residential and Social Mobility in Omaha, 1880–1920* (New York: Oxford University Press, 1972). For discussions of the impact of industrialization or urbanization on immigrants, see Josef J. Barton, *Peasants and Strangers: Italians, Rumanians, and Slovaks in an American City, 1890–1950* (Cambridge: Harvard University Press, 1975); John Bodnar, *Immigration and Industrialization: Ethnicity in an American Mill Town, 1870–1940* (Pittsburgh: University of Pittsburgh Press, 1977); idem *The Transplanted: A History of Immigrants in Urban America* (Bloomington: Indiana University Press, 1985); Francis G. Couvares, *The Remaking of Pittsburgh: Class and Culture in an Industrializing City, 1877–1919* (Albany: State University of New York Press, 1984); Caroline Golab, *Immigrant Destinations* (Philadelphia: Temple University Press, 1977); Jeffrey S. Gurock, *When Harlem Was Jewish: 1870–1930* (New York: Columbia University Press, 1979); Virginia Yans-McLaughlin, *Family and Community: Italian Immigrants in Buffalo, 1880–1930* (Ithaca, NY: Cornell University Press, 1977); Olivier Zunz, *The Changing Face of Inequality: Urbanization, Industrial Development, and Immigrants in Detroit, 1880–1920* (Chicago: University of Chicago Press, 1982); John Bodnar, Roger Simon, and Michael P. Weber, *Lives of Their Own: Blacks, Italians, and Poles in Pittsburgh, 1900–1960* (Urbana: University of Illinois Press, 1982).

9. For a classic statement of this view, see Oscar Handlin, *The Uprooted: The Epic Story of the Great Migrations that Made the American People* (Boston: Little, Brown, 1951). See also, W. Lloyd Warner and Leo Srole, *The Social Systems of American Ethnic Groups* (New Haven: Yale University Press, 1945), pp. 156–219.

10. Eric L. McKitrick and Stanley Elkins, "Institutions in Motion," *American Quarterly* 12 (Summer 1980): 188–97.

11. See, e.g., Victor Greene, *For God and Country: The Rise of Polish and Lithuanian Ethnic Consciousness in America, 1860–1910* (Madison: State Historical Society of Wisconsin, 1975); Anthony J. Kuzniewski, *Faith and Fatherland: The Polish Church War in Wisconsin, 1896–1918* (Notre Dame: University of Notre Dame Press, 1980); Joseph John Parot, *Polish Catholics in Chicago, 1850–1920* (DeKalb: Northern Illinois University Press, 1981); William J. Galush, "Faith and Fatherland: Dimensions of Polish-American Ethnoreligion, 1875–1975," in *Immigrants and Religion in Urban America*, ed. Randall M. Miller and Thomas D. Marzik (Philadelphia: Temple University Press, 1977), pp. 84–102; M. Mark Stolarik, "Lay Initiative in American-Slovak Parishes, 1880–1930," *Records of the American Catholic Historical Society of Philadelphia* 83 (Sep.– Dec., 1972): 151–58; Rudolph J. Vecoli, "Prelates and Peasants: Italian Immigrants and the Catholic Church," *Journal of Social History* 2 (Spring 1969): 217–68; Richard M. Linkh, *American Catholicism and European Immigrants (1900–1924)* (New York: Center for Migration Studies, 1975). For traditional histories that minimize or ignore conflicts between immigrants and the Catholic church, see, e.g., John Tracy Ellis,

American Catholicism (Chicago: University of Chicago Press, 1956); Thomas T. McAvoy, *A History of the Catholic Church in the United States* (Notre Dame: University of Notre Dame Press, 1969); Theodore Maynard, *The Catholic Church and the American Idea* (New York: Appleton-Century-Crofts, 1953).

12. For notable exceptions, see, e.g., Jay P. Dolan, *The American Catholic Experience: A History from Colonial Times to the Present* (Garden City, NY: Doubleday, 1985); idem, *The Immigrant Church;* Parot, *Polish Catholics in Chicago;* Raymond A. Mohl and Neil Betten, "The Immigrant Church in Gary, Indiana: Religious Adjustment and Cultural Defense," *Ethnicity* 8 (1981): 1–17.

13. Vecoli, "Prelates and Peasants"; idem, "Cult and Occult in Italian-American Culture: The Persistence of a Religious Heritage," in *Immigrants and Religion in Urban America,* ed. Randall M. Miller and Thomas D. Marzik (Philadelphia: Temple University Press, 1977), pp. 25–47.

14. See, e.g., Timothy L. Smith, "Lay Initiative in the Religious Life of American Immigrants, 1880–1950," in *Anonymous Americans: Explorations in Nineteenth-Century Social History,* ed. Tamara K. Hareven (Englewood Cliffs, NJ: Prentice-Hall, 1971), pp. 214–49; Stolarik, "Lay Initiative," p. 151; Galush, "Faith and Fatherland," pp. 85–86.

15. For theories on the relationship between religion and ethnicity, see Martin E. Marty, "Ethnicity: The Skeleton of Religion in America," *Church History* 41 (Mar. 1972): 5–21; Timothy L. Smith, "Religion and Ethnicity in America," *American Historical Review* 83 (Dec. 1978): 1155–85.

16. This term is used by Tamotsu Shibutani and Kian M. Kwan in their discussion of ethnic stratification. See Tamotsu Shibutani and Kian M. Kwan, *Ethnic Stratification: A Comparative Approach* (New York: Macmillan, 1965).

Chapter 1. From Village to City

1. See n. 6, Introduction, for how the term *Pittsburgh* is defined.

2. R. W. Seton-Watson [Scotus Viator], *Racial Problems in Hungary* (London: Archibald Constable, 1908), p. 434.

3. Ibid., pp. 8–14; C. A. Macartney, *Hungary and Her Successors: The Treaty of Trianon and Its Consequences, 1919–1937* (London: Oxford University Press, 1937), pp. 76–78.

4. *Slovenská Vlastiveda,* 4 vols. (Bratislava, Czechoslovakia: Slovenská Akadémia Vied, 1943), vol. 1, p. 197. These statistics are for 1910.

5. C. A. Macartney, *The Habsburg Empire, 1790–1918* (London: Weidenfeld & Nicolson, 1968), pp. 121, 502 (nn. 3, 4), 503 (n. 1), 530, 698–99, 723–24; *The Catholic Encyclopedia, 1913,* s. v. "Hungary," by A. Aldasy (hereafter, Aldasy, "Hungary"); Seton-Watson, *Racial Problems in Hungary,* pp. 110–13.

6. *Jednota,* 9 Jan. 1907; interviews with Paul Granatir, Bloomingdale, OH, 21 June 1978; Andrew Holovanisin, Pittsburgh, 30 Nov. 1978; John Ciganik, 17 May 1977; and Ferdinand Dvorsky, 28 Nov. 1978.

7. Aldasy, "Hungary."

8. Interviews with Andrew Holovanisin, 30 Nov. 1978, and Ferdinand Dvorsky, 28 Nov. 1978. The "fame" of some churches is still evident today even in publications in Czechoslovakia. See *Vlastivedný slovník obcí na Slovensku* [Historical and Geographic Dictionary of Communities in Slovakia], 3 vols. (Bratislava, Czechoslovakia: Slovenská Akadémia Vied, 1977).

9. Interviews with Ferdinand Dvorsky, 28 Nov. 1978; Andrew Holovanisin, 30

Nov. 1978; John Ciganik, 17 May 1977; and Margaret Kuzma, Homestead, PA, 13 May 1977, 27 Nov. 1978. Description of prayers is also based on an analysis of four Slovak prayer books in the author's possession.

10. No comprehensive study of Slovak folklore and superstitions is available. The best analysis of the religious folklore and customs of a Slavic people is in William I. Thomas and Florian Znaniecki, *The Polish Peasant in Europe and America*, 4 vols. (Boston: Gorham, 1918–1920), vol. 1, pp. 205–88. Darina Krausová discusses Slovak superstitions, folklore, and peasant customs in "Zvykoslovie a ľudové umenie" [Mores and folk art], in *Vlastivedný slovník obcí*, vol. 1, pp. 73–74 (hereafter, Krausová, "Zvykoslovie a ľudové umenie").

11. Interviews with Andrew Holovanisin, 30 Nov. 1978; John Ciganik, 17 May 1977; and Ferdinand Dvorsky, 28 Nov. 1978; Krausová, "Zvykoslovie a ľudové umenie," p. 74; Father Andrew V. Pier, "Christmas Customs in Slovakia," in *Jednota Annual Furdek 1974*, ed. FCSU (Middletown, PA: Jednota, 1974; reprint); *NN*, 15 Dec. 1981.

12. Emily Greene Balch, *Our Slavic Fellow Citizens* (New York: New York Charities, 1910), pp. 88, 90. Interviews with Andrew Holovanisin, 30 Nov. 1978; John Ciganik, 17 May 1977; and Ferdinand Dvorsky, 28 Nov. 1978.

13. Balch, *Our Slavic Fellow Citizens*, pp. 90–93; Krausová, "Zvykoslovie a ľudové umenie," pp. 73–74; Jarmila Pátková, "Ľudová výroba" [Folk craft], in *Vlastivedný slovník obcí*, vol. 1, pp. 71–72 (hereafter, Pátková, "Ľudová výroba").

14. Peter Brock, *The Slovak National Awakening: An essay in the intellectual history of east central Europe*, (Toronto: University of Toronto Press, 1976), pp. 53–54; M. Mark Stolarik, "Immigration and Eastern Slovak Nationalism," *Slovakia* 26 (1976): 13–20.

15. Balch, *Our Slavic Fellow Citizens*, pp. 42–43, 85, 96–97. For a concise description of these classes and their plight as early as the 1830s, see Macartney, *Habsburg Empire*, pp. 273–75.

16. Balch, *Our Slavic Fellow Citizens*, pp. 97–99; Ján Hanzlík, "Začiatky vysťahovalectva zo Slovenska do USA a jeho priebeh až do roku 1918, jeho príčiny a následky" [Beginnings and course of emigration from Slovakia to the United States to 1918, its course and results], in *Začiatky českej a slovenskej emigrácie do USA* [Beginnings of Czech and Slovak emigration to the United States], ed. Josef Polišenský (Bratislava, Czechoslovakia: Slovenská Akadémia Vied, 1970), pp. 50–55; Konštantín Čulen, *Dejiny Slovákov v Amerike* [History of the Slovaks in America], 2 vols. (Bratislava, Czechoslovakia: Slovenská Liga na Slovensku, 1942), vol. 1, pp. 53–55; Emil Lengyel, *Americans from Hungary* (Philadelphia: Lippincott, 1948), p. 100; Julianna Puskás, *From Hungary to the United States (1880–1914)* (Budapest: Akadémiai Kiadó, 1982), p. 62. Interview with John Ciganik, 17 May 1977.

17. Puskás, *From Hungary to the United States*, pp. 45–60; Macartney, *Habsburg Empire*, pp. 703–07; I. T. Berend and G. Ranki, *Hungary: A Century of Economic Development* (London: David & Charles, 1974), pp. 24–90; Scott M. Eddie, "The Changing Pattern of Landownership in Hungary, 1867–1914," *Economic History Review*, 2d ser., 20 (Apr. 1967): 293–309.

18. Balch, *Our Slavic Fellow Citizens*, pp. 100–101, 217–18, 220–21; Yeshayahu Jelinek, "Self-identification of First Generation Hungarian Jewish Immigrants," *American Jewish Historical Quarterly* 61 (Mar. 1972): 217–18, 220–21.

19. Balch, *Our Slavic Fellow Citizens*, pp. 52–53, 238–39; Minister of the Interior to the people of Spiš County, 24 Apr. 1884, in *Slovenské vysťahovalectvo Dokumenty I do roku 1918* [Slovak emigration, Documents I, to 1918], comp. František Bielik and Elo Rákoš (Bratislava, Czechoslovakia: Slovenská Akadémia Vied, 1969), Document 26; Alois B. Koukol, "A Slav's a Man for a' That," in *Wage-Earning Pittsburgh*, ed. Paul

Underwood Kellogg (New York: Russell Sage, 1914), p. 63. See also Čulen, *Dejiny Slovákov*, vol. 1, p. 38.

20. Balch, *Our Slavic Fellow Citizens*, pp. 99, 106, 113, 119; Čulen, *Dejiny Slovákov*, vol. 1, pp. 53–55; Hanzlík, "Začiatky vyst'ahovalectva zo Slovenska," pp. 50–55; Julianna Puskás, *Emigration from Hungary to the United States Before 1914* (Budapest: Akadémiai Kiadó, 1975), p. 14.

21. Immigration Commission, *Statistical Review*, p. 359.

22. Puskás, *Emigration from Hungary*, pp. 15–16.

23. Marian Mark Stolarik, "Immigration and Urbanization: The Slovak Experience, 1870–1918" (Ph.D. diss., University of Minnesota, 1974), pp. 8–20. The *matriky* (registers) of sample village churches reveal a high frequency of marriages between persons from different villages. *Matriky*, Spišská Nová Ves, 1883–1893; *Matriky*, Majerka, 1884–1899; *Matriky*, Krížová Ves, 1881–1897. All of these *matriky* are housed in the State Regional Archives, Levoča, Czechoslovakia.

24. Puskás, *Emigration from Hungary*, p. 18; József Gellén, "Emigration in a Systems Framework: The Case of Hungary, 1899–1913," unpublished paper in author's possession.

25. These statistics are actually for fiscal year 1907–1908. U.S. Department of Commerce and Labor, Commissioner General of Immigration, *Report of the Commissioner General of Immigration, 1908*, in *Reports of the Department of Commerce and Labor, 1908*, pp. 110–11.

26. Interview with Paul Granatir, 21 June 1978; Balch, *Our Slavic Fellow Citizens*, pp. 118–19.

27. Balch, *Our Slavic Fellow Citizens*, pp. 103–104, 265–66; Puskás, *From Hungary to the United States*, pp. 29, 31.

28. U.S. Department of Labor, Bureau of Immigration, *Annual Report of the Commissioner General of Immigration to the Secretary of Labor, for the Fiscal Year ended June 30, 1918*, in *Reports of the Secretary of Labor and Reports of Bureaus, 1918*, pp. 376–77. Statistics are for fiscal years 1899–1913.

29. Immigration Commission, *Statistical Review*, pp. 51, 372.

30. Interview with Andrew Holovanisin, 30 Nov. 1978. Andrew Holovanisin's father sent his wife and infant son, Andrew, back to northern Hungary because he could not afford to keep them in America. He planned to send for his family once he could support them again but met an untimely death.

31. U.S. Congress, Senate, Immigration Commission, *Reports of the Immigration Commission: Immigrants in Industry*, pt. 2: *Iron and Steel Manufacturing*, S. Doc. 633, 61st Cong., 2d sess., 1911, vol. 8, p. 249 (hereafter, Immigration Commission, *Iron and Steel*); Peter Roberts, "Immigrant Wage-Earners," p. 38; Jozef A. Kushner, *Slováci Katolíci Pittsburghského Biskupstva* [Slovak Catholics of the Pittsburgh Diocese] (Passaic, NJ: Slovak Catholic Sokol, 1946), pp. 15–18.

32. *SvA*, 15 May 1900, 28 Mar. 1905.

33. Letters from Slovaks describing working conditions where they lived were published regularly in Slovak newspapers, especially in *SvA*. For representative examples, see *ASN*, 3 and 8 Nov. 1894, 4 July 1901, 27 Aug., 10 Sep., and 15 Oct. 1902, 14 Sep. 1904, 22 Jan. 1908; *NN*, 13 Jan. 1910, 18 July 1912; *SH*, 9 July 1908, 6 Mar. 1913.

34. P. V. Rovnianek, *Zápisky za živa pochovaného* [Notes from one buried alive] (N.p.: 1924), pp. 111–13.

35. Ibid.; Konštantín Čulen, *J. Slovenský: Životopis zakladatel'a prvých slovenských novín v Amerike* [J. Slovensky: A biography of the founder of the first Slovak newspaper in America] (Winnepeg: Canadian Slovak, 1946), pp. 92, 94.

36. Balch, *Our Slavic Fellow Citizens*, p. 114; Frank J. Sheridan, "Italian, Slavic, and Hungarian Unskilled Immigrant Laborers in the United States," U.S. Department of Commerce and Labor, *Bulletin of the Bureau of Labor* 15 (Sep. 1907): 407–08; Puskás, *Emigration from Hungary*, pp. 14–18.

37. Kushner, *Slováci Katolíci*, p. 100.

38. Ibid., pp. 100–101.

39. SGC, marriage records, 1903–1910; SGC, burial records, 1903–1910. The record series (baptismal, marriage, burial) are contained in separate registers with a variety of titles and include a number of years. For this study, the registers are cited as "records." The citations include the name of the appropriate record series and list only the inclusive dates for which relevant data was derived. (See the Bibliographical Essay for descriptions and full citations of all church records used in this study.) A number of Slovaks from Zemplín County later settled in the Frankstown neighborhood (currently the Greenfield section of Pittsburgh), but these Slovaks, who also chain migrated by region, came from a clearly different section of Zemplín than did those who moved to western Allegheny City. See, June Granatir Alexander, "Staying Together: Chain Migration and Patterns of Slovak Settlement in Pittsburgh Prior to World War I," *Journal of American Ethnic History* 1 (Fall 1981): 63–65.

40. SMC, *Zlaté Jubileum Kostola Sv. Matúša* [Golden Jubilee of Saint Matthew Church] (N.p.: 1955), p. 34. This remarkably well researched church jubilee book relied on some oral interviews with Slovak immigrants who had settled in the South Side as early as 1888.

41. *ASN*, 24 Dec. 1896. Church records confirm that Slovaks were living in different sections of the Pittsburgh area. SEC, baptismal records, 1895; SEC, marriage records, 1895.

42. Joel A. Tarr, *Transportation Innovation and Changing Spatial Patterns: Pittsburgh, 1850–1910* (Pittsburgh: Transportation Research Institute, Carnegie-Mellon University, 1972), pp. 17, 26–28; Josephine McIlvain, "Twelve Blocks: A Study of One Segment of Pittsburgh's South Side, 1880–1915," *Western Pennsylvania Historical Magazine* 60 (Oct. 1977): 353.

43. For extensive documentation and a detailed discussion of Slovak chain migration patterns into pre-World War I Pittsburgh, see Alexander, "Staying Together," pp. 56–83; idem, "The Immigrant Church and Community: The Formation of Pittsburgh's Slovak Religious Institutions, 1880–1914" (Ph.D. diss., University of Minnesota, 1980), pp. 66–157.

44. Immigration Commission, *Iron and Steel*, 8: 249; Roberts, "Immigrant Wage-Earners," pp. 37–39; Bodnar, Simon, and Weber, *Lives of Their Own*, pp. 56–63.

45. Roberts, "Immigrant Wage-Earners," pp. 37–39; H. F. J. Porter, "Industrial Hygiene of the Pittsburgh District," in *Wage-Earning Pittsburgh*, ed. Paul Underwood Kellogg (New York: Russell Sage, 1914), pp. 218–21; John Bodnar, Michael Weber, and Roger Simon, "Migration, Kinship, and Urban Adjustment: Blacks and Poles in Pittsburgh, 1900–1930," *Journal of American History* 66 (Dec. 1979): 558, 562–65; interviews with John Ciganik, 17 May 1977, and Ferdinand Dvorsky, 12 Apr. 1977.

46. *ASN*, 26 Dec. 1901.

47. Ibid., 24 Dec. 1896. This challenge to the figures reported in *ASN* is based on the 1897 census of the Saint Elizabeth Church that listed the number of "souls" as 2,780. Even this total was most likely an adjusted estimate. The church census included Slovaks who lived in Pittsburgh and a few nearby areas and probably also a small number of non-Slovaks. Given these facts, the estimate reported in the newspaper is much too high. Church Reports, City of Pittsburgh, entry for Saint Elizabeth,

OVGC. Censuses are listed by church in a register (hereafter referred to as Church Reports, OVGC, followed by the name of the relevant church).

48. *ASN*, 17 Oct., 23 Nov., and 26 Dec. 1895, 13 Feb. and 24 Dec. 1896. These issues included either lists of Slovak businessmen or ads for their wares or services. The city directories for Pittsburgh and Allegheny City are not reliable sources for determining Slovak businesses. With the exception of Rovnianek's, the Slovak businesses listed in the city's Slovak newspapers were not listed in the directories, 1895–1897.

49. Kushner, *Slováci Katolíci*, p. 93; SMC, *Zlaté Jubileum*, p. 34. At least one Slovak Catholic lodge even gave substantial contributions to Saint Wenceslaus Church. Branch 2, FCSU, Zápisnice (minutes), meetings of 10 Dec. 1893, 13 May and 9 Dec. 1894, 13 Jan. and 10 Feb. 1895, Branch 2 Collection, SMA.

50. Bureau of Census, *Thirteenth Census*, 1: 991.

Chapter 2. From Self-Help to Community Development

1. Rovnianek, *Zápisky*, pp. 118–40.

2. Čulen, *Dejiny Slovákov*, vol. 1, pp. 110, vol. 2, pp. 202–09.

3. Ibid., vol. 2, p. 202; Jozef Paučo, *Štefan Furdek a Slovenské Prisťahovalectvo* [Stephen Furdek and the Slovak Immigration] (Middletown, PA: Jednota, 1955), pp. 97–101; Kenneth Baka, "The First Catholic Slovak Ladies Association," in *Slovaks in America: A Bicentennial Study*, comp. Joseph C. Krajsa et al. (Middletown, PA: Jednota Slovak American, 1978), pp. 172–73.

4. Štefan Zeman ml., "Päťdesiať rokov šľachetnej práce slov. evanjelikov v Amerike" [Fifty years of the noble work of Slovak Lutherans in America], in SEU, *Zlatá Kniha, 1893–1943* [Golden (Anniversary) Book] (Pittsburgh: Slovenský Hlásnik, 1943), p. 34.

5. Pavel Hibbler, "Vývin Slovenskej Evanjelickej A. V. Jednoty" [Development of the Slovak Evangelical Union of the Augsburg Confession], in SEU, *Slovenský Evanjelický Kalendár, 1929*, pp. 134–35. See the Bibliographical Essay for a discussion and full citation of all fraternal publications and yearly almanacs [*kalendár*] used in this study.

6. *SvA*, 7 May 1901.

7. P. Ďurovčik, "Dvadsať päť rokov vzporníenok" [Twenty-five-year overview], in SCPU, *Kalendár pre Slovenských Kalvínov, 1927*, p. 32.

8. NSS, *Dejiny a Pamätnica Národného Slovenského Spolku, 1890–1950* [History and Souvenir Book of the National Slovak Society) (Pittsburgh: NSS, 1950), p. 214; Jozef Paučo, *75 Rokov Prvej Katolíckej Slovenskej Jednoty* [75 Years of the First Catholic Slovak Union] (Middletown, PA: Jednota, 1965), pp. 16–82, passim; *NN*, 10 Mar. 1910; Frank Uherka, "Krátky prehľad S.K.P. Jednoty" [Short overview of the Slovak Calvinistic Presbyterian Union], in SCPU, *Kalendár pre Slovenských Kalvínov, 1927*, pp. 40, 42. These totals do not include the members of the Pennsylvania Slovak Catholic Union, which had a membership in 1910 of approximately 15 thousand (*NN*, 10 Mar. 1910); nor do they include a small number of splinter groups not associated with the national organizations described above.

9. *ASN*, 28 Feb. 1895.

10. Interview with John Ciganik, 17 May 1977; *Jednota*, 16 Oct. 1912.

11. *ASN*, 16 Dec. 1903.

12. Ignac Gessay, "Spolky pred organisáciami" [Societies before the organizations], in NSS, *Národny Kalendár, 1911*, pp. 66–77, with quotation on p. 66.

13. Peter V. Rovnianek, "The Slovaks in America," *Charities* 13 (Dec. 1904): 242; Seton-Watson, *Racial Problems in Hungary*, pp. 274–77.

14. Rev. Ján Method Liščinský, "Katolícka Slovenská Ženská Jednota" [Catholic Slovak Ladies Union], in FSCU, *Kalendár Jednota, 1911*, p. 180. Accent marks on persons' names are rendered inconsistently in the sources, and sources also inconsistently Americanize spellings. I have therefore dropped accents from names when used in the text. In addition, I use the common English spelling for more well known names. In source citations, however, the names of the authors appear as given in the original publication.

15. For a differing conclusion—that Slovak mutual aid societies were based on Old World societies, see Stolarik, "Immigration and Urbanization," pp. 69–73; Barton, *Peasants and Strangers*, pp. 64, 67–69, 70; see also, Smith, "Lay Initiative," pp. 22, 226, 241–43. See and cf., Robert T. Anderson and Gallatin Anderson, "The Indirect Social Structure of European Village Communities," *American Anthropologist* 64 (Oct. 1962): 1016–26 (whose evidence and conclusions about Yugoslavia suggest that voluntary associations were not part of "Slavic" village life); idem, "Voluntary Associations and Urbanization: A Diachronic Analysis," *American Journal of Sociology* 65 (Nov. 1959): 265–73.

16. Rovnianek, *Zápisky*, p. 136.

17. *SH*, 20 Aug. 1908.

18. Interview with Ferdinand Dvorsky, 28 Nov. 1978.

19. *SH*, 20 Aug. 1908.

20. Gessay, "Spolky pred organisáciami," pp. 66–77.

21. Martin Slanina, "Historia čísla 2 Prvej Kat. Slov. Jednoty" [History of Branch 2 of the First Catholic Slovak Union], in FCSU, *Pamätník Zlatého Jubilea a 27 Konvencie Prvej Katolíckej Slovenskej Jednoty* [Memorial Album of the Golden Jubilee and 27th Convention of the First Catholic Slovak Union] (Middletown, PA: Jednota, 1940), p. 139. Slanina does not give the date when this celebration took place, but given the information he does provide, it occurred before 1888.

22. Ibid. Andrew Holovanisin insisted that there was nothing comparable to fraternals in his village or in neighboring villages in Zemplín. He vividly remembered his mother describing the fraternal that Andrew's father joined before he was killed as being uniquely American. Andrew recalled that the stories of fraternalists, their activities, and gala dress caused him to resolve to join one if he ever came to the United States. He recalled that "Martin Slanina was like a hero to me." When he came to the United States in the 1920s, Andrew did join a fraternal and remained an active member throughout his life. (Interview, 30 Nov. 1978).

23. Slanina, "Historia čísla 2," p. 139; Saint Michael Society, *75th Anniversary* (Pittsburgh: N.p., 1964), unpaged.

24. Rovnianek, *Zápisky*, p. 120; NSS, *Dejiny a Pamätnica*, p. 234.

25. NSS, *Dejiny a Pamätnica*, passim; FCSU, *Pamätník Zlatého Jubilea*, passim; Uherka, "Krátky prehľad S.K.P. Jednoty," pp. 40, 42; Michal Janošov, "Úryvky z dejín Spolku 'Sv. Emmanuela,' čísla 65. S.E.J., v Pittsburgh, Pa." [Excerpts from the history of the Society of Holy Emmanuel, Branch 65 of the Slovak Evangelical Union in Pittsburgh, Pa.], in SEU, *Zlatá Kniha, 1893–1943*, p. 126.

26. A more detailed discussion of the origins of Slovak fraternalists as well as documentation for this claim is provided in the latter part of chapter 7.

27. *ASN*, 28 Feb. 1895.

28. NSS, *Dejiny a Pamätnica*, p. 304. NSS lodges are called assemblies, but to avoid confusion, I refer to individual lodges of all Slovak fraternal organizations as *branch* with the appropriate lodge number.

29. Membership ledgers, branches 2, 4, 97, 159, First Catholic Slovak Union Papers, IHRC (hereafter, Membership ledgers, FCSU); NSS, Menoslov [Membership roster], odbor 2–odbor 17, 1892–1894, NSSH (hereafter, NSS, Menoslov, 1892–1894).

30. Estimates of membership are derived from monthly reports published in 1910 isues of *NN, Jednota*, and *SH*. Additional data was derived from SMA, Učtovníca Sp. sv. Antona z Padua, Č. 50, P.K.S.J., 1902–1912 [Account book of the Society of St. Anthony of Padua, Branch 50, FCSU], in Branch 50 Collection (hereafter, Branch 50 Učtovníca). The estimate of 50 percent is based upon censuses of Slovak Catholic churches in Pittsburgh, which listed a total of 750 families belonging to Pittsburgh's churches. The total number of persons (adults and children) listed as belonging to these churches in 1910 was 4,109. Not all of these persons were Slovaks, nor did all live in Pittsburgh. (Branch 50 Učtovníca indicates that, throughout the period to 1910, a significant number of its members did not live in Pittsburgh. This was probably the case in other lodges as well.) Based on the number of "families" who belonged to Slovak churches, it is reasonable to assume that at least 1,400 Slovak men and women qualified for membership in fraternal societies. Given the fact that the city's Slovak population contained a number of either single men over the age of sixteen or married men over that age whose families were in Europe, it is reasonable to assume that the number of fraternalists should have been larger. In addition to Catholics included in the parish censuses referred to above, the city's Slovak Lutherans added to the number of potential eligible members. (Catholic statistics are derived from Church Reports, OVGC, separate entries for SEC, SGC, SJC, SMC.)

31. Branch 2, FCSU, Zápisnice, meetings of 9 Mar. and 8 June 1913 (Branch 2 minutes, 1911–1923, are held by officers of Branch 2 and were made available to me by the former president, Andrew Holovanisin, now deceased). Branch 50, FCSU, Zápisnice, meetings of 2 Sep. 1900, 21 Jan. 1906, 17 Feb. 1907 (Branch 50 Collection, SMA); Albert Mamatey to Andrej Halaša, 2 July 1907, Archives of the Matica Slovenská, Correspondence of U.S. Slovaks with leaders in Slovakia, reel 1, Slovak Collection, IHRC (hereafter, AMS, IHRC).

32. *Jednota*, 22 Jan. 1908.

33. Interviews with Ferdinand Dvorsky, 28 Nov. 1978, and John Ciganik, 17 May 1977.

34. Membership ledgers, FCSU, entries for branches 2, 4, 21, 97, 159, 185, 254; NSS, Menoslov, 1892–1894.

35. M. Mark Stolarik, "A Place for Everyone: Slovak Fraternal Benefit Societies," in *Self-Help in Urban America: Patterns of Minority Business Enterprise*, ed. Scott Cummings (Port Washington, NY: Kennikat, 1980), pp. 130–41.

36. Branch 2, FCSU, Zápisnice, meeting of 9 Aug. 1891; *Stanovy Sv. Michala Spolok* [By-laws of the St. Michael Society] (N.p., n.d.), pp. 22–23.

37. Branch 50, FCSU, Zápisnice, meetings of 31 Mar. 1901, 28 Dec. 1902, 3 Jan. 1904.

38. *Stanovy Sv. Michala Spolok*, pp. 37–38.

39. *ASN*, 9 Apr. 1901. The notice published in the paper did not indicate whether the man was a member of the sponsoring lodge.

40. Branch 50, FCSU, Zápisnice, meeting of 4 Nov. 1900. Funeral costs were deducted from the deceased's death benefits and, occasionally, the beneficiary received considerably less than was anticipated. One Pittsburgh Slovak who died in 1894 had an insurance policy worth $600.00, but after the lodge paid medical and funeral costs, his mother received only $280.69. P. V. Rovnianek to Pavel Mudron, 2 Jan. 1895, AMS, IHRC.

41. *ASN*, 11 Oct. 1894; *Jednota*, 24 Apr. and 7 Aug. 1907; *NN*, 10 Feb. 1910; *SvA*, 24 May 1910.

42. Branch 2, FCSU, Zápisnice, meetings of 9 and 14 Aug. 1892, 11 Feb. and 10 June 1894, 18 Dec. 1898; *ASN*, 6 Sep. and 3 Dec. 1894, 19 Feb. 1895, 24 Sep., 8 Oct., and 3 Dec. 1896.

43. Branch 2, FCSU, Zápisnice, meetings of 10 Apr. and 4 July 1892, 1 Sep. 1895, 10 Nov. 1912, 12 Jan., 13 Apr., 18 May, 14 Aug., and 11 Oct. 1913; Branch 50, FCSU, Zápisnice, meetings of 1 Sep. 1895, 18 Oct. 1896, 2 May and 4 July 1897, 1 May 1898, 2 Sep. 1900, 2 June 1901, 2 Aug. 1903.

44. Branch 2, FCSU, Zápisnice, meetings of 21 Apr. and 6 Oct. 1895, 6 Sep. 1896; Branch 50, FCSU, Zápisnice, meetings of 6 Oct. 1895, 8 Oct. 1896, 7 Mar., 2 May, 4 July 1897, 2 Sep. 1900, 2 June 1901, 2 Aug. 1903, 18 Sep. 1904, 1 Sep. 1907, 6 June 1909, 7 Aug. 1910; *NN*, 14 Apr. and 15 Sep. 1910.

45. Branch 2, FCSU, Zápisnice, meetings of 21 Apr., 1 Sep., and 6 Oct. 1895. This was a Slovak Greek Catholic church in Pittsburgh's South Side. The Greek Catholics and their separate churches are not included in this study because their history merits separate and special examination that is beyond the scope of this present work.

46. The term *fellow feeling* is used by Helen Lopata in reference to Polish immigrants. Helen Lopata, *Polish Americans: Status Competition in an Ethnic Community* [Englewood Cliffs, NJ: Prentice-Hall, 1976).

47. Branch 2, FCSU, Zápisnice, meeting of 14 Feb. 1894.

48. For discussions of the changing role and activities of immigrant self-help societies in the United States, see essays contained in Scott Cummings, ed., *Self-Help in Urban America: Patterns of Minority Business Enterprise* (Port Washington, NY: Kennikat, 1980).

Chapter 3. Creating Neighborhood Institutions

1. U.S. Department of the Interior, Census Office, *Report on the Statistics of Churches in the United States at the Eleventh Census: 1890*, vol. 16, pp. 91, 96, 98 (hereafter, Census Office, *Church Statistics: 1890*) The population totals include only "communicants"; this excluded children under nine years of age—and estimated 15 percent of the total entered in the census; see ibid., p. 233.

2. Rev. George J. Bullion, "Bishop Phelan," in *Catholic Pittsburgh's One Hundred Years*, ed. Catholic Historical Society of Western Pennsylvania (Chicago: Loyola University Press, 1943), pp. 55–56; Rev. Thomas F. Coakley, "Archbishop Canevin," in ibid., p. 68; St. Regis Association, ed., *Catholic Yearbook of the Pittsburgh Diocese, 1908–1909* (Pittsburgh: St. Regis Association, 1909), p. 15.

3. Census Office, *Church Statistics: 1890*, p. 98; U.S. Department of Commerce and Labor, Bureau of the Census, *Religious Bodies 1906*, pt. 1, *Summary and General Tables*, vol. 1, pp. 408, 409 (hereafter, Bureau of Census, *Religious Bodies*).

4. See, e.g., *PC*, 3 May, 26 June, and 10 July 1890, 9 Nov. 1893, 27 Sep. and 1 Nov. 1894, 19 Nov. 1896, 20 May and 23 Sep. 1897, 13 Jan. 1898, 16 Aug. 1899, 18 Sep. 1901, 4 June 1902, 5 Mar. and 20 Aug. 1903, 7 Dec. 1905, 14 Nov. and 25 July 1907, 30 Dec. 1909, 5 May and 22 Sep. 1910, 19 Oct. 1911, 15 Aug. 1912, 25 Sep. 1913. These representative articles reveal the ongoing concern by diocesan spokesmen over issues pertaining to immigration and to the question of the patriotism of Catholics in the United States.

5. Rt. Rev. Regis Canevin, *An Examination Historical and Statistical into Losses and Gains of the Catholic Church* (N.p., 1912).

6. McAvoy, *A History of the Catholic Church*, pp. 231–34; Aaron I. Abell, *American Catholicism and Social Action: A Search for Social Justice, 1865–1950* (Garden City, NY: Doubleday, 1960), pp. 37–39; Thomas Čapek, *The Čechs (Bohemians) in America* (Boston: Houghton Mifflin, 1920), p. 25; Thomas and Znaniecki, *Polish Peasant*, vol. 2, pp. 1593–97.

7. *PC*, 24 May 1899, 19 Apr. 1906.

8. Colman J. Barry, *The Catholic Church and German Americans* (Milwaukee: Bruce, 1953), pp. 131–82ff.; *PC*, 1 Oct. 1891, 31 Mar. 1892, 4 Oct. 1894, 21 May 1896, 24 May 1899, 28 Apr. 1904, 25 May 1905, 14 July 1910.

9. Linkh, *American Catholicism and European Immigrants*, pp. 51–52.

10. *PC*, 22 Sep. 1910.

11. Ibid., 16 May 1895.

12. Ibid., 25 July 1895.

13. Ibid., 23 May 1895. The Reverend Raymond Wider, who was chosen president of the First Catholic Slovak Union in 1893 and who was pastor of Saint Michael Slovak Roman Catholic Church in Braddock, probably helped influence this favorable attitude toward the First Catholic Slovak Union. During an earlier convention, Wider submitted an article to the *Pittsburgh Catholic* that praised the fraternal and claimed its goals were to encourage Slovaks to become U.S. citizens while not forgetting their homeland and, also, to encourage them to "be true to their religion"; see ibid., 19 May 1892.

14. Rev. Joseph V. Adamec, "The Slovak Catholic Federation: A 65 Year Perspective," in *Slovaks in America: A Bicentennial Study*, comp. Joseph C. Krajsa et al. (Middletown, PA: Slovak American, 1978); p. 224; *Jednota*, 15 and 22 Mar. 1911, 7 May 1913; *SvA*, 2 and 7 Mar. 1911, 13 May 1913.

15. *SvA*, 7 Mar. 1911.

16. Liščinský, "Katolícka Slovenská Ženská Jednota," p. 183.

17. *Jednota*, 20 Mar. 1902.

18. Ibid., 18 July, 7 and 14 Oct. 1906, 12 June 1910.

19. Ibid., 16 Mar. 1910.

20. Ibid., 18 July 1906, described a "good Catholic" as "every baptized person who believes strongly everything the Pope and bishops . . . instruct about the Saviour [and] who keeps the laws of the Church."

21. Ibid., 20 Jan. 1904, 3 Jan. 1906: Bl. Tatranský, "Zo zápiskov Amerického farára" [From the notes of an American pastor], in FCSU, *Kalendár Jednota, 1902*, pp. 120–21.

22. *Jednota*, 26 Sep. 1906.

23. Ibid., 26 Aug. 1908, 3 Nov. 1909, 28 Sep. 1910, 28 Feb. and 5 June 1912, 15 Apr. 1915.

24. Branch 2, FCSU, Zápisnice, meetings of 10 Dec. 1893, 13 May and 9 Dec. 1894. The focus on Branch 2 and other male lodges is not meant to exclude women from this analysis. Female religious associations did not come into existence in Pittsburgh until after the churches were founded. Also, the evidence indicates that men and women had the same general attitudes toward religion and their churches, although men did hold the positions as lay officers in the churches. Because of these similar attitudes toward religion, general terms such as lay persons, congregations, church members, Slovaks, and similar general descriptions are meant, unless otherwise indicated, to include both men and women.

25. Ibid., 24 Apr. 1894; SEC, *Pamätník Zlatého Jubilea to jest Päťdesiat Ročnej Slávnosti Slovenskej Rímsko-Katolíckej Osady Svätej Alžbety Pittsburgh, Pa., 1894–1944* [Me-

morial Album of the Golden Jubilee being the Celebration of the Fifty-Year Anniversary of the Slovak Roman Catholic Parish of Saint Elizabeth, Pittsburgh, Pa., 1894–1944] (N.p., 1944), p. 11.

26. Branch 2, FCSU, Zápisnice, meeting of 24 Apr. 1894; Kushner, *Slováci Katolíci,* p. 94; SEC, *Pamätník,* p. 11.

27. Branch 2, FCSU, Zápisnice, meeting of 24 Apr. 1894; Kushner, *Slováci Katolíci,* p. 94; SEC, *Pamätník,* pp. 11–12.

28. Branch 2, FCSU, Kniha prijímania údov v testamentov od 14 April 1907 [Register of members accepted with testaments since April 14 1907]. This register is held by officers of Branch 2 and was made available to me by Andrew Holovanisin. With the exception of Branch 2, none of the available fraternal records listed members' occupations. Branch 2's records are spotty. Consequently, virtually the only sources for occupations were Pittsburgh's city directories. Unfortunately, these directories do not include a large number of Slovak workers who participated in the early church ventures. On the general weaknesses of Pittsburgh's city directories, see June Granatir Alexander, "City Directories as 'Ideal' Censuses: Slovak Immigrants and Pittsburgh's Early Twentieth-Century Directories as a Test Case," *Western Pennsylvania Historical Magazine* 65 (July 1982): 203–20.

29. Stephan Thernstrom, *The Other Bostonians: Poverty and Progress in the American Metropolis, 1880–1970* (Cambridge: Harvard University Press, 1973), pp. 283–88. Thernstrom argues that persons of low socioeconomic status were more likely to be excluded from Boston's city directories until they had remained in the city for several years. However, an examination of a sample of Slovak laborers in Pittsburgh reveals that Pittsburgh's directories regularly failed to include them even after they had remained in the city for several years. Still, by including Slovak businessmen and overlooking laborers, the Pittsburgh city directories did reveal some socioeconomic bias in the early twentieth century. See, Alexander, "City Directories," pp. 212–14.

30. Membership ledgers, FCSU, branches 2, 4, 21, 97; NSS, Menoslov (1892–1894).

31. Membership ledgers, FCSU, branches 2, 4, 21, 97.

32. Kushner, *Slováci Katolíci,* p. 94; SEC, *Pamätník,* pp. 13, 15; ASN, 8 Jan. 1895.

33. ASN, 27 Dec. 1894, 8 Jan. 1895.

34. Ibid., 11 Oct., 8 and 17 Nov. 1894.

35. SEC, *Pamätník,* p. 15; Kushner, *Slováci Katolíci,* pp. 95–96.

36. ASN, 27 Dec. 1894.

37. Ibid. The issue of obtaining a pastor was advertised as one that Slovaks would have to discuss at the upcoming January meeting.

38. Kushner, *Slováci Katolíci,* pp. 24, 96, 99–100; SEC, *Pamätník,* p. 15.

39. W. Kittel, Chancellor, to Reverend Coloman Gasparik, 3 Mar. 1895, in DA, Church Files, SEC folder; Kushner, *Slováci Katolíci,* pp. 99–100.

40. 11 Apr. 1895.

41. ASN, 17 Oct. 1895.

42. Ibid., 27 Dec. 1894, 8 Jan. 1895.

43. Church Reports, OVGC, entry for SEC.

44. *Jednota,* 9 Jan. 1907; interviews with John Ciganik, 17 May 1977; Andrew Holovanisin, 30 Nov. 1978; and Paul Granatir, 21 June 1978.

45. Kushner, *Slováci Katolíci,* p. 101; SGC, *Pamätník Zlatého Jubilea Slovenskej Rímsko Katolíckej Osady Sv. Gabriela, N. S.* [Memorial Album of the Golden Jubilee of the Slovak Roman Catholic Parish of Saint Gabriel, North Side] (Pittsburgh; N. p., 1953), unpaged.

46. *ASN*, 22 Oct. 1902.

47. Branch 50, FCSU, Zápisnice, meeting of 5 Oct. 1902. There is no clear evidence that Branch 159 called for the first organizational meeting for a church.

48. Ibid., meeting of 2 Nov. 1902.

49. St. Regis Association, ed., *Catholic Yearbook and Directory of the Pittsburgh Diocese, 1913* (Pittsburgh: St. Regis Association, 1913), p. 242. Some of the churches listed in this book were Greek Catholic, but they were not listed separately nor explicitly identified as Greek Rite churches.

50. *ASN*, 29 Oct. 1902; Kushner, *Slováci Katolíci*, pp. 105–07; DA, Priests' Biographies, 1899–1905, entry for Father Matthew Pekar. Pekar left Saint Matthew's in April 1903, and a replacement was not found until August 1905 (ibid., entry for Father John Gurecky).

51. Kushner, *Slováci Katolíci*, p. 107; Branch 50, FCSU, Zápisnice, meeting of 1 Mar. 1903; SMC, cash book, 1903–1911, entries for 1903–1905, passim [hereafter, SMC, cash book (1903–1911)]. The parish petitioned the diocese in 1904 for permission to borrow money. Permission was granted to borrow money but not to begin construction of a church building. In 1905, the parish sought the bishop's permission to begin construction on a building. Permission was granted. [Father] Joannes Gurecky, Andy Pekar, and Joseph Gurcak to Bishop Phelan, 2 June 1904 (original in Latin); Rev. John Gurecky to Rt. Rev. Regis Canevin, 8 Apr. 1905; Application of 14 Apr. 1905; Sara Elleir to Rt. Rev. Bishop Canevin, 22 Mar. 1905. (Elleir informed the bishop that the parish had paid a deferred payment on its mortgage. She worked for the mortgagers.) All documents contained in SMC, FB file.

52. Church Reports, OVGC, entry for SMC.

53. *ASN*, 5 Apr. 1900; Kushner, *Slováci Katolíci*, pp. 101–02. Kushner claims the first organizational meeting for a Slovak Catholic church in western Allegheny City was held in 1901. The published report in *ASN* shows that the first meeting was actually held in 1900.

54. *ASN*, 24 July 1902; Kushner, *Slováci Katolíci*, p. 103.

55. *ASN*, 24 July 1902; SGC, *Pamätník*.

56. Father Gasparik's opposition to a fourth Slovak church will be discussed later in this chapter.

57. SGC, *Pamätník*. According to Saint Gabriel's history, the required number of families was eventually found. In 1903, when the first official census of Saint Gabriel congregation was taken, the parish had 109 families and 843 "souls." So the first official record of the parish did report it as having the requisite number of families. Church Reports, OVGC, entry for SGC.

58. *PC*, 10 Nov. 1904.

59. *Jednota*, 3 July 1907.

60. Alexander, "Staying Together," pp. 69–70.

61. *Jednota*, 2 Mar. 1910.

62. Resolution of 17 Mar. 1907 in DA, Church Files, SEC folder; SEC, *Pamätník*, pp. 19, 21; Kushner, *Slováci Katolíci*, pp. 98–99.

63. Frank Benkovsky to Rt. Rev. J. F. Regis Canevin, 20 Oct. 1909, in SJC, EB file.

64. Ibid.

65. *SvA*, 22 Dec. 1909; *NN*, 15 Sep. and 20 Oct. 1910; *Jednota*, 27 Mar. 1912; Kushner, *Slováci Katolíci*, p. 32.

66. *Jednota*, 3 Nov. 1909, 4 May and 28 Sep. 1910; interview with Margaret Kuzma, 27 Nov. 1978; Kushner, *Slováci Katolíci*, p. 61.

67. Letter to Rev. C. Gasparik, 23 October 1909, in SJC, EB file. The extant letter

is an unsigned carbon with no letterhead but it was written by Bishop Canevin or the diocesan chancellor at the bishop's direction.

68. Letter to Frank Benkovsky, 23 Oct. 1909, in SJC, EB file. The extant letter is an unsigned carbon; see explanation in n. 67.

69. Church Reports, OVGC, entries for SEC, SGC, SMC, and SJC.

70. *Jednota*, 2 Mar. 1910.

71. Ibid.

72. Chancellor to Rev. Jos[eph]. Vrhunec, 23 Nov. 1909, in SJC, EB file. The contents of this letter indicate that Frankstown Slovaks did not even try to name their own church; instead, through Father Vrhunec, they asked the bishop what the church should be called.

73. Interview with Anastasia Dvorsky, Pittsburgh, 12 Apr. 1977. Miss Dvorsky recalled her mother relating that when she was pregnant and tried to attend a non-Slovak church, she was asked to leave and go to her own church. She did not recall who asked her mother to leave.

74. Names of founders were derived from SEC, *Pamätnik;* SGC, *Pamätnik;* SMC, *Zlaté Jubileum;* SJC, *Golden Jubilee* (Pittsburgh: n.p., 1960), unpaged. Occupations were derived from the Pittsburgh city directories (but see nn. 28 and 29 of this chapter). It should also be noted that, since the overwhelming majority of Slovaks were laborers, it is not surprising that laborers constituted the majority of persons involved in church founding efforts. The key point here is that the formation of ethnic institutions did not rely on the leadership of entrepreneurs made up of a business or professional elite.

75. Membership ledgers, FCSU, branches 2, 4, 21, 97, 159, 185, 254; Branch 50, FCSU, Účtovníca; *ASN*, 1893–1904, passim; *Jednota*, 1902–1911, passim.

76. *ASN*, 24 July 1902.

77. *Jednota*, 3 July 1907.

Chapter 4. Maintaining Catholic Churches

1. Interviews with Margaret Kuzma, 27 Nov. 1978, 13 May 1977; Ferdinand Dvorsky, 12 Apr. 1977; Mary Ciganik, 17 May 1977; and Ann Jacobs, Pittsburgh, 17 May 1977; interview with Michael Zahorsky by Peter Gottlieb, Aliquippa, PA, 21 June 1974, as part of the Pennsylvania Historical and Museum Commission Project, 1974, Series 1, Tape 16; *Jednota*, 21 Aug. 1912, Sep. 1914, and 31 Mar. 1915.

2. Interviews with Ferdinand Dvorsky, 12 Apr. 1977; Margaret Kuzma, 13 May 1977, 27 Nov. 1978; and John and Mary Ciganik, 17 May 1977. Another man recalls that when he immigrated to the North Side in 1929, immigrants from the same villages and regions still often clustered together after church services (interview with Andrew Holovanisin, 30 Nov. 1978).

3. This description is a composite of Slovak weddings described in Pittsburgh's Slovak newspapers. Smaller weddings or those of Slovaks who did not belong to a well-known family went unnoticed in the papers, so there is no clear description of how they were celebrated. See also Rovnianek, "Slovaks in America," p. 244.

4. *Jednota*, 8 Nov. 1911.

5. Branch 50, FCSU, Zápisnice, meetings of 6 May 1900, 1 June 1902; Branch 2, FSCU, Zápisnice, meetings of 31 Mar. 1897, 18 Sep. 1898, 17 Feb. 1901, 12 Feb. and 12 Mar. 1911, 11 Feb. 1912, 9 Feb. 1913; *Jednota*, 16 Jan. 1907, 10 Nov. 1915.

6. *Jednota*, 20 July 1904, 3 Jan. 1906, 2 Jan. 1907; Š[tefan] Furdek, "Vel'konočná spoved' " [Easter confession], in FCSU, *Kalendár Jednota, 1913*, pp. 105–107; j [pseud.],

"Tie kňazské dôchodky, bohatstvá" [Priestly income, wealth], in FCSU, *Kalendár Jednota, 1911,* p. 54; Tatranský, "Zo zápiskov," p. 121; Aldasy, "Hungary."

7. This is a composite derived from documents contained in the records of several county governments and housed in three regional and one district archives in Czechoslovakia. Citations for the following documents include collection titles and the call number of specific documents; the numbers that follow slashes are document dates (years) or dates with an additional identifying number. Documents in the county records indicate that the practice of instituting temporary collections for churches among neighboring villages differed among the counties. Requests for collections were more common in Spiš County and in the Bratislava district. State Regional Archives, Levoča, Hlavný župan, 601/1887, 309/1891, 318/1891, 140/1898, 498/1899; Podžupan, 826/1894. Bratislava District Archives, Bratislava, Zápisnice municipalného výboru, 1867–1918, 1634/455–1868, 281/43–1868, 75/42–1869, 116/78–1869, 116/19–1869. I could find petitions for only two collections in the Prešov region (State Regional Archives, Prešov), Župan, 169/1894, 208/1898. In the Košice region, I found no recorded petitions for collections. Documents pertaining to government involvement in the administration of financial affairs of churches include Podžupan (Levoča), 103–118/1873; Podžupan (Prešov), 18/1873; Zápisnice municipalného výboru, 1867–1918 (Bratislava), 174/53-1868, 1070/325-1869, 75/42-1869, 478/233-1869. There is some evidence that Slovaks became so accustomed to receiving support for churches that in the early years of immigration to the United States some priests may have requested help from bishops in northern Hungary. In 1899, a Slovak pastor in McKeesport, Pennsylvania, asked the Bishop of Košice for money to buy an organ for the McKeesport Slovak Catholic church. Letter to the Bishop of Košice, 29 Mar. 1899, Diocesan Archives, Košice.

8. This discussion is a composite derived from interviews with Ferdinand Dvorsky, 12 Apr. 1977, 28 Nov. 1978; John Ciganik, 17 May 1977; and Andrew Holovanisin, 30 Nov. 1978. These three men came from three different counties in northern Hungary, and their descriptions of lay involvement and church support suggest that there was a uniformity of the laity's roles.

9. *PC,* 10 Nov. 1904.

10. Kushner, *Slováci Katolíci,* p. 103; SGC, *Pamätník;* SMC, cash book (1903–1911); SMC, financial ledger, entry entitled Pôžičky [loans].

11. SMC, cash book (1903–1911), entry for December 1909.

12. A more detailed discussion of this issue is provided later in this chapter.

13. SMC, financial ledger, entries for 1903–1906, passim; SMC, cash book (1903–1911), passim; SMC, cash book (1912–1918), passim.

14. Kushner, *Slováci Katolíci,* p. 94; SEC, *Pamätník,* pp. 12, 15; ASN, 11 Oct., 8 Nov., and 27 Nov. 1895; *Jednota,* 23 Mar. 1904.

15. SMC, cash book (1903–1911), entries for month of Feb. and 31 Mar. 1903.

16. *Jednota,* 23 Mar. 1904.

17. SMC, cash book (1903–1911), passim; interview with Ferdinand Dvorsky, 12 Apr. 1977.

18. SMC, cash book (1903–1911), entries for month of Oct. 1903 and 20 July 1904; interview with Ferdinand Dvorsky, 12 Apr. 1977; *Jednota,* 23 Oct. 1907, 23 Sep. and 26 Oct. 1909. These are only a few examples of newspaper accounts of church collections at baptisms or marriages.

19. SMC, financial ledger; SMC, cash book (1903–1911), passim.

20. SMC, cash book (1903–1911), entries for 7 Jan., 4 Mar., and 9 Sep. 1906, 17 Feb. 1907. One parishioner described the blessing of the church monstrance, a cere-

mony that drew over one hundred people, as an occasion that "both young and old would always remember." *Jednota,* 25 Jan. 1905.

21. *PC,* 7 June 1906.

22. SMC, cash book (1903–1911), entry for 23 Sep. 1906.

23. *ASN,* 11 Oct. and 8 Nov. 1894, 17 Nov. 1895, 6 Aug. 1902, 7 Oct. 1903.

24. Ibid., 28 Feb. and 7 Nov. 1895, 30 Jan. and 21 May 1896, 31 Oct. and 5 Dec. 1901, 20 Feb. and 8 May 1902; *Jednota,* 21 Sep. 1904, 25 Oct. 1905, 6 Mar. 1907, 24 Feb. 1909.

25. This observation is made with caution, because issues of the *ASN* for the period after June 1904 are missing. However, if Saint Gabriel's or its fraternals did publicize their activities in this newspaper after 1904, this would have been a different procedure than had been followed in the previous years when the Saint Gabriel congregation did not advertise socials in *Jednota.*

26. This conclusion is based on a close analysis of the minutes of branches 2 and 50 of FCSU and a careful reading of the four extant Slovak newspapers that carried ads for social functions at Slovak Catholic churches.

27. SMC, cash book (1903–1911), passim; SMC, cash book (1912–1918), passim.

28. Interviews with Margaret Kuzma, 27 Nov. 1978; John and Mary Ciganik, 17 May 1977; Ferdinand Dvorsky, 12 Apr. 1977 and 28 Nov. 1978; and Ann Jacobs, 17 May 1977.

29. Interview with Ferdinand Dvorsky, 28 Nov. 1978; Ray Dvorsky to June Alexander, 12 Sept. 1979.

30. *Jednota,* 23 Oct. 1907.

31. Ibid., 2 Jan. 1907.

32. Ibid., 20 Jan. 1909.

33. Interview with Ferdinand Dvorsky, 12 Apr. 1977.

34. Interview with Father George Jurica, Pittsburgh, 12 April 1977.

35. Jay Dolan (*Immigrant Church,* p. 71) uses the phrase "a church within a church" to describe a German Catholic parish established in New York City earlier in the nineteenth century.

36. *Jednota,* 2 Aug. 1905, 8 Jan. and 5 Aug. 1908, 17 Mar. 1909, 7 Sep. 1910, 20 Mar., 22 May, 24 July, and 21 Aug. 1912; *PC,* 7 June and 27 Sep. 1906, 7 May and 6 Aug. 1908. Father Gasparik of Saint Elizabeth Church was the only Slovak pastor who occasionally asked non-Slavic priests to assist him. (*PC,* 7 May 1908; *Jednota,* 17 Mar. 1909, 20 Mar. 1912.) It is impossible, however, to ascertain the names of all the priests who assisted Slovak pastors during the early decades of the twentieth century. The available information strongly indicates that Slovak priests relied on one another or on Slavic priests, such as Father Vrhunec at Saint Joachim's, who were pastors of Slovak parishes.

37. *Jednota,* 4 Sep. 1907, 2 Feb. 1910. These observations pertain to Pittsburgh, not to the entire diocese. In small towns, it may have been difficult to get a Slovak pastor to substitute for an extended period for a Slovak priest absent on vacation or due to illness. In 1909, in Homestead, Bishop Canevin assigned an Irish priest to serve a Slovak parish while the pastor was in Hungary, but the parish resisted, and the bishop temporarily closed the church. Kushner, *Slováci Katolíci,* p. 62.

38. *PC,* 24 Aug. 1893, 17 Aug. 1905, 31 Dec. 1908; Diocese of Pittsburgh, *Statuta Dioeceseos Pittsburgensis In Synodis Dioecesanis, Habitas Lata, Et Prout Nunc Prostant Promulgata In Synodo Dioecesana Sexta Dubus 7, 8 et 9 Febuarii 1893* [Statutes of the Pittsburgh Diocese] (Pittsburgh: N. p., 1893), p. 69 (hereafter, Pittsburgh Diocese, *Statutes 1893*).

39. Pittsburgh Diocese, *Statutes 1893*, p. 69.

40. SEC, SGC, SMC, and SJC, FB files (separate files for each church).

41. *PC*, 10 Nov. 1904; Diocese of Pittsburgh, *Statuta Dioeceseos Pittsburgensis In Synadis Dioecesanis Lata, Et Prout Nune Prostant Promulgata In Synodo Dioecesana Decima Die 10 Mensis Octobris, A.D. 1905* [Statutes of the Pittsburgh Diocese] (Pittsburgh: N. p., 1906), p. 83 (hereafter, Pittsburgh Diocese, *Statutes 1905*).

42. Application of 15 Dec. 1910, in SMC, FB file. The difficulties Saint Matthew Church encountered are discussed later in this chapter.

43. SMC, cash book (1912–1918), entries for 28 Sep. 1913 and 19 Jan. 1914.

44. *PC*, 24 Aug. 1893, 25 Jan. 1894. Pittsburgh Diocese, *Statutes 1893*, pp. 68–69; Pittsburgh Diocese, *Statutes 1905*, pp. 82, 84.

45. *PC*, 25 Jan. 1894; Pittsburgh Diocese, *Statutes 1893*, p. 68; Pittsburgh Diocese, *Statutes 1905*, p. 82. Initially, trustee elections were to be held annually; by 1905, trustees were serving three-year terms.

46. Pittsburgh Diocese, *Statutes 1893*, pp. 67–69; Pittsburgh Diocese, *Statutes 1905*, p. 83. Cautious church officials apparently wanted to squelch any possibility that the new system might create trustee battles reminiscent of those that had occurred earlier in the century. Correspondingly, titles to Catholic churches in the Pittsburgh diocese remained in the name of their respective congregations, with the bishop as trustee.

47. Pittsburgh Diocese, *Statutes 1905*, pp. 83–84.

48. Testimony of Saint Elizabeth's parishioners to the bishop, October 1916, in SEC, CC file (hereafter, SEC, Testimony, 1916).

49. Interview with Ferdinand Dvorsky, 12 Apr. 1977.

50. SMC, cash book (1903–1911), passim; SMC, cash book (1912–1918), passim.

51. SMC, cash book (1903–1911), entry for 3 June 1908; SMC, Audit Report, 3 July 1908, in SMC, FB file.

52. Assistant Chancellor to Rev. John Uhlyarik, 3 Feb. 1911, in SMC, FB file. This letter informed Uhlyarik that the diocesan audit had found the church's financial accounts in order.

53. Pittsburgh Diocese, *Statutes 1893*, p. 69; Pittsburgh Diocese, *Statutes 1905*, p. 84.

54. Pittsburgh Diocese, *Statutes 1893*, p. 68; Pittsburgh Diocese, *Statutes 1905*, p. 84.

55. SEC, Testimony, 1916.

56. Petition from Saint Elizabeth's Parishioners to Bishop Regis Canevin, 21 Jan. 1915, in SEC, CC file. The petition referred explicitly to the diocesan statutes regarding trustee elections.

57. Ibid. The petition was written in English, and while parishioners who signed it undoubtedly knew that it referred to the 1915 trustee election, some may not have been able to read the entire petition and thus were not aware of all of the grievances listed.

58. SEC, Testimony, 1916.

59. Petition to the Right Reverend Regis Canevin, n.d., in SEC, CC file.

60. SEC, Testimony, 1916.

61. Bishop Canevin to Rev. Coloman Gasparik, 4 Dec. 1916, in SEC, CC file.

62. Rev. Coloman Gasparik to the Right Reverend R. J. Canevin, 7 Dec. 1916, in SEC, CC file.

63. Bishop Regis Canevin to Rev. Coloman Gasparik, 9 Dec. 1916; Church Committee list, 1916. Both documents in SEC, CC file.

64. Church Committee lists, 1915, 1916, in SEC, CC file.

65. Letter [unsigned carbon, author not identified] to John Kulamer, attorney at law, 28 Dec. 1909; letter [unsigned carbon] to Rev. J. Uhlyarik, 23 Dec. 1909. Both documents in SMC, FB file.

66. Rev. John Uhlyarik to Rt. Rev. Bishop Canevin [Apr. 1911 (?)], in SMC, CC file. Original in Latin.

67. Asst. Chancellor to Rev. John Uhlyarik, 21 Apr. 1911, in SMC, CC file.

68. *Jednota*, 7 Feb. 1912.

69. Assistant Chancellor to trustee, 29 July 1911, in SMC, CC file.

70. *Jednota*, 24 Jan. and 7 Feb. 1912.

71. Both trustees remained members of Saint Matthew Church. There was no serious decline afterward in the membership of Saint Matthew's. The number of individuals increased from 1,130 in 1911 to 1,385 in 1912; the number of families decreased from 214 to 203. Church Reports, OVGC, entry for SMC.

72. June Granatir Alexander, "The Laity in the Church: Slovaks and the Catholic Church in Pre-World War I Pittsburgh," *Church History* 53 (Sep. 1984): 363–78.

73. For example, the founders of Saint Gabriel Church persuaded a Slovak priest in Olyphant, Pennsylvania, to write to priests in Hungary on their behalf. Kushner, *Slováci Katolíci*, pp. 102–03.

74. *Katolícke Noviny*, 5 Mar. 1903.

75. Pastors' daily schedules can be partially reconstructed from entries in baptismal, marriage, and burial records. The following discussion of priests' activities is based on an analysis of the ecclesiastical records for Pittsburgh's four Slovak Roman Catholic churches.

76. This description of priests' activities is based on ecclesiastical records and on interviews with Margaret Kuzma, 13 May 1977 and 27 Nov. 1978; John and Mary Ciganik, 17 May 1977; and Ann Jacobs, 17 May 1977. All of these interviewees witnessed activities of pastors in the early twentieth century.

77. *Jednota*, 16 Dec. 1908.

78. Gurecky recorded this assessment in a short history of the parish which he wrote on the first page of SMC, financial ledger.

79. SMC, cash book (1903–1911), passim. Gurecky did not keep for himself all of the money he received for signing "verification cards," which certified that Catholics had made their yearly confession. Ibid., entries for months of Sep. 1903 and Jan. 1904; SMC, financial ledger, entries for 1903–1906, passim.

80. Father Ján Gurecký to Father V. Sasinek, 15 June 1903, AMS, IHRC.

81. Father Ján Gurecký to Father V. Sasinek, 9 Sep. 1903, AMS, IHRC.

82. *Jednota*, 25 Jan. 1905.

83. SMC, *Zlaté Jubileum*, p. 42.

84. *Jednota*, 12 Oct. 1902, 8 Aug. 1906, 5 Aug. 1908, 14 Dec. 1910; Furdek, "Vel'konočná spoved'," pp. 105–08; Tatranský, "Zo zápiskov," pp. 120–21; j, "Tie kňazské dôchodky, bohatstvá," pp. 53–55.

85. *NN*, 22 Sep. 1910. He did not say who the priest was, but since Saint Elizabeth's was the only church in Pittsburgh at the time, it was most likely Father Gasparik.

86. *PC*, 10 Nov. 1904.

87. Ibid., 20 Oct. 1910, 12 Oct. 1911; *Jednota*, 19 Oct. 1910, 8 Nov. 1911.

88. Vecoli, "Cult and Occult," pp. 25–47; idem, "Prelates and Peasants," pp. 217–68.

Chapter 5. Preserving the Faith

1. The Lutheran Church of Hungary did not maintain jurisdiction over members who emigrated. George Dolak, *A History of the Slovak Evangelical Lutheran Church in the United States, 1902–1927* (St. Louis: Concordia, 1955), pp. 15–16, 54, 68, 70, 107–

108, 142–45; Fedor Ruppeldt, *Slovenské-Evangelici v Amerike* [Slovak Lutherans in America] (Ružomberok, Czechoslovakia: Cirkev Evanj. a.v. na Slovensku, 1932), pp. 53–55; Ján Body, *Pamätník Rev. A. L. Ramer Ph.D.* [Memorial to Rev. A. L. Ramer, Ph.D.] (N.p.: Slovak Zion Synod, n.d.), pp. 5–7; S. G. Mazak "A Brief History of the Slovak Lutheran Synod of the United States," *Concordia Historical Institute Quarterly* 3 (1930): 83 (this article appeared in two parts, the conclusion was published in ibid. 4 [1931]: 105–12).

2. Dolak, *A History*, pp. 17–68. The Evangelical Lutheran Synodical Conference of America, hereafter referred to by the shortened title, Synodical Conference.

3. Ibid., pp. 33–34.

4. Ibid., pp. 33–35. They actually tried to form a *seniorate*, a term used to refer to administrative districts of the Lutheran Church in Hungary.

5. *SvA*, 23 June 1899; Ján Bajus, "Historický náčrt Slovenskej evanjelicko-luteránskej cirkvi" [Historical sketch of the Slovak Evangelical Lutheran Church], in SELC, *Jubilejný Evanjelicko-Luteránsky Kalendár, 1952* (Pittsburgh: Slavia, 1952), pp. 32–34, 46.

6. *SvA*, 19 June 1906; "Tranoscius" Spolok, "Zo života našich bratov v Amerike" [From the life of our brothers in America], in *Tranovský Evanjelický Kalendár, 1907* (Sv. Mikuláš, Czechoslovakia: N.p., 1907), p. 154. At an 1899 pastoral meeting, the clergymen adopted a resolution opposing social events to raise money for Lutheran churches. Bajus, "Historický náčrt," pp. 32, 34.

7. Dolak, *A History*, pp. 52, 63–64, 74–75.

8. Ibid., pp. 69, 76–78.

9. Ibid., p. 72.

10. It is tempting to view the disagreements as being between nationalists and nonnationalists. Supporters of the Slovak Synod may well have been nationalists; nevertheless, the disagreements that divided the Lutheran clergy were based on confessional disputes. (The issue of nationalism versus religious and ethnic identities is discussed in more depth later in this study.) Moreover, I could not find evidence that the disagreements were a continuation of religious disputes among Slovaks in Hungary. Even so, the key concern here is the impact that conditions in America had on immigrants. It was the question of the Synodical Conference's beliefs that stirred problems among Lutheran immigrants in America.

11. *SH*, 3 Dec. 1908, 17 June 1909, 23 June 1910, 28 Sep. 1911.

12. Ibid., 23 Nov. 1911; Dolak, *A History*, p. 66.

13. *SH*, 25 Feb. 1909, 7, 4, 21, and 28 Sep. 1911, 9 Dec. 1915.

14. For a subjective discussion of the synod's view toward the Lutheran Church of Hungary and to its successor in Czechoslovakia after World War I, see Dolak, *A History*, pp. 71–72, 106–27.

15. Ibid., pp. 58–62, 159–60; Lutheran Church in America, *A History of the Slovak Zion Synod, LCA* (N.p.: Lutheran Church in America, 1977), pp. 119–20 (hereafter, LCA, *A History*).

16. Ibid., p. 119; Dolak, *A History*, pp. 61, 142, 149, 159, 162. By 1913, the Synod had achieved qualified success in convincing congregations to accept announcement. In 1913, twenty-seven of the forty-one Slovak Lutheran congregations served by synod pastors had introduced the practice. However, there were perhaps as many as thirty-four American Slovak churches that were either independent or affiliated with another synod. Some of them had left the Slovak Synod specifically because of disagreements with its newly instituted practices.

17. Dolak, *A History*, pp. 81–82. Pastors pointed out that the *Tranoscius* had actually

predated the *Spevník*. The *Tranoscius* was apparently being used in some places in Hungary.

18. Ibid., p. 162. Most Slovak congregations rejected the *Tranoscius*. In 1913, only thirteen of the forty-one congregations served by synod pastors had adopted the hymnal.

19. NSS, *Dejiny and Pamätnica, 1890–1950*, p. 291.

20. SEU, *Zlatá Kniha, 1893–1943*, pp. 126–27.

21. For a lengthy description of where Slovak Lutherans settled in Pittsburgh, see Alexander, "Immigrant Church and Community," pp. 116–28.

22. In 1890, a few Slovak Lutherans in Pittsburgh did join with Slovak Calvinists and Hungarians of the Reformed faith in an attempt to found a church. However, most if not all of the Slovak Lutherans withdrew from the effort and became charter members of Braddock's Slovak Lutheran congregation. *SH,* 9 Nov. 1911; First Hungarian Reformed Church (Hazelwood), collection book. I am grateful to Bertalon Olah for making this book available to me and for translating for me.

23. The liturgical language of Slovak Lutheran services was the same as that used in the Kralice Bible, the Czech translation of the Holy Book. LCA, *A History,* p. 107.

24. HEC, *A History of Holy Emmanuel Church, 1904–1964* (N.p.: 1964), p. 6; SEU, "Z činnosti 65 čísla. SEJ v N. S. Pittsburgh, Pa." [From the activities of Branch 65 of the Slovak Evangelical Union in the North Side, Pittsburgh, Pa.], in *Slovenský Evanjelický Kalendár, 1926,* p. 116. This article contains a series of excerpts from the lodge's minutes.

25. SEU, "Z činnosti 65 čísla," p. 116; HEC, *A History,* p. 6.

26. It is not clear if the elections and initiation of money assessments occurred in 1902 or 1903. The church history, which was written from Branch 65 minutes, claims that the introduction of a dues system occurred in 1903 (p. 6). However, the published excerpts from the lodge minutes suggest that both the introduction of the dues system and the elections took place in 1902. This discrepancy could be due to the imprecise format used for publishing the minutes for 1902 and 1903. SEU, "Z činnosti 65 čísla," p. 117.

27. As far as can be determined, in this formative period, Branch 65 did not call a general meeting of Pittsburgh's Slovak Lutherans. There is no record of the type of interlodge cooperation that had accompanied the early founding efforts of the city's Slovak Catholic churches.

28. SEU, "Z činnosti 65 čísla," p. 117. Church inspectors existed in Hungary and, in general, they were charged with overseeing church properties. Dolak, *A History,* pp. 50–51.

29. *ASN,* 20 Apr. 1904; Alexander, "Immigrant Church and Community," pp. 118–26.

30. *ASN,* 20 Apr. 1904.

31. Ibid., 11 May 1904.

32. HEC, Zápisnice, meeting of 31 Aug. 1913. There are no records that outline the precise duties of the trustees during the early years of the church. Moreover, there are no records that clearly describe who was eligible to vote and who did vote.

33. SEU, "Z činnosti 65 čísla," pp. 117, 122; other Slovak Lutheran lodges in America adopted similar procedures, see Dolak, *A History,* pp. 25, 131.

34. *SvA,* 20 July 1906; *SH,* 20 Feb. and 23 July 1908, 11 Nov, 1909, 27 Apr. 1911.

35. SEU, "Z činnosti 65 čísla," pp. 117, 122. Between 1903 and 1906, Branch 65 also lent the Holy Emmanuel congregation at least $700.

36. Although from 1908 to 1915, Pittsburgh's Lutheran lodges advertised dances,

picnics, and other events, none of them published an invitation for Slovak Lutherans to attend a social sponsored for the church. And, given the scattered residences of the city's Slovak Lutherans, together with the recognition that not all of them regularly attended religious services, public advertisements were necessary in order to reach the largest segment of the population.

37. HEC, *A History*, p. 7. Balent performed every funeral, marriage, and baptism recorded in the church records from April 1904, when ecclesiastic records were first kept for the congregation. However, the church history claims he did not become the permanent pastor until the fall of 1905.

38. Dolak, *A History*, p. 31, n. 50.

39. Janošov, "Úryvky z dejín Spolku," p. 127.

40. *SvA*, 23 Nov. 1906; Konštantín Čulen, *Slovenské Časopisy v Amerike* [Slovak Periodicals in America] (Middletown, PA: Jednota, 1970), p. 164.

41. *SvA*, 20 July 1906.

42. *SH*, 14 May and 4 June 1908.

43. Ibid., 4 June 1908.

44. Ibid.; Dolak, *A History*, pp. 31 (n. 50), 114–15.

45. *SH*, 14 and 21 May 1908.

46. Ibid., 14 May 1908.

47. Ibid., 4 June 1908

48. Ibid., 14 May 1908. Although not explicitly stated, this comment strongly suggests that Balent did try to prevent some fraternal activities, especially those involving use of the church. The charges that fraternals and their activities were "sinful" were common allegations of synod clergy.

49. Ibid.

50. Ibid., 4 June 1908. Holy Emmanuel's baptismal and marriage records (1904–1908) show that a few Lutherans were married to Slovak Calvinists, but there is no way to determine if Balent's allegations about Calvinists receiving communion at the church are correct.

51. *SH*, 28 Jan. 1909.

52. Ibid., 2 Dec. 1909.

53. Janošov, "Úryvky z dejín Spolku," pp. 126–27. Names of lodge officers were regularly published in issues of *SH*.

54. *SH*, 6 Aug. 1908. George Teraj had been an officer of the church. Another person who claimed to be a lodge and church member wrote a letter similar to Teraj's, but he did not sign his name. Ibid., 4 Feb. 1909.

55. Ibid. 6 Aug. 1908.

56. There is no record of the vote on these issues. Ambivalence among lay persons is further discussed in chapter 6.

57. HEC, *A History*, p. 7; Uherka, "Kratký prehľad S.K.P. Jednota," p. 52.

58. HEC, Zápisnice, meetings of 27 Sep., 26 Oct., and 23 Nov. 1913, 1 Mar. 1914.

59. Ibid., meeting of 5 Apr. 1914.

60. Ibid.

61. These fears and specific lay actions to allay them are discussed in chapter 6.

62. *SH*, 1 Oct. 1914. The Reverend John Pelikan, who as president of the Slovak Synod had earlier been the object of severe criticisms by Holy Emmanuel's spokesmen, attended the Reverend John Marcis's formal installation as Holy Emmanuel's pastor. The Holy Emmanuel congregation was not the only Slovak Lutheran congregation in the United States that relented and accepted a synod pastor after initially rejecting the Synodical Conference. (See Dolak, *A History*, pp. 159–60.) However,

Holy Emmanuel congregation continued to use the *Spevník* even after Marcis became pastor. HEC, Zápisnice, meeting of 19 June 1921.

63. *SH*, 22 Apr. 1915.

64. Ibid., 2 Dec. 1915.

65. HEC, Zápisnice, meetings of 19 and 26 June 1921.

Chapter 6. Taking Charge

1. Alexander, "Staying Together," pp. 71–73; HEC, baptismal, marriage, burial records, 1904–1910.

2. *SH*, 2 Sep. and 9 Dec. 1909, 31 Mar., 16 June, 29 Sep., and 24 Nov. 1910, 11 May and 12 Oct. 1911, 28 Mar. 1912.

3. Ibid., 2 Nov. and 9 Dec. 1909, 24 Nov. 1910, 21 Dec. 1911, 19 Dec. 1912.

4. On two research trips to Czechoslovakia (1982 and 1985), I attempted to obtain solid information about how regularly Slovak Lutherans attended Sunday services in the villages at the turn of the century. The information I received was conflicting. The immigrants I interviewed in Pittsburgh, who had left their homeland in the early twentieth century, could not offer comments on this subject with any certainty. One immigrant did claim that in villages where there was no Lutheran church some Lutherans did not go to regular Sunday services. Sometimes they attended the Catholic church in their villages. Interview with Paul Granatir, 21 June 1978. (His mother was Lutheran.)

5. *SH*, 3 Feb. 1910.

6. Ibid., 19 May 1910. Teraj's original letter was published in the Cleveland *Hlas*. I could not locate a copy. A description of his complaints was determined by information provided in three letters written in response to his letter. These letters contain systematic rebuttals to specific allegations and statements that Teraj had made. Teraj's call was not related to the synod-church conflicts that had plagued Holy Emmanuel congregation in 1908. Indeed, Teraj had been a staunch critic of the synod, and there was nothing in any of the letters that suggest that Teraj wanted to start another church affiliated with the Slovak Synod.

7. Three letters appear in the same issue of *SH* (19 May 1910). One letter was signed by Anton Miller on behalf of Holy Emmanuel's officers; a second was submitted by Anton Miller alone; and a third was written by Karol Salva-Cebratsky, a youth of Holy Emmanuel congregation who was studying for the ministry.

8. Ibid., 12 June 1913.

9. Ibid.; HEC, *A History*, p. 7.

10. HEC, Zápisnice, meeting of 17 Aug. 1913.

11. Ibid., meeting of 12 Oct. 1913. There were ninety-nine "active" male and fifteen "active" female members. It is not clear why the female total was so small. There is no indication that *men* meant, in fact, families and thus would have included women. In October 1913, fifty-four Slovak women belonged to Pittsburgh Slovak Lutheran lodges (*SH*, 13 Nov. 1913). I could not determine why there was such a great discrepancy between the number of women belonging to fraternals and the number listed as active members of the church.

12. *SH*, 1913, passim. Membership statistics for local Slovak Lutheran lodges were published in various issues of this paper.

13. Ibid., 21 Aug. 1913.

14. HEC, Zápisnice, meeting of 31 Aug. 1913.

15. The conclusion that eight of these men belonged to a fraternal is based on

information that they had previously or were at present serving as local or national fraternal officers. Seven of the men belonged to the Slovak Evangelical Union (*SH*, Jan. 1908 to Sep. 1913, passim) and one belonged to the National Slovak Society (*NN*, 20 Jan. 1910). Another man had formerly been a treasurer for the National Slovak Society, but it could not be determined if he was still a member in 1913 (*ASN*, 3 Oct. 1901).

16. HEC, Zápisnice, meetings of 23 Nov. 1913 and 1 Mar. 1914.

17. Ibid., meeting of 31 Aug. 1913. Nonmembers probably included transients as well as persons who, for various reasons, were reluctant to contribute.

18. Ibid. The minutes do not record whether or not the collectors actually performed as recruiters.

19. This conclusion is based on the letters that commented on and complained about support for the church. Letters noted that there was a larger attendance on particularly important feasts. Neither the letters nor the minutes included any estimates of the number of Lutherans who regularly attended services.

20. Ibid., meeting of 4 Jan. 1914.

21. *SH*, 22 Apr. 1915.

22. Ibid., 9 Apr. 1914.

23. Ibid., 6 Nov. 1913. In 1914, besides Holy Emmanuel, at least six other Slovak Lutheran churches claimed such groups. (Ibid., 12 Mar. 1914). The effort at Holy Emmanuel's may also have reflected the nationalism that was intensifying among Slovaks on the eve of World War I (discussed in depth in chapter 8). Nevertheless, the group was certainly part of an effort to revive the church and to make it a social center.

24. Ibid., 12 Feb., 12 Mar., 23 Apr., 27 Aug., and 29 Oct. 1914, 30 Sep. 1915.

25. Ibid., 29 Oct. 1914.

26. For an incisive discussion of the meaning of *community* with which this chapter and subsequent discussions of "community" in this study are in agreement, see Thomas Bender, *Community and Social Change in America* (New Brunswick, NJ: Rutgers University Press, 1978).

27. Holy Emmanuel Church has remained a Slovak Lutheran church to the current day. Why and how it has survived as an ethnic church merit separate and careful consideration, beyond the scope of this study.

28. *NN*, 4 Jan. 1912.

29. Ibid.

30. On settlement patterns in the South Side, see Alexander, "Immigrant Church and Community," pp. 133–45; idem, "City Directories," pp. 217–18.

31. *NN*, 4 Jan. 1912.

32. Ibid.; *Jednota*, 24 Jan. 1912.

33. *NN*, 4 Jan. 1912.

34. SMC, cash book (1912–1918) entries for January to March 1912.

35. For other examples of lay assertiveness, see Stolarik, "Lay Initiative."

36. Branch 2, FCSU, Zápisnice, meeting of 9 Dec. 1894.

37. This does not mean that Lutheran lodges did not feel they should help the church. Although a small amount, in 1908, one Pittsburgh lodge donated five dollars to the church in the hope that other lodges would follow the example. *SH*, 30 July 1908.

38. Pittsburgh Diocese, *Statutes 1905*, p. 85.

39. SMC, cash book (1903–1911), passim; SMC, cash book (1912–1918), passim; SEC, SGC, SJC, and SMC, CC files (separate files for each church). Committee lists for some years are missing from some of the church files.

40. Occupations derived from Pittsburgh city directories, but, on the weaknesses of these directories, see chapter 3, nn. 28 and 29. *Diffenbacher's Directory of Pittsburgh and Allegheny Cities* (Pittsburgh: Stevens & Foster, 1894–1897); Polk & Co., *Pittsburgh and Allegheny Directory* (R. L. Dudley, 1898–1907); Polk & Co., *Pittsburgh Directory* (Pittsburgh: R. L. Dudley, 1908–1915).

41. SMC, cash book (1903–1911), passim; SMC, financial ledger.

42. Three men are not listed in city directories. Ibid. and SMC, cash book (1912–1918), passim.

43. SMC, cash book (1912–1918), passim; SMC, financial ledger.

44. For other conclusions about the economic status of ethnic leaders, see Josef J. Barton, "Eastern and Southern Europeans," in *Ethnic Leadership in America*, ed. John Higham (Baltimore: Johns Hopkins University Press, 1978), pp. 163–64, 169–71; Ewa Morawska, "The Internal Status Hierarchy in the East European Communities in Johnstown, PA, 1890–1930s," *Journal of Social History* 16 (Fall 1982): 75–107.

45. Data on fraternal membership were derived from a number of sources. Membership and insurance applications, 1908–1912 (FCSU), branches 2, 4, 21, 97, 185, 254, 460 in First Catholic Slovak Union Papers, IHRC (hereafter, Membership applications, FCSU); Branch 2, FCSU, Kniha prijímania údov; Branch 50, FCSU, Účtovníca; *Jednota*, 1903–1915, passim; *SH*, 1908–1915, passim; *NN*, 1910–1915, passim.

46. Data derived from lists regularly published in official newspapers of Slovak organizations. See newspaper citations in n. 45.

47. In addition, two men had been both a president and a subordinate officer before their elections to a Church Committee; two became president after their elections to trustee positions; and one became a subordinate officer in his lodge after he was elected to a Church Committee post.

48. *ASN*, 17 Apr. 1902; Polk, *Pittsburgh Directory*, 1908–1913; *SH*, Jan. 1908 to Dec. 1913, passim. Subsequent information given here regarding fraternal membership and occupations of Slovak Lutherans was derived from these sources and from *NN*, 1910–1914, passim; *SvA*, 27 Jan. 1914.

49. See, e.g., Robert D. Cross, *The Emergence of Liberal Catholicism in America* (Cambridge: Harvard University Press, 1958), pp. 63–64, 69–70, 162–81, 213–14.

50. See, e.g., Rowland Berthoff, "The American Social Order: A Conservative Hypothesis," *American Historical Review* 65 (Apr. 1960): 495–514; idem, *An Unsettled People: Social Order and Disorder in American History* (New York: Harper & Row, 1971).

Chapter 7. Diversity Within Unity

1. *Jednota*, 7 Sep. 1910; Branch 50, FCSU, Zápisnice, meeting of 7 Aug. 1910.

2. *Jednota*, 7 Sep. 1910.

3. For an explanation of the problems and limitations of using marriage records for determining regional persistence, see appendix.

4. *Region* refers to an area consisting of several counties where the same dialect was spoken.

5. For an explanation of persons included in and excluded from the total marriages, see appendix.

6. Slovak families are defined here and throughout this chapter as those families in which at least one parent was Slovak.

7. Saint Gabriel Church is excluded from this analysis because the church's pastors did not record parents' origins in baptismal records. The format of Saint Mat-

thew's baptismal records, in which godparents' names were often written close to the center binding, together with the nearly illegible handwriting of Fathers Janusek and Uhlyarik, who served the parish in succession from August 1905 to 1918, made it impossible to record godparents' names and then to locate them in other records. Besides having dismally poor handwriting, Father Uhlyarik often either Magyarized or mispelled names and used inconsistent spellings for the same name; hence it was impossible to try to locate and identify godparents with any degree of certainty in the church's records. For a discussion of the problems of utilizing church records, see appendix.

8. *Village area* refers to the villages and towns that lay clustered together or in close proximity (usually less than ten miles) to one another.

9. As previously discussed, intercounty marriages were infrequent, and when they did occur, the partners often came from neighboring counties in the same region.

10. These totals include persons listed in the category "one from parents' county, one not." Also, these totals include instances when information could not be found on the origin of one godparent.

11. This total differs from that given earlier for families having two or more children, because the data presented here are for all Slovak families with two or more children listed in church records, not just for those for whom the godparents' origins could be determined.

12. There is no practical way to tabulate the selection of godparents for more than two children in order to show the number and characteristics of those who served more than once.

13. Traditions that may have affected the choice of godparents differed among Slovaks. For example, some families may have agreed to sponsor each other's children; other families may have traditionally selected relatives as godparents. Regardless of what customs persons might have followed in Europe, these traditions would have been disrupted by the emigration process in which some persons remained behind while others emigrated.

14. In one instance, the godfather was from the parents' village area, but the godmother was from a different county. Origins could not be determined for the godparents in seven entries.

15. For a more detailed analysis of fraternal membership, see Alexander, "Immigrant Church and Community," pp. 186–200.

16. Branch 50, FCSU, Účtovníca. All data on origins of Branch 50 members are derived from this account book.

17. Membership applications, FCSU, Branch 159. All data on Branch 159 membership are derived from these applications.

18. FCSU, *Pamätník Zlatého Jubilea*, p. 150. Origins from SMC, baptismal and burial records, 1903–1910; Branch 50, FCSU, Účtovníca.

19. Membership applications, FCSU, branches 2, 4, 21, 97, 185, 460.

20. FCSU, *Pamätník Zlatého Jubilea*, pp. 157–58.

21. Membership applications, FCSU, branches 4, 21, 460.

22. See, e.g., *ASN*, 13 Aug. 1896, 4 July 1901; *Jednota*, 3 Sep. 1902, 23 Mar. 1904, 10 July 1907; *SH*, 30 Apr. 1914; *SvA*, 26 Sep. 1899, 21 Dec. 1911; A. G. Toth, "Jako máme žiť' v Amerike," [How we should live in America] in NSS, *Národný Kalendár, 1899*, p. 131.

23. The following discussion and segments of chapter 8 are parts of my unpublished paper, "The Slovaks of Pittsburgh," that was originally prepared for an anthology on immigrant communities edited by John Bodnar.

24. *Jednota*, 3 Sep. 1902.
25. Ibid., 18 Dec. 1907.
26. Interview with Mary Ciganik, 17 May 1977.
27. *Jednota*, 10 and 31 Jan. 1912.
28. Ibid., 10 Jan. 1912.

Chapter 8. The Slovak Church and Community

1. *Jednota*, 21 Dec. 1910. They could also have been concerned about Hungarian Catholics living in or near Frankstown. Chain migrations caused a number of Hungarians and Slovaks from the same regions to settle in the Frankstown-Hazelwood area. First Hungarian Reformed Church (Hazelwood), baptismal and marriage records, 1891–1903 (microfilm), HSWP; Alexander, "Immigrant Church and Community," pp. 128–32.
2. *Jednota*, 21 Dec. 1910. As early as 1902, Bohacek had publicly expressed his nationalism and denounced the Hungarian government for its Magyarization policies. Ibid., 1 Oct. 1902.
3. Ibid., 21 Aug. 1912.
4. Vrhunec had served a Slovak parish before the bishop transferred him full time to Saint Joachim's. Kushner, *Slováci Katolíci*, p. 109. Margaret Kuzma, who knew Father Vrhunec, confirmed that he was fluent in Slovak. Interview, 27 Nov. 1978.
5. *Jednota*, 21 Aug. 1912.
6. Ibid. and 30 Aug. 1911. Bohacek claimed on other occasions that Vrhunec was popular with most of the Saint Joachim parishioners. Ibid., 8 Nov. 1911, 3 Mar. 1915.
7. SJC, *Golden Jubilee*.
8. *Jednota*, 21 Dec. 1910.
9. *ASN*, 16 Sep. and 17 Aug. 1895; *NN*, 14 Apr., 16 July, 8 Sep., and 15 Sep. 1910; Čulen, *Dejiny Slovákov*, vol. 2, p. 206.
10. *Jednota*, 21 Sep. 1904.
11. Ibid.
12. Gasparik's certificate for service in the Hungarian army is in DA, Church Files, SEC folder. Interviews with Margaret Kuzma, 13 May 1977 and 27 Nov. 1978. Mrs. Kuzma was a personal friend of Father Gasparik's and, as a child—and later, as an adult—visited him at the rectory. Interviews with Ferdinand Dvorsky, 12 Apr. 1977, and John Ciganik, 17 May 1977.
13. *Jednota*, 2 Jan. 1907; *SvA*, 8 Feb. 1907. Father Uhlyarik signed a letter that Father Joseph Kossalko sent to Cardinal Gibbons that accused Slovaks who attended the Slovak Congress in Wilkes-Barre of trying to establish an independent Slovak church in the United States. By sending this letter, Kossalko and others were trying to work against what they saw as the development of Slovak nationalism in the United States. Čulen, *Dejiny Slovákov*, vol. 1, pp. 71–86; Stolarik, "Immigration and Urbanization," pp. 210–12.
14. SGC, *Pamätník*.
15. Kushner, *Slováci Katolíci*, p. 103.
16. *Jednota*, 21 Sep. 1904.
17. Ibid., 11 Sep. 1912.
18. SMC, *Zlaté Jubileum*, p. 46.
19. At Holy Emmanuel Lutheran Church, despite all the problems it faced in the prewar years, the question of a pastor's nationalism never publicly surfaced.

20. *Jednota*, 20 Dec. 1911; Kushner, *Slováci Katolíci*, p. 103; interview with Mary Ciganik, 17 May 1977.

21. See chapter 7, n. 23; *Jednota*, 10 Sep. and 6 Oct. 1912.

22. See, e.g., ibid., 7 Feb. 1906, 19 and 26 Aug., 9 and 23 Sep. 1908, 2, 10, 17, 24, and 31 Aug. 1910, 5 Apr. 1911.

23. *PC*, 10 Nov. 1904, 28 Dec. 1905.

24. *ASN*, 22 Oct. 1902.

25. *Jednota*, 31 July 1907.

26. See John Bodnar, "Schooling and the Slavic-American Family 1900–1940," in *American Education and the European Immigrant, 1840–1940*, ed. Bernard J. Weiss (Urbana: University of Illinois Press, 1982), pp. 78–95; idem, "Immigration and Modernization: The Case of Slavic Peasants in Industrial America," *Journal of Social History* 10 (Fall 1976): 44–49, 55–58.

27. It is difficult to determine exactly who the nationalists and nonnationalists were. Some letters to newspapers were not signed; nor could I locate information on the socioeconomic status or background of most of those who did sign their names. As a result, at the parish level, the available evidence allows for only a description of differing attitudes or positions on issues that involved Slovak cultural or political nationalism.

28. *Jednota*, 30 Aug. 1911. Bohacek was a laborer. He was also from Bratislava County in the western part of northern Hungary—a region that tended to be more nationalistic than the eastern counties. Church records also reveal that Bohacek had children of school age; thus he was making this plea for his own children and was apparently willing himself to donate money for a school.

29. Application of 9 May 1913 in SJC, FB file.

30. The failure to build a school in 1913 was not due to heavy financial indebtedness. In 1910, the parish had borrowed only $3,000 in order to build a church. Application of 28 Mar. 1910 in SJC, FB file.

31. *Jednota*, 15 Mar. 1911.

32. Ibid., 26 Apr. 1911.

33. Ibid., 24 July 1912. Father Uhlyarik was instrumental in finally establishing a school. SMC, *Zlaté Jubileum*, pp. 46–47.

34. Kushner, *Slováci Katolíci*, pp. 103–04, 150–51; SGC, *Pamätník*.

35. Church Reports, OVGC, entry for SGC.

36. Interviews with Ferdinand Dvorsky, 28 Nov. 1978, and Ann Jacobs, 17 May 1977.

37. *Jednota*, 20 Dec. 1911.

38. Ibid., 9 Apr. 1913.

39. *SH*, 6 Nov. 1913, 12 Feb., 23 Apr., 27 Aug., and 29 Oct. 1914.

40. For a discussion of Slovak leaders' attitudes toward education, see M. Mark Stolarik, "Immigration, Education, and the Social Mobility of Slovaks 1870–1930," in *Immigrants and Religion in Urban America*, ed. Randall M. Miller and Thomas D. Marzik (Philadelphia: Temple University Press, 1977), pp. 103–16.

41. See, e.g., Greene, *For God and Country;* Parot, *Polish Catholics in Chicago, 1850–1920*.

42. The public invitation to Slovaks to participate in the dedication of Saint Elizabeth Church exemplified ethnic pride in only a few persons. This attitude did not evolve into ethnocentrism among parishioners once the church began functioning. Nor did the ethnocentric position of the layman who revelled in the idea that Saint Gabriel Church was to be "purely Slovak" with "purely Slovak parishioners" presage

the rise of strong nationalism or ethnocentrism in that church or in the city's other Slovak churches.

43. *Jednota*, 7 Aug. 1907 ("grieves" in the original). Spilka was not specific about what he meant by "national causes," but he was probably concerned about a lack of support for the recently organized Slovak League of America. Its goals included collecting money and also garnering support for Slovak nationalists in Hungary.

44. Ibid., 4 Sep. 1907.

45. Ibid., 18 Dec. 1907.

46. Seton-Watson, *Racial Problems in Hungary*, pp. 334–39.

47. *Jednota*, 29 May and 5 June 1907; Čulen, *Dejiny Slovákov*, vol. 2, pp. 108–09, 113–24. For a brief history of the Slovak League and a description of its goals, see Constantine Čulen, "Beginnings of the Slovak League of America," in *Sixty Years of the Slovak League of America*, ed. Joseph Paučo (Middletown, PA: Jednota, 1967), pp. 26–36.

48. *Jednota*, 20 Feb. 1907. The report also noted that the attendance was not limited solely to Pittsburgh Slovaks, but that Slovaks from various towns in western Pennsylvania as well as eastern Ohio attended.

49. Seton-Watson, *Racial Problems in Hungary*, pp. 339–43.

50. *Jednota*, 30 Oct. and 13 Nov. 1907; *SvA*, 12 Nov. 1908; Stolarik, "Immigration and Urbanization," p. 217.

51. *Jednota*, 6 Dec. 1911.

52. *NN*, 8 Sep. 1910. Since he lived in the North Side, he referred most often to Slovaks living in that section of the city.

53. *Jednota*, 14 Dec. 1910, 21 Aug. 1912.

54. Ibid., 7 Aug. 1912.

55. Ibid., 11 Sep. 1912.

56. *NN*, 3 and 10 Oct. 1912.

57. Ibid., 31 Oct. 1912; *SH*, 31 Oct. 1912.

58. Representatives from a few non-Pittsburgh organizations also participated. *SH*, 31 Oct. and 7 Nov. 1912; *NN*, 31 Oct. 1912.

59. *SH*, 7 Nov. 1912.

60. The criticism stemmed from disagreements between Blaho and Father Andrew Hlinka, who was a prominent Slovak Catholic nationalist in Hungary. Stolarik, "Immigration and Urbanization," pp. 218–20. Criticisms by Slovak priests were published in some Slovak newspapers in the United States; see, e.g., *SH*, 2 Jan. 1913.

61. *SH*, 10 Oct. 1912.

62. Ibid.

63. Ibid., 2 Jan. 1913, estimated that 2,500 persons came to hear Blaho speak and 300 attended a banquet for him. There is no way to verify these figures. They may reflect the exuberance of the event's organizers as well as be an attempt to show that Pittsburgh's Slovaks surpassed Slovaks in other cities in their support for "nationalist causes." Also, Slovaks who did not reside in Pittsburgh attended the affair.

64. Branch 2, FCSU, Zápisnice, meeting of 9 Mar. 1913.

65. *SH*, 26 June 1913, 23 June 1914.

66. Branch 2, FCSU, Zápisnice, meeting of 9 Mar. 1913.

Conclusion

1. Warner and Srole, *Social Systems*, p. 160.

2. See Bender, *Community and Social Change*, especially, pp. 5–10, 143–50.

3. The use of the phrase "Slovak neighborhoods" is not meant to deny the ethnic diversity that existed in Pittsburgh neighborhoods or in those of other cities, but, instead, refers to the interaction among Slovaks in the neighborhoods.

4. For examples of analyses that call for broader or more flexible definitions of *ethnic community*, see Bender, *Community and Social Change;* Kathleen Neils Conzen, "Immigrants, Immigrant Neighborhoods, and Ethnic Identity: Historical Issues," *Journal of American History* 66 (Dec. 1979): 603–15; Timothy L. Smith, "Religious Denominations as Ethnic Communities: A Regional Case Study," *Church History* 35 (June 1966): 207–26.

5. Traditional histories of American Catholicism that minimize conflict within the church and describe happy relations with its immigrants sorely need reassessment. However, corrective studies cannot easily generalize about "conflicts" between immigrants and the American Catholic church. Such generalizations can overlook the fundamental differences among ethnic groups that influenced church-immigrant relations. Also, different dioceses adopted different policies regarding national churches. An overemphasis on conflicts in Catholic or Protestant bodies risks focusing on dramatic and, perhaps, sporadic incidents in the religious lives of immigrants. This can skew a broader perspective of the relationship between various immigrant groups and American bodies.

6. M. Mark Stolarik, *Growing Up on the South Side: Three Generations of Slovaks in Bethlehem, Pennsylvania, 1880–1976* (Lewisburg, PA: Bucknell University Press, 1985).

7. SEC, marriage records, 29 June 1914.

8. Israel Zangwill, *The Melting-Pot: Drama in Four Acts* (New York: Macmillan, 1909).

9. *Jednota,* 8 Nov. 1911.

Bibliographical Essay

Unpublished Sources

As the footnotes and appendix indicate, the baptismal, marriage, and burial records for each of Pittsburgh's Slovak churches were indispensable sources for this study. They offer information on the characteristics of church members and are also crucial for determining the origins of persons. In addition, the pastors' daily lives can be partially reconstructed from these records. For the early twentieth century, administrative materials such as financial records or minutes are available for only the Saint Matthew and Holy Emmanuel churches. With the exception of Saint Elizabeth Church, all church records cited are maintained at their respective churches. Saint Elizabeth's records are kept at Saint Wenceslaus Church (North Side). The records of Saint Elizabeth Church have also been microfilmed and deposited in the Archives of Industrial Society, University of Pittsburgh. All church records are restricted and can be used only with the permission of the pastor.

In addition to local church records, information on individual Catholic parishes can be found in the Archives of the Diocese of Pittsburgh. It contains files on individual churches in the diocese. The archives also have files on former pastors and house the Bishop Richard Phelan Collection. There is no separate collection for Bishop Regis Canevin. Many materials from the early twentieth century are still kept in active files at the Pittsburgh Diocesan Office and are not open for public research. Special permission must be obtained to examine them. For this study, files of the Office of the Vicar-General Chancellor were consulted. The materials in these files provided vital information on the interaction between diocesan officials and lay Catholics.

Important information on Slovak fraternalists and the social life of Pittsburgh Slovaks can be found in the early records of the lodges. These materials are often only available by contacting local lodge officers. Local records cited in the text that are held by individuals include early membership lists [*Kniha prijímania údov*] (to 1907) and minutes (1911–1923) of Branch 2 of the First Catholic Slovak Union. Some fraternal records have been entrusted to repositories. The Slovak Museum and Archives (Middletown, Pa.) have the records of some lodges of the First Catholic Slovak Union. The Branch 2 and Branch 50 Collections, which contain minutes and membership 181 information, were especially important for this study. The Immigration History Research Center, University of Minnesota, houses a rich collection of materials on Slovak immigrants. The First Catholic Slovak Union Papers offer particularly valuable data. These papers include membership ledgers for individual lodges in the late nineteenth century. The collection also has membership applications which contain extensive and diverse information on individuals. The Archives of Industrial Society, University of Pittsburgh, house several collections that contain valuable material on immigrant and ethnic groups in the Pittsburgh area. Although not cited in this work, two collections were consulted and are particularly valuable for examinations of Pittsburgh's immigrant groups. These collections are (1) Neighborhood Centers Association, Pittsburgh, Records, 1890–1954; and (2) the American Service Institute, Pittsburgh, Records, 1941–1961. In addition, descriptions of collections housed in the Archives of Industrial Society as well as guides to source materials on ethnic groups in the Pittsburgh area have been compiled under the auspices of the Hillman Foundation to the Ethnic Studies Committee, Pittsburgh Council on Higher Education.

The state archives in Czechoslovakia house a variety of materials that are useful for studying emigration. The records of three State Regional Archives, in Levoča, Prešov, and Košice, were consulted, as were materials deposited in the Bratislava District Archives. Among the valuable materials in these archives are reports on economic and social conditions. In addition, the records contain petitions and other correspondence that dealt with individual villages or towns. Since religion was a state matter in prewar Hungary, information can also be garnered on churches. The materials consulted are contained in the papers of the Hlavný Župan or the Podžupan for the Levoča, Prešov, and Košice regions and in the Zápisnice municipalného výboru for the Bratislava district. Most of the late nineteenth-century documents contained in the various collections are in Hungarian.

Oral Interviews

The study also relied on oral interviews with eleven different people. The persons selected were either immigrants or the children of immigrants. Except for Andrew Holovanisin, all of the immigrants immigrated to America before World War I. Andrew Holovanisin was born in the United States but as an infant was sent back to his native village with his mother. He returned to the United States and settled in Pittsburgh in 1929. With one exception, all interviews were conducted by the author; those that could be taped are in the possession of the author. The following are interviews cited in the text.

Ciganik, John. Pittsburgh. 17 May 1977.
Ciganik, Mary. Pittsburgh. 17 May 1977.
Dvorsky, Anastasia. Pittsburgh. 12 Apr. 1977.
Dvorsky, Ferdinand. Pittsburgh. 12 Apr. 1977.
———. Pittsburgh. 28 Nov. 1978.
Granatir, Paul. Bloomingdale, OH. 21 June 1978.
Holovanisin, Andrew. Pittsburgh. 30 Nov. 1978.
Jacobs, Ann. Pittsburgh. 17 May 1977.
Jurica, Father George. Pittsburgh. 12 Apr. 1977.
Kuzma, Margaret. Homestead, PA. 13 May 1977.
———. Homestead, PA. 27 Nov. 1978.

Zahorsky, Michael, by Peter Gottlieb. Aliquippa, PA. 21 June 1974. Pennsylvania Historical and Museum Commission Project, 1974. Series 1, Tape 16.

Newspapers

Newspapers were crucial sources for this study. They provided information not available elsewhere. The fraternal publications listed the names of local officers. Newspapers also reported church and local community activities not recorded elsewhere. They contained letters from local Slovaks that discussed issues and conditions in their neighborhoods or churches. These letters proved invaluable for an analysis of Pittsburgh's prewar Slovak Lutheran and Catholic populations. Newspapers used in this study are:

Amerikánsko-Slovenské Noviny [American Slovak News]. 1893–1904. *(ASN)*
Jednota [The Union]. 1893, 1902–1915.
Národné Noviny [National News]. 1910–1915. *(NN)*
Pittsburgh Catholic. 1890–1915. *(PC)*
Slovák v Amerike [Slovak in America]. 1894–1915. *(SvA)*
Slovenský Hlásnik [Slovak Herald]. 1908–1915. *(SH)*

Fraternal, Church, and Religious Society Publications

Each Pittsburgh Slovak parish published a church history to commemorate the fiftieth anniversary of its founding. These jubilee books vary in quality but all contain important events in the churches' histories and information on pastors who served them. In addition to official newspapers, anniversary albums, and miscellaneous publications, Slovak fraternal organizations published a yearly almanac (*kalendár*). These contain articles touching upon a wide variety of topics. Several of the articles were vital for this study because they were written by immigrants. Although typically referred to as the *kalendár* of an organization, the titles of these yearly publications could vary slightly, and indeed, sometimes different titles were used in the same issue. The most useful way to cite material from these almanacs is to list the articles by organization and by year. Every *kalendár* cited in this work is housed in the Slovak Collection of the Immigration History Research Center. The following are fraternal publications and articles cited in the text that appeared in a fraternal *kalendár* or other church or fraternal publications.

First Catholic Slovak Union (FCSU)

Furdek, Š[tefan]. "Veľkonočná spoveď' " [Easter confession]. *Kalendár Jednota, 1913,* pp. 105–07.
j [pseud]. "Tie kňazské dôchodky, bohatstvá" [Priestly income, wealth]. *Kalendár Jednota, 1911,* pp. 53–55.
Liščinský, Rev. Ján Method. "Katolícka Slovenská Ženská Jednota" [Catholic Slovak Ladies Union]. *Kalendár Jednota, 1911,* pp. 180–84.
Pamätník Zlatého Jubilea a 27 Konvencie Prvej Katolíckej Slovenskej Jednoty [Memorial Album of the Golden Jubilee and 27th Convention of the First Catholic Slovak Union]. Middletown, PA: Jednota, 1940.
Slanina, Martin. "Historia čísla 2 Prvej Kat. Slov. Jednoty" [History of Branch 2 of the First Catholic Slovak Union]. In *Pamätník Zlatého Jubilea a 27 Konvencie Prvej Katolíckej Slovenskej Jednoty* [Memorial Album of the Golden Jubilee and 27th

Convention of the First Catholic Slovak Union], p. 139. Middletown, PA: Jednota, 1940.

Tatranský, Bl. "Zo zápiskov Amerického farára" [From the notes of an American pastor]. *Kalendár Jednota, 1902*, pp. 120–23.

National Slovak Society (NSS)

Dejiny a Pamätnica Národného Slovenského Spolku, 1890–1950 [History and Memorial Album of the National Slovak Society, 1890–1950]. Pittsburgh: National Slovak Society, 1950.

Gessay, Ignac. "Spolky pred organisáciami" [Societies before the organizations]. *Národný Kalendár, 1911*, pp. 66–77.

Toth, A. G. "Jako máme žiť' v Amerike" [How we should live in America]. *Národný Kalendár, 1899*, pp. 129–31.

St. Michael Society (Branch 2, First Catholic Slovak Union)

Stanovy Sv. Michala Spolok [By-laws of the St. Michael Society]. N.p., n.d. *75th Anniversary*. Pittsburgh: N.p., 1964. Unpaged.

Slovak Calvinistic Presbyterian Union (SCPU)

Ďurovčik, P. "Dvadsať päť rokov vzpomienok" [Twenty-five-year overview]. *Kalendár pre Slovenských Kalvínov, 1927*, pp. 32–36.

Uherka, Frank. "Krátky prehľad S.K.P. Jednoty" [Short overview of the Slovak Calvinistic Presbyterian Union]. *Kalendár pre Slovenských Kalvínov, 1927*, pp. 37–56.

Slovak Evangelical Union (SEU)

Hibbler, Pavel. "Vývin Slovenskej Evanjelickej A. V. Jednoty" [Development of the Slovak Evangelical Union of the Augsburg Confession]. *Slovenský Evanjelický Kalendár, 1929*, pp. 55–130.

Janošov, Michal. "Úryvky z dejín Spolku 'Sv. Emmanuela' čísla 65. S.E.J., v Pittsburgh, Pa." [Excerpts from the history of the society of Holy Emmanuel, Branch 65 of the Slovak Evangelical Union in Pittsburgh, Pa.]. *Zlatá Kniha, 1893–1943* [Golden (Anniversary) Book]. Pittsburgh: Slovenský Hlásnik, 1943, pp. 125–27.

"Z činnosti 65 čísla SEJ v N. S. Pittsburgh, Pa." [From the activities of Branch 65 of the Slovak Evangelical Union in the North Side, Pittsburgh, Pa.]. *Slovenský Evanjelický Kalendár, 1926*, pp. 116–23.

Zeman, Štefan, ml. "Päťdesiať rokov šľachetnej práce slov. evanjelikov v Amerike" [Fifty years of the noble work of Slovak Lutherans in America]. *Zlatá Kniha, 1893–1943* [Golden (Anniversary) Book]. Pittsburgh: Slovenský Hlásnik, 1943, pp. 32–40.

Slovak Evangelical Lutheran Church (SELC)

Bajus, Ján. "Historický náčrt Slovenskej evanjelicko-luteránskej cirkvi" [Historical sketch of the Slovak Evangelical Lutheran Church]. *Jubilejný Evanjelicko-Luteránsky Kalendár, 1952*, pp. 28–48.

"Transocius" Spolok

"Zo života našich bratov v Amerike" [From the life of our brothers in America]. *Tranovský Evanjelický Kalendár, 1907*.

Government Publications

Census and other government publications provide useful statistical data on the for-eign-born populations in the United States and in Pittsburgh. But because immigrants were not listed separately by mother tongue in the census until 1910, census publications were of secondary importance to this work. More important to this study were the census reports on religious bodies in the United States. These publications include statistics as well as brief histories of the numerous religious bodies in the United States. This data is especially valuable for information concerning Protestant denominations. The government publications cited in this work are

Sheridan, Frank J. "Italian, Slavic, and Hungarian Unskilled Immigrant Laborers in the United States." U.S. Department of Commerce and Labor. *Bulletin of the Bureau of Labor* 15 (Sep. 1907): 403–86.

U.S. Congress. Senate. Immigration Commission. *Reports of the Immigration Commission.* Vols. 8 and 9, *Immigrants in Industries.* Pt. 2, *Iron and Steel Manufacturing.* S. Doc. 633, 61st Cong., 2d sess., 1911.

———. Senate. Immigration Commission. *Reports of the Immigration Commission.* Vol. 3, *Statistical Review of Immigration 1820–1910—Distribution of Immigrants 1850–1900.* S. Doc. 756, 61st Cong., 3d sess., 1911.

U.S. Department of Commerce and Labor. Bureau of the Census. *Thirteenth Census of the United States Taken in the Year 1910.* Vol. 1, *Population 1910: General Report and Analysis.*

———. Bureau of the Census. *Thirteenth Census of the United States Taken in the Year 1910.* Vol. 3, *Population: Reports by States, with Statistics for Counties, Cities and Other Civil Divisions: Nebraska-Wyoming, Alaska, Hawaii, and Porto Rico.*

———. Bureau of the Census. *Religious Bodies 1906.* Pt. 1, *Summary and General Tables.*

———. Commissioner General of Immigration. *Report of the Commissioner General of Immigration, 1908.* In *Reports of the Department of Commerce and Labor, 1908.*

U.S. Department of Interior. Census Office. *Compendium of the Eleventh Census: 1890.* Pt. 3, *Population.*

———. Census Office. *Report on the Statistics of Churches in the United States at the Eleventh Census: 1890.*

———. Census Office. *Twelfth Census of the United States Taken in the Year 1900.* Vol. 1, *Population.*

U.S. Department of Labor. Bureau of Immigration. *Annual Report of the Commissioner General of Immigration to the Secretary of Labor, for the Fiscal Year ended June 30, 1918.* In *Reports of the Secretary of Labor and Reports of Bureaus, 1918.*

Books

The standard histories of religion in America as well as histories of Pittsburgh were among the most useful works consulted for this study. Any examination of ethnic churches should begin with a reading of such works. While these works provided necessary background for this case study, many are not included in this bibliography because it is limited to the works cited. The following lists contain scholarly works in both English and Slovak that are cited in the text.

Abell, Aaron I. *American Catholicism and Social Action: A Search for Social Justice, 1865–1950.* Garden City, NY: Doubleday, 1960.

Balch, Emily Greene. *Our Slavic Fellow Citizens.* New York: New York Charities, 1910.

Barry, Colman J. *The Catholic Church and German Americans*. Milwaukee: Bruce, 1953.

Barton, Josef J. *Peasants and Strangers: Italians, Rumanians, and Slovaks in an American City, 1890–1950*. Cambridge: Harvard University Press, 1975.

Bender, Thomas. *Community and Social Change in America*. New Brunswick, NJ: Rutgers University Press, 1978.

Berend, I. T., and Ranki, G. *Hungary: A Century of Economic Development*. London: David & Charles, 1974.

Berthoff, Rowland. *An Unsettled People: Social Order and Disorder in American History*. New York: Harper & Row, 1971.

Bielik, František, and Elo Rákoš, comps. *Slovenské vysťahovalectvo Dokumenty I do roku 1918* [Slovak emigration, Documents I, to 1918]. Bratislava, Czechoslovakia: Slovenská Akadémie Vied, 1969.

Bodnar, John. *Immigration and Industrialization: Ethnicity in an American Mill Town, 1870–1940*. Pittsburgh: University of Pittsburgh Press, 1977.

———. *The Transplanted: A History of Immigrants in Urban America*. Bloomington: Indiana University Press, 1985.

Bodnar, John, Roger Simon, and Michael P. Weber. *Lives of Their Own: Blacks, Italians, and Poles in Pittsburgh, 1900–1960*. Urbana: University of Illinois Press, 1982.

Body, Ján. *Pamätník Rev. A. L. Ramer, Ph.D.* [Memorial to Rev. A. L. Ramer, Ph.D.]. N.p.: Slovak Zion Synod, n.d.

Briggs, John W. *An Italian Passage: Immigrants to Three American Cities, 1890–1930*. New Haven: Yale University Press, 1978.

Brock, Peter. *The Slovak National Awakening: An Essay in the Intellectual History of East Central Europe*. Toronto: University of Toronto Press, 1976.

Canevin, Rt. Rev. Regis. *An Examination Historical and Statistical into Losses and Gains of the Catholic Church*. N.p., 1912.

Čapek, Thomas. *The Čechs (Bohemians) in America*. Boston: Houghton Mifflin, 1920.

Chudacoff, Howard P. *Mobile Americans: Residential and Social Mobility in Omaha, 1880–1920*. New York: Oxford University Press, 1972.

Couvares, Francis G. *The Remaking of Pittsburgh: Class and Culture in an Industrializing City, 1877–1919*. Albany: State University of New York Press, 1984.

Cross, Robert D. *The Emergence of Liberal Catholicism in America*. Cambridge: Harvard University Press, 1958.

Čulen, Konštantín. *Dejiny Slovákov v Amerike* [History of Slovaks in America]. 2 Vols. Bratislava, Czechoslovakia: Slovenská Liga na Slovensku, 1942.

———. *J. Slovenský: Životopis zakladateľa prvých slovenských novín v Amerike* [J. Slovensky: A biography of the founder of the first Slovak newspaper in America]. Winnipeg: Canadian Slovak, 1946.

———. *Slovenské Časopisy v Amerike* [Slovak Periodicals in America]. Middletown, PA: Jednota, 1970.

Cummings, Scott, ed. *Self-Help in Urban America: Patterns of Minority Business Enterprise*. Port Washington, NY: Kennikat, 1980.

Dolak, George. *A History of the Slovak Evangelical Lutheran Church in the United States of America, 1902–1927*. St. Louis: Concordia, 1955.

Dolan, Jay P. *The American Catholic Experience: A History from Colonial Times to the Present*. Garden City, NY: Doubleday, 1985.

———. *The Immigrant Church: New York's Irish and German Catholics, 1815–1865*. Baltimore: Johns Hopkins University Press, 1975.

Ellis, John Tracy. *American Catholicism*. Chicago: University of Chicago Press, 1956.

Golab, Caroline. *Immigrant Destinations*. Philadelphia: Temple University Press, 1977.

Greene, Victor. *For God and Country: The Rise of Polish and Lithuanian Ethnic Conscious-ness in America, 1860–1910.* Madison: State Historical Society of Wisconsin, 1975.

Gurock, Jeffrey S. *When Harlem Was Jewish, 1870–1930.* New York: Columbia University Press, 1979.

Handlin, Oscar. *The Uprooted: The Epic Story of the Great Migrations That Made the American People.* Boston: Little, Brown, 1951.

Kessner, Thomas. *The Golden Door: Italian and Jewish Immigrant Mobility in New York City, 1880–1915.* New York: Oxford University Press, 1977.

Kushner, Jozef A. *Slováci Katolíci Pittsburghského Biskupstva* [Slovak Catholics of the Pittsburgh Diocese]. Passaic, NJ: Slovak Catholic Sokol, 1946.

Kuzniewski, Anthony J. *Faith and Fatherland: The Polish Church War in Wisconsin, 1896–1918.* Notre Dame: University of Notre Dame Press, 1980.

Lengyel, Emil. *Americans from Hungary.* Philadelphia: Lippincott, 1948.

Linkh, Richard M. *American Catholicism and European Immigrants (1900–1924).* New York: Center for Migration Studies, 1975.

Lopata, Helen. *Polish Americans: Status Competition in an Ethnic Community.* Englewood Cliffs, NJ: Prentice-Hall, 1976.

Lutheran Church in America. *A History of the Slovak Zion Synod, LCA.* N.p.: Lutheran Church in America, 1977.

Macartney, C. A. *The Habsburg Empire, 1790–1918.* London: Weidenfeld & Nicolson, 1968.

———. *Hungary and Her Successors: The Treaty of Trianon and Its Consequences, 1919–1937.* London: Oxford University Press, 1937.

McAvoy, Thomas T. *A History of the Catholic Church in the United States.* Notre Dame: University of Notre Dame Press, 1969.

Maynard, Theodore. *The Catholic Church and the American Idea.* New York: Appleton-Century-Crofts, 1953.

Nelli, Humbert S. *The Italians in Chicago, 1880–1930: A Study in Ethnic Mobility.* New York: Oxford University Press, 1970.

Parot, Joseph John. *Polish Catholics in Chicago, 1850–1920.* DeKalb: Northern Illinois University Press, 1981.

Paučo, Jozef. *75 Rokov Prvej Katolíckej Slovenskej Jednoty* [75 Years of the First Catholic Slovak Union]. Middletown, PA: Jednota, 1965.

———. *Štefan Furdek a Slovenské Prisťahovalectvo* [Stephen Furdek and the Slovak Immigration]. Middletown, PA: Jednota, 1955.

Puskás, Julianna. *Emigration from Hungary to the United States Before 1914.* Budapest: Akadémiai Kiadó, 1975.

———. *From Hungary to the United States (1880–1914).* Budapest: Akadémiai Kiadó, 1982.

Rovnianek, P. V. *Zápisky za živa pochovaného* [Notes from one buried alive]. N.p., 1924.

Ruppeldt, Fedor. *Slovenský-Evanjelici v Amerike* [Slovak Lutherans in America]. Ružomberok, Czechoslovakia: Cirkev Evanj. a.v. na Slovensku, 1932.

Seton-Watson, R. W. [Scotus Viator]. *Racial Problems in Hungary.* London: Archibald Constable, 1908

Shibutani, Tamotsu, and Kian M. Kwan. *Ethnic Stratification: A Comparative Approach.* New York: Macmillan, 1965.

Slovenská Vlastiveda. 4 Vols. Bratislava, Czechoslovakia: Slovenská Akadémia Vied, 1943.

Stolarik, M. Mark. *Growing Up on the South Side: Three Generations of Slovaks in Bethlehem, Pennsylvania, 1880–1976.* Lewisburg, PA: Bucknell University Press, 1985.

Tarr, Joel A. *Transportation Innovation and Changing Spatial Patterns: Pittsburgh, 1850–1910*. Pittsburgh: Transportation Research Institute, Carnegie-Mellon University, 1972.

Thernstrom, Stephan. *The Other Bostonians: Poverty and Progress in the American Metropolis, 1880–1970*. Cambridge: Harvard University Press, 1973.

———. *Poverty and Progress: Social Mobility in a Nineteenth Century City*. Cambridge, Mass.: Harvard University Press, 1964.

Thomas, William I., and Florian Znaniecki. *The Polish Peasant in Europe and America*. 4 Vols. Boston: Gorham, 1918–1920.

Vlastivedný slovník obcí na Slovensku [Historical and Geographical Dictionary of Communities in Slovakia]. 3 Vols. Bratislava, Czechoslovakia: Slovenská Akadémia Vied, 1977.

Warner, W. Lloyd, and Leo Srole. *The Social Systems of American Ethnic Groups*. New Haven: Yale University Press, 1945.

Yans-McLaughlin, Virginia. *Family and Community: Italian Immigrants in Buffalo, 1880–1930*. Ithaca, N.Y.: Cornell University Press, 1977.

Zangwill, Israel. *The Melting-Pot: Drama in Four Acts*. New York: Macmillan, 1909.

Zunz, Olivier. *The Changing Face of Inequality: Urbanization, Industrial Development, and Immigrants in Detroit, 1880–1920*. Chicago: University of Chicago Press, 1982.

Articles

Adamec, Rev. Joseph V. "The Slovak Catholic Federation: A 65 Year Perspective." In *Slovaks in America: A Bicentennial Study*, comp. Joseph C. Krajsa et al., pp. 223–32. Middletown, PA: Jednota Slovak American, 1978.

Alexander, June Granatir. "City Directories as 'Ideal' Censuses: Slovak Immigrants and Pittsburgh's Early Twentieth-Century Directories as a Test Case." *Western Pennsylvania Historical Magazine* 65 (July 1982): 203–20.

———. "The Laity in the Church: Slovaks and the Catholic Church in Pre-World War I Pittsburgh." *Church History* 53 (Sep. 1984): 363–78.

———. "Staying Together: Chain Migration and Patterns of Slovak Settlement in Pittsburgh Prior to World War I." *Journal of American Ethnic History* 1 (Fall 1981): 56–83.

Anderson, Robert T., and Gallatin Anderson. "Voluntary Associations and Urbanization: A Diachronic Analysis." *American Journal of Sociology* 65 (Nov. 1959): 265–73.

———. "The Indirect Social Structure of European Village Communities." *American Anthropologist* 64 (Oct. 1962): 1016–26.

Baka, Kenneth. "The First Catholic Slovak Ladies Association." In *Slovaks in America: A Bicentennial Study*, comp. Joseph C. Krajsa et al., pp. 169–95. Middletown, PA: Jednota Slovak American, 1978.

Barton, Josef J. "Eastern and Southern Europeans." In *Ethnic Leadership in America*, ed. John Higham, pp. 150–75. Baltimore: Johns Hopkins University Press, 1978.

Berthoff, Rowland. "The American Social Order: A Conservative Hypothesis." *American Historical Review* 65 (Apr. 1960): 495–514.

Bodnar, John. "Immigration and Modernization: The Case of Slavic Peasants in Industrial America." *Journal of Social History* 10 (Fall 1976): 44–67.

———. "Schooling and the Slavic-American Family, 1900–1940." In *American Education and the European Immigrant, 1840–1940*, ed. Bernard J. Weiss, pp. 78–95. Urbana: University of Illinois Press, 1982.

Bodnar, John, Michael Weber, and Roger Simon. "Migration, Kinship, and Urban Adjustment: Blacks and Poles in Pittsburgh, 1900–1930." *Journal of American History* 66 (Dec. 1979): 548–65.

Bullion, Rev. George J. "Bishop Phelan." In *Catholic Pittsburgh's One Hundred Years*, ed. Catholic Historical Society of Western Pennsylvania, pp. 53–67. Chicago: Loyola University Press, 1943.

Coakley, Rev. Thomas F. "Archbishop Canevin." In *Catholic Pittsburgh's One Hundred Years*, ed. Catholic Historical Society of Western Pennsylvania, pp. 68–72. Chicago: Loyola University Press, 1943.

Conzen, Kathleen Neils. "Immigrants, Immigrant Neighborhoods, and Ethnic Identity: Historical Issues." *Journal of American History* 66 (Dec. 1979): 603–15.

Čulen, Constantine. "Beginnings of the Slovak League in America." In *Sixty Years of the Slovak League of America*, ed. Joseph Paučo, pp. 26–36. Middletown, PA: Jednota, 1967.

Eddie, Scott M. "The Changing Pattern of Landownership in Hungary, 1867–1914." *Economic History Review*, 2d ser., 20 (Apr. 1967): 293–309.

Galush, William J. "Faith and Fatherland: Dimensions of Polish-American Ethnoreligion, 1875–1975." In *Immigrants and Religion in Urban America*, ed. Randall M. Miller and Thomas D. Marzik, pp. 84–102. Philadelphia: Temple University Press, 1977.

Hanzlík, Ján. "Začiatky vysťahovalectva zo Slovenska do USA a jeho priebeh až do roku 1918, jeho príčiny a následky" [Beginnings and course of emigration from Slovakia to the United States to 1918, its course and results]. In *Začiatky českej a slovenskej emigrácie do USA* [Beginnings of Czech and Slovak emigration to the United States], ed. Josef Polišenský, pp. 49–75. Bratislava, Czechoslovakia: Slovenská Akadémia Vied, 1970.

Jelinek, Yeshayahu. "Self-identification of First Generation Hungarian Jewish Immigrants." *American Jewish Historical Quarterly* 61 (Mar. 1972): 214–22.

Koukol, Alois B. "A Slav's a Man for a' That." In *Wage-Earning Pittsburgh*, ed. Paul Underwood Kellogg, pp. 61–77. New York: Russell Sage, 1914.

McIlvain, Josephine. "Twelve Blocks: A Study of One Segment of Pittsburgh's South Side, 1880–1915." *Western Pennsylvania Historical Magazine* 60 (Oct. 1977): 351–70.

McKitrick, Eric L., and Stanley Elkins. "Institutions in Motion." *American Quarterly* 12 (Summer 1960): 188–97.

Marty, Martin E. "Ethnicity: The Skeleton of Religion in America." *Church History* 41 (Mar. 1972): 5–21.

Mazak, S. G. "A Brief History of the Slovak Lutheran Synod of the United States." *Concordia Historical Institute Quarterly* 3 (1930): 80–86.

——. "A Brief History of the Slovak Lutheran Synod of the United States." *Concordia Historical Institute Quarterly* 4 (1931): 105–12.

Mohl, Raymond A., and Neil Betten. "The Immigrant Church in Gary, Indiana: Religious Adjustment and Cultural Defense." *Ethnicity* 8 (1981): 1–17.

Morawska, Ewa. "The Internal Status Hierarchy in the East European Communities in Johnstown, PA, 1890–1930s." *Journal of Social History* 16 (Fall 1982): 75–107.

Pier, Father Andrew V. "Christmas Customs in Slovakia." In *Jednota Annual Furdek, 1974*, ed. F.C.S.U., Middletown, PA: Jednota, 1974, reprint.

Porter, H. F. J. "Industrial Hygiene of the Pittsburgh District." In *Wage-Earning Pittsburgh*, ed. Paul Underwood Kellogg, pp. 217–78. New York: Russell Sage, 1914.

Roberts, Peter. "Immigrant Wage-Earners." In *Wage-Earning Pittsburgh*, ed. Paul Underwood Kellogg, pp. 33–60. New York: Russell Sage, 1914.

Rovnianek, Peter V. "The Slovaks in America." *Charities* 13 (Dec. 1904): 239–44.

Smith, Timothy L. "Religion and Ethnicity in America." *American Historical Review* 83 (Dec. 1978): 1155–85.

———. "Lay Initiative in the Religious Life of American Immigrants, 1880–1950." In *Anonymous Americans: Explorations in Nineteenth-Century Social History*, ed. Tamara K. Hareven, pp. 214–49. Englewood Cliffs NJ: Prentice-Hall, 1971.

———. "Religious Denominations as Ethnic Communities: A Regional Case Study." *Church History* 35 (June 1966): 207–26.

Stolarik, M. Mark. "Immigration, Education, and the Social Mobility of Slovaks, 1870–1930." In *Immigrants and Religion in Urban America*, ed. Randall M. Miller and Thomas D. Marzik, pp. 103–16. Philadelphia: Temple University Press, 1977.

———. "Immigration and Eastern Slovak Nationalism" *Slovakia* 26 (1976): 13–20.

———. "Lay Initiative in American-Slovak Parishes, 1880–1930." *Records of the American Catholic Historical Society of Philadelphia* 83 (Sep.–Dec. 1972): 151–58.

———. "A Place for Everyone: Slovak Fraternal-Benefit Societies." In *Self-Help in Urban America: Patterns of Minority Economic Development*, ed. Scott Cummings, pp. 130–41. Port Washington, NY: Kennikat, 1980.

Vecoli, Rudolph J. "Cult and Occult in Italian-American Culture: The Persistence of a Religious Heritage." In *Immigrants and Religion in Urban America*, ed. Randall M. Miller and Thomas D. Marzik, pp. 25–47. Philadelphia: Temple University Press, 1977.

———. "Ethnicity: A Neglected Dimension of American History." In *The State of American History*, ed. Herbert J. Bass, pp. 70–88. Chicago: Quadrangle, 1970.

———. "Prelates and Peasants: Italian Immigrants and the Catholic Church." *Journal of Social History* 2 (Spring 1969): 217–68.

City Directories, Encyclopedias, Yearbooks, and Religious Statutes

The Catholic Encyclopedia, 1913. S.v. "Hungary," by A. Aldasy.

Diffenbacher's Directory of Pittsburgh and Allegheny Cities. Pittsburgh: Stevens & Foster, 1894–1897.

Diocese of Pittsburgh. *Statuta Dioeceseos Pittsburgensis in Synodis Dioecesanis, Habitas Lata, et Prout Nunc Prostant Promulgata in Synodo Dioecesana Sexta Dubus 7, 8 et 9 Febuarii 1893* [Statutes of the Pittsburgh Diocese . . .]. Pittsburgh: N.p., 1893.

———. *Statuta Dioeceseos Pittsburgensis in Synodis Dioecesanis Lata, et Prout Nunc Prostant Promulgata in Synodo Dioecesana Decima Die 10 Mensis Octobris, A.D. 1905* [Statutes of the Pittsburgh Diocese . . . 1905]. Pittsburgh: N.p., 1906.

Polk & Co. *Pittsburgh and Allegheny Directory*. Pittsburgh: R. L. Dudley, 1898–1907.

———. *Pittsburgh Directory*. Pittsburgh: R. L. Dudley, 1908–1915.

St. Regis Association, ed. *Catholic Yearbook and Directory of the Pittsburgh Diocese, 1913*. Pittsburgh: St. Regis Association, 1913.

———. *Catholic Yearbook of the Pittsburgh Diocese, 1908–1909*. Pittsburgh: St. Regis Association, 1909.

Theses and Unpublished Papers

Several theses and doctoral dissertations, in addition to those cited below, have been written on the Pittsburgh area. Although these works are not cited in this bibliography, any study of the Pittsburgh metropolitan area should include an examination of the unpublished theses on the subject.

Alexander, Sylvia June Granatir. "The Immigrant Church and Community: The Formation of Pittsburgh's Slovak Religious Institutions, 1880–1914." Ph.D. dissertation, University of Minnesota, 1980.

Gellén, József. "Emigration in a Systems Framework: The Case of Hungary, 1899–1913." Unpublished paper in author's possession.

Stolarik, Marian Mark. "Immigration and Urbanization: The Slovak Experience, 1870–1918." Ph.D. dissertation, University of Minnesota, 1974.

Index

193